PHILIP'S Red Books

OXFORD

www.philips-maps.co.uk

First published in 2007 as *Philip's Street Atlas Oxford* by
Philip's, a division of Octopus Publishing Group Ltd
www.octopusbooks.co.uk
Endeavour House, 189 Shaftesbury Avenue
London WC2H 8JY
An Hachette UK Company
www.hachette.co.uk

First Red Books edition 2010, first impression 2010

ISBN 978-1-84907-118-5

© Philip's 2010

Ordnance Survey®

This product includes mapping data licensed from
Ordnance Survey®, with the permission of the
Controller of Her Majesty's Stationery Office.

© Crown copyright 2010. All rights reserved.
Licence number 100011710

Printed and bound in China

Contents

II **Key to**

III **Key to map pages**

IV **Route planning**

2 **Street maps** at 4½ inches to 1 mile

58 **Street maps** at 7 inches to 1 mile

60 **Index**

▼ Radcliffe Camera, *John Woodworth / iStockphoto.com*

Key to map symbols

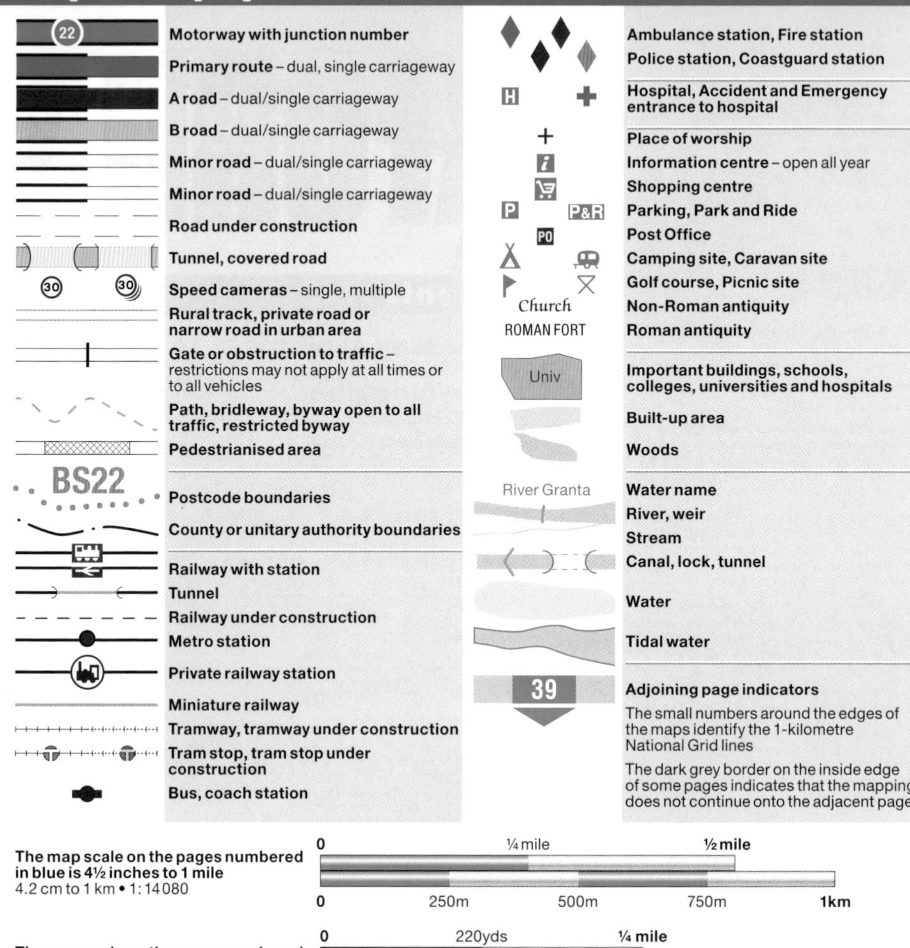

Motorway with junction number	Ambulance station, Fire station
Primary route – dual, single carriageway	Police station, Coastguard station
A road – dual/single carriageway	Hospital, Accident and Emergency entrance to hospital
B road – dual/single carriageway	Place of worship
Minor road – dual/single carriageway	Information centre – open all year
Minor road – dual/single carriageway	Shopping centre
Road under construction	Parking, Park and Ride
Tunnel, covered road	Post Office
Speed cameras – single, multiple	Camping site, Caravan site
Rural track, private road or narrow road in urban area	Golf course, Picnic site
Gate or obstruction to traffic – restrictions may not apply at all times or to all vehicles	Non-Roman antiquity
	Roman antiquity
Path, bridleway, byway open to all traffic, restricted byway	Important buildings, schools, colleges, universities and hospitals
Pedestrianised area	Built-up area
	Woods
Postcode boundaries	Water name
County or unitary authority boundaries	River, weir
	Stream
Railway with station	Canal, lock, tunnel
Tunnel	
Railway under construction	Water
Metro station	
Private railway station	Tidal water
Miniature railway	Adjoining page indicators
Tramway, tramway under construction	The small numbers around the edges of the maps identify the 1-kilometre National Grid lines
Tram stop, tram stop under construction	The dark grey border on the inside edge of some pages indicates that the mapping does not continue onto the adjacent page
Bus, coach station	

Church
ROMAN FORT
Univ
River Granta

The map scale on the pages numbered in blue is 4½ inches to 1 mile
4.2 cm to 1 km • 1:14080

0   ¼ mile   ½ mile
0   250m   500m   750m   1km

The map scale on the pages numbered in red is 7 inches to 1 mile
8.4 cm to 1 km • 1:9050

0   220yds   ¼ mile
0   125m   250m   375m   500m

Abbreviations

Acad	Academy	Ind Est	Industrial Estate	Meml	Memorial	Ret Pk	Retail Park
Allot Gdns	Allotments	IRB Sta	Inshore Rescue Boat Station	Mon	Monument	Sch	School
Cemy	Cemetery			Mus	Museum	Sh Ctr	Shopping Centre
C Ctr	Civic Centre	Inst	Institute	Obsy	Observatory	TH	Town Hall/House
CH	Club House	Ct	Law Court	Pal	Royal Palace	Trad Est	Trading Estate
Coll	College	L Ctr	Leisure Centre	PH	Public House	Univ	University
Crem	Crematorium	LC	Level Crossing	Recn Gd	Recreation Ground	W Twr	Water Tower
Ent	Enterprise	Liby	Library			Wks	Works
Ex H	Exhibition Hall	Mkt	Market	Resr	Reservoir	YH	Youth Hostel

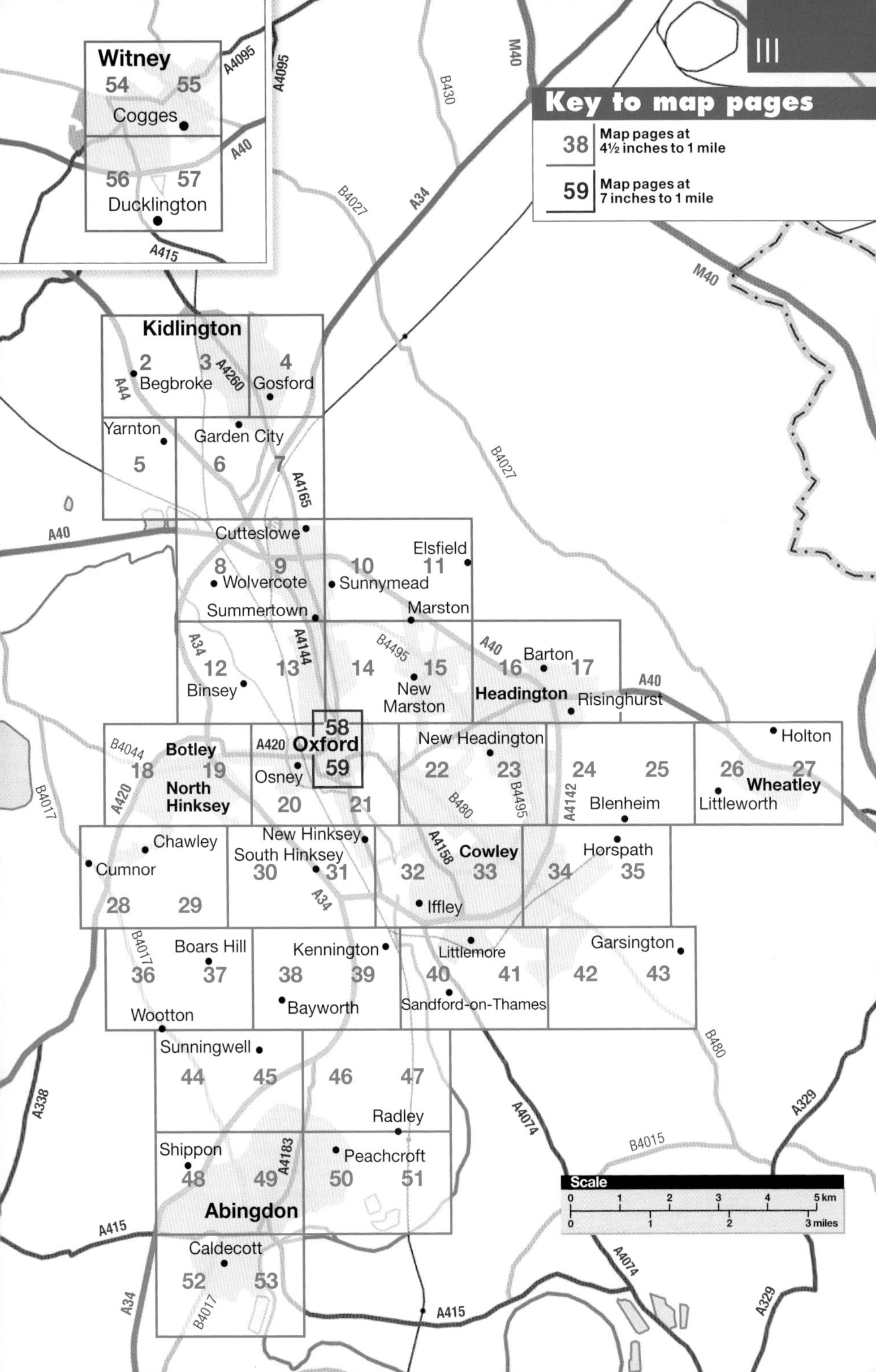

Witney

54 55

Cogges

56 57

Ducklington

A4095
A4095
A40
A415
M40
B430
A34
B4027
A4027

Key to map pages

| 38 | Map pages at 4½ inches to 1 mile |

| 59 | Map pages at 7 inches to 1 mile |

M40

Kidlington

2 3 4
Begbroke Gosford

A44
A4260

Yarnton

5 6 7
Garden City

A4165

A40

Cutteslowe

8 9 10 11
Wolvercote Sunnymead Elsfield

Summertown Marston

A34
A4144
B4495
A40

12 13 14 15 16 17
Binsey New Headington Barton Risinghurst
Marston

Headington

A40

Oxford
58
59

18 19 20 21
Botley Osney

North
Hinksey

New Headington 22 23 24 25 26 27
Holton

Blenheim Wheatley
Littleworth

A420
B4044
A420
A4017
B490
B4495
A4142
A40

28 29 30 31 32 33 34 35
Chawley New Hinksey Cowley Horspath
Cumnor South Hinksey

Iffley

A4158
A34

36 37 38 39 40 41 42 43
Boars Hill Kennington Littlemore Garsington

Wootton Bayworth Sandford-on-Thames

B4017
B480

44 45 46 47
Sunningwell Radley

A338
A4074
A329
B4015

48 49 50 51
Shippon Peachcroft

Abingdon

Caldecott

52 53

A415
A4183
A34
B4017
A415
A4074
A329

Scale

| 0 | 1 | 2 | 3 | 4 | 5 km |
| 0 | | 1 | | 2 | 3 miles |

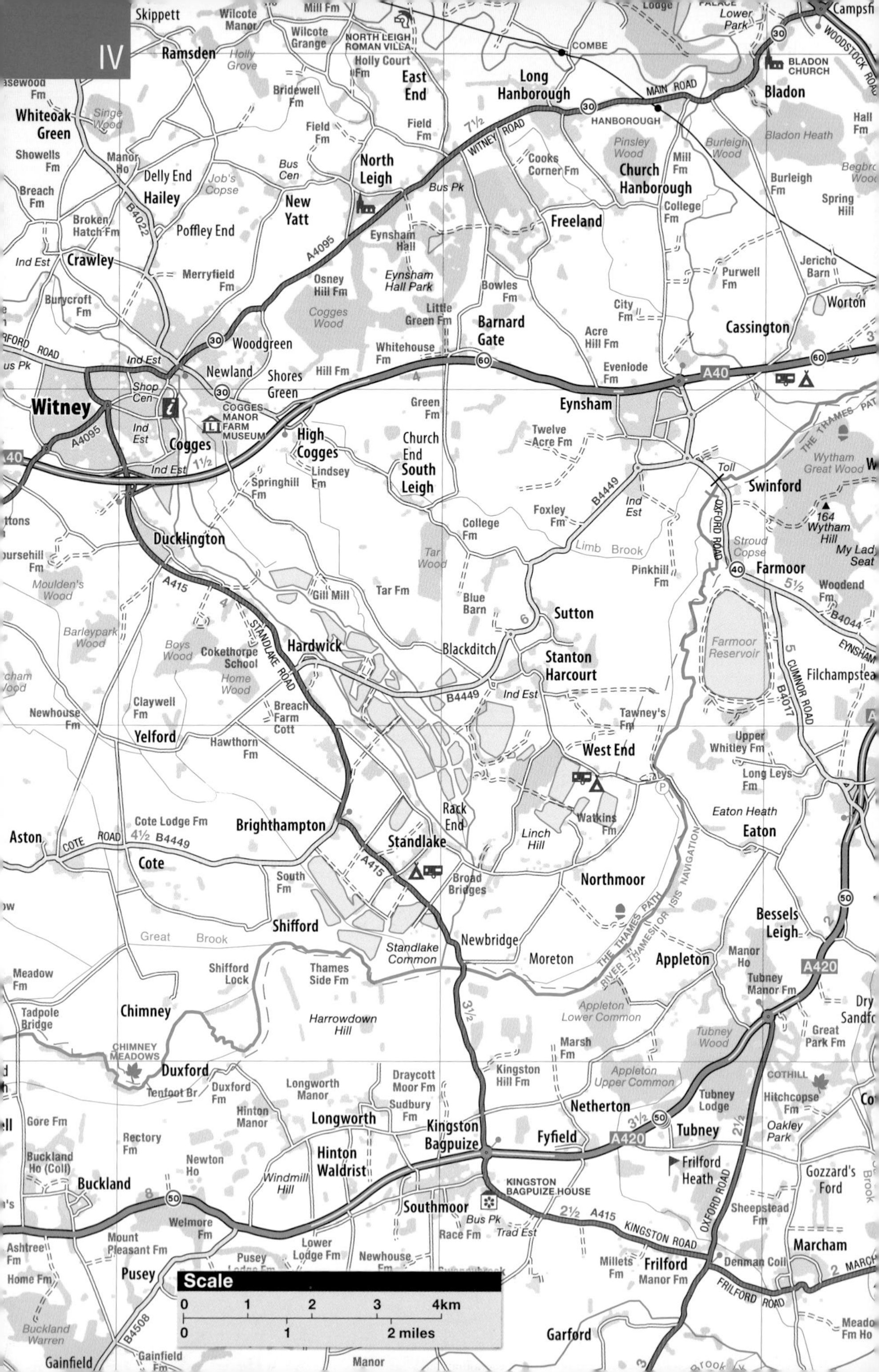

IV
Skippett
Wilcote Manor
Mill Fm
Wilcote Grange
NORTH LEIGH ROMAN VILLA
Lodge
PALACE
Lower Park
Campsfi
COMBE
Ramsden
Holly Grove
Holly Court Fm
East End
Long Hanborough
BLADON CHURCH
WOODSTOCK ROAD
Bladon
MAIN ROAD
HANBOROUGH
Whiteoak Green
Singe Wood
Bridewell Fm
Field Fm
Field Fm
7½
WITNEY ROAD
Hall Fm
Bladon Heath
Pinsley Wood
Burleigh Wood
Showells Fm
Manor Ho
Delly End
Job's Copse
Bus Cen
North Leigh
Cooks Corner Fm
Church Hanborough
Mill Fm
Burleigh Fm
Begbro Wood
Breach Fm
Hailey
New Yatt
Bus Pk
College Fm
Spring Hill
Broken Hatch Fm
B4022
Poffley End
Freeland
Eynsham Hall
Ind Est
Crawley
A4095
Merryfield Fm
Eynsham Hall Park
Osney Hill Fm
Purwell Fm
Jericho Barn
Bowles Fm
Burycroft Fm
Cogges Wood
Little Green Fm
Barnard Gate
City Fm
Worton
Acre Hill Fm
Cassington
RFORD ROAD
Woodgreen
Whitehouse Fm
Ind Est
Evenlode Fm
us Pk
Newland
Shores Green
Hill Fm
A40
Shop Cen
Witney
Eynsham
COGGES MANOR FARM MUSEUM
Green Fm
THE THAMES PATH
A4095
Ind Est
High Cogges
Church End
Twelve Acre Fm
Cogges
Wytham Great Wood
A40
Ind Est
1½
Lindsey Fm
South Leigh
Toll
Swinford
Springhill Fm
B4449
Ind Est
OXFORD ROAD
ttons
Ducklington
College Fm
Foxley Fm
164 Wytham Hill
Stroud Copse
My Lady Seat
Limb Brook
ursehill Fm
Tar Wood
Pinkhill Fm
Farmoor
5½
Woodend Fm
Moulden's Wood
A415
Gill Mill
Tar Fm
Blue Barn
B4044
Sutton
Farmoor Reservoir
EYNSHAM
Barleypark Wood
Boys Wood
Cokethorpe School
STANDLAKE ROAD
Hardwick
Blackditch
Stanton Harcourt
CUMNOR ROAD
cham Wood
Home Wood
Filchampstea
Breach Farm Cott
B4449
Ind Est
B4017
Claywell Fm
Tawney's Fm
Newhouse Fm
Yelford
Upper Whitley Fm
Hawthorn Fm
West End
Long Leys Fm
Rack End
Watkins Fm
Eaton Heath
Cote Lodge Fm
Brighthampton
Linch Hill
Aston
COTE ROAD
4½
B4449
Standlake
Eaton
ISIS NAVIGATION
Cote
A415
South Fm
Broad Bridges
Northmoor
Bessels Leigh
Shifford
THE THAMES PATH
RIVER THAMES OR ISIS NAVIGATION
Great Brook
Standlake Common
Newbridge
Moreton
Appleton
Manor Ho
A420
Meadow Fm
Shifford Lock
Thames Side Fm
Tubney Manor Fm
Dry Sandfo
Tadpole Bridge
Chimney
3½
Harrowdown Hill
Appleton Lower Common
Great Park Fm
CHIMNEY MEADOWS
Marsh Fm
Tubney Wood
Duxford
Draycott Moor Fm
Kingston Hill Fm
Appleton Upper Common
COTHILL
Tenfoot Br
Duxford Fm
Longworth Manor
Tubney Lodge
Hitchcopse Fm
Gore Fm
Hinton Manor
Sudbury Fm
Netherton
Rectory Fm
Longworth
Kingston Bagpuize
Fyfield
3½
Tubney
Oakley Park
Buckland Ho (Coll)
Hinton Waldrist
A420
Frilford Heath
Newton Ho
Windmill Hill
Gozzard's Ford
Buckland
KINGSTON BAGPUIZE HOUSE
OXFORD ROAD
Southmoor
2½
A415
Sheepstead Fm
Welmore Fm
Bus Pk
KINGSTON ROAD
Mount Pleasant Fm
Race Fm
Trad Est
Marcham
Ashtree Fm
Lower Lodge Fm
Newhouse Fm
Millets Fm
Frilford
Denman Coll
Pusey
Pusey Lodge Fm
Manor Fm
FRILFORD ROAD
Home Fm
Scale
0 1 2 3 4km
0 1 2 miles
Buckland Warren
B4508
Garford
Meado Fm Ho
Gainfield
Gainfield Fm
Manor

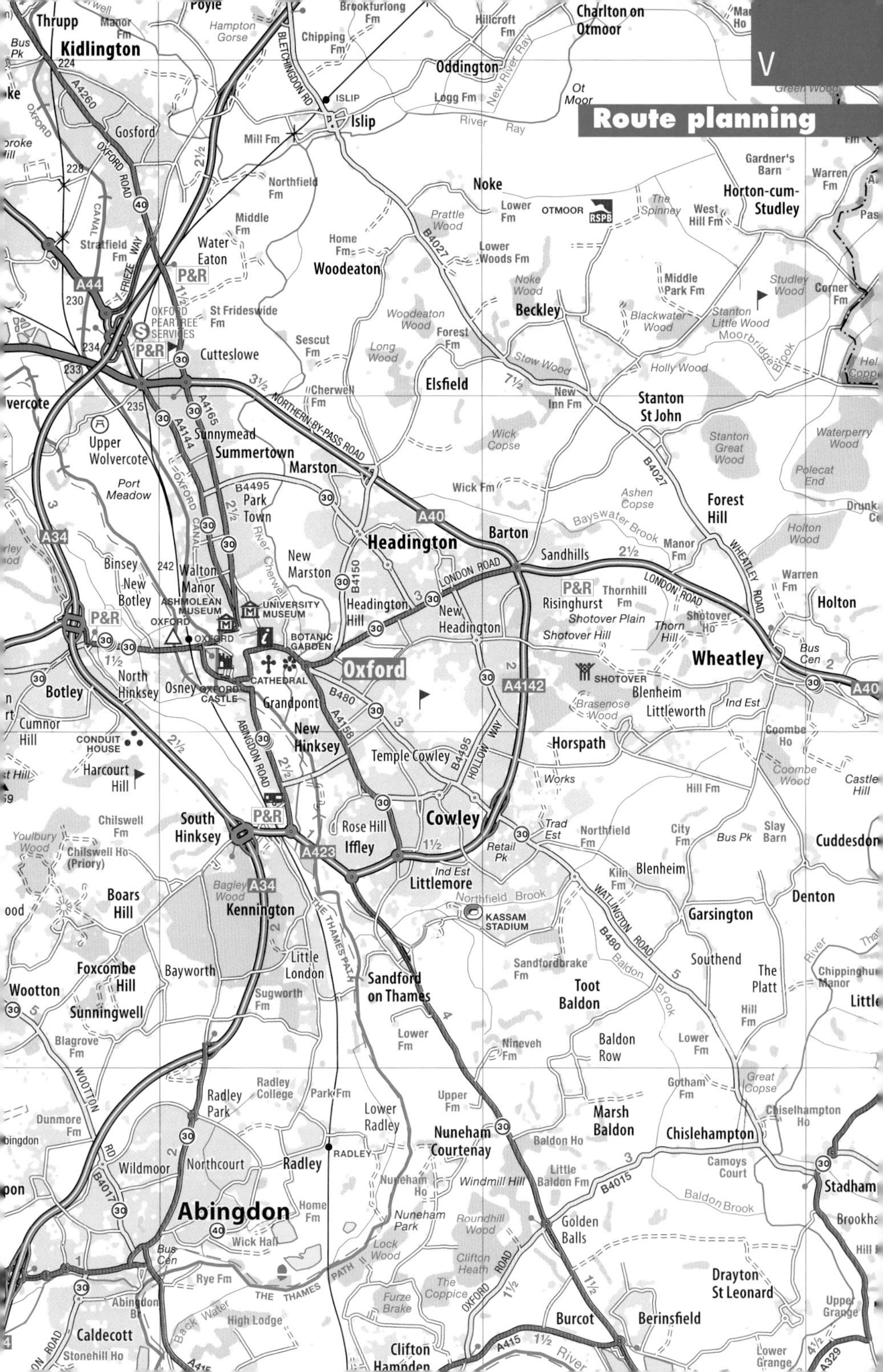
Thrupp
Manor Fm
Poyle
Hampton Gorse
Brookfurlong Fm
Hillcroft Fm
Charlton on Otmoor
Bus Pk
Kidlington
Chipping Fm
BLETCHINGDON RD
Oddington
New River Ray
A4260
ISLIP
Logg Fm
Ot Moor
Islip
River Ray
OXFORD CANAL
Gosford
Mill Fm
OXFORD ROAD
Gardner's Barn
Warren Fm
Northfield Fm
Noke
Horton-cum-Studley
Middle Fm
Lower Fm
OTMOOR
RSPB
The Spinney
West Hill Fm
Prattle Wood
Stratfield Fm
Water Eaton
Home Fm
B4027
Lower Woods Fm
Woodeaton
P&R
FRIEZE WAY
Noke Wood
Middle Park Fm
Studley Wood
Corner Fm
A44
OXFORD PEARTREE SERVICES
St Frideswide Fm
Woodeaton Wood
Beckley
Blackwater Wood
Stanton Little Wood
Sescut Fm
Forest Fm
Moorbridge Brook
Long Wood
Stow Wood
Holly Wood
Cutteslowe
Elsfield
Cherwell Fm
NORTHERN-BY-PASS ROAD
New Inn Fm
Stanton St John
Wolvercote
A4165
A4144
Upper Wolvercote
Sunnymead
Summertown
Wick Copse
Stanton Great Wood
Waterperry Wood
Port Meadow
Marston
B4027
Polecat End
B4495
Park Town
Wick Fm
Ashen Copse
Forest Hill
A40
Bayswater Brook
A34
Headington
Barton
Holton Wood
Binsey
Walton Manor
New Marston
River Cherwell
Manor Fm
Sandhills
New Botley
B4150
LONDON ROAD
P&R
Thornhill Fm
Warren Fm
ASHMOLEAN MUSEUM
UNIVERSITY MUSEUM
Headington Hill
New Headington
Risinghurst
WHEATLEY ROAD
Holton
OXFORD
Shotover Plain
Shotover Ho
Thorn Hill
Shotover Hill
BOTANIC GARDEN
Wheatley
Bus Cen
Oxford
Botley
North Hinksey
Osney
CATHEDRAL
OXFORD CASTLE
A4142
SHOTOVER
Blenheim
Brasenose Wood
Littleworth
Ind Est
Grandpont
B480
Cumnor Hill
CONDUIT HOUSE
New Hinksey
A4158
Temple Cowley
B4495
HOLLOW WAY
Horspath
Coombe Ho
Harcourt Hill
ABINGDON ROAD
Works
Coombe Wood
Hill Fm
Castle Hill
Chilswell Fm
South Hinksey
P&R
Rose Hill
Cowley
Trad Est
Northfield Fm
City Fm
Bus Pk
Slay Barn
Cuddesdon
Youlbury Wood
Chilswell Ho (Priory)
Iffley
Retail Pk
A423
Ind Est
Littlemore
Kiln Fm
Blenheim
Boars Hill
Bagley Wood
A34
Northfield Brook
KASSAM STADIUM
WATLINGTON ROAD
Garsington
Denton
Kennington
THE THAMES PATH
B480
Baldon Brook
Little London
Sandfordbrake Fm
Southend
Foxcombe Hill
Bayworth
Sandford on Thames
Toot Baldon
The Platt
Chippinghurst Manor
Wootton
Sugworth Fm
Hill Fm
Sunningwell
Lower Fm
Nineveh Fm
Baldon Row
Lower Fm
Blagrove Fm
WOOTTON RD
Radley College
Park Fm
Gotham Fm
Great Copse
Radley Park
Lower Radley
Upper Fm
Marsh Baldon
Chiselhampton Ho
Dunmore Fm
Nuneham Courtenay
Chislehampton
Baldon Ho
Wildmoor
Northcourt
Radley
RADLEY
Camoys Court
Nuneham Ho
Windmill Hill
Little Baldon Fm
B4015
Stadhampton
B4017
Abingdon
Home Fm
Nuneham Park
Baldon Brook
Roundhill Wood
Golden Balls
Wick Hall
Lock Wood
Bus Cen
Clifton Heath
OXFORD ROAD
Rye Fm
THE THAMES PATH
The Coppice
Drayton St Leonard
Abingdon Br
Furze Brake
Back Water
High Lodge
Burcot
Berinsfield
Upper Grange
Caldecott
Clifton Hampden
A415
River
Lower Grange
A329
Stonehill Ho

A44 Woodstock, Evesham
WOLSEY CT
Campsfield
OX20
WOODSTOCK RD
A44
Rowel Brook
WOODSTOCK RD E
WOODSTOCK RD W
Sparrowgap Bridge
Oxford Spires Bsns Pk
THE BOULEVARD
Langford Hall
LANGFORD LA
The Langf Bsns Pk
Oxford Motor Pk
EVENLODE CRES
EVENLODE CRES
Detention Ctr
OX5
BEGBROKE CRES
SANDHILL RD
BEGBROKE LA
WILLOW WAY
ROWEL DR
FOXGLOVE RD
QUARRY END
PO
FERNHILL RD
Rowel Brook
ST MICHAEL'S LA
Priory
Hall Farm
SPRING HILL RD
PH
1 WOODSTOCK RD E
2 WOODSTOCK RD W
3 WOODSTOCK RD
Begbroke
Dolton Lane
Begbroke Hill
Begbroke Science Park
Begbroke Wood
POPPY CL
LIVINGSTONE CL
STANLEY CL
BROAD FIELD RD
A44
THE SPEARS
WOODSTOCK ROAD
GRAVEL PITS LA
WILLOW CL
AYSGARTH RD
FIELD CL
OX29
Spring Hill
Yarnton
College Farm
A
B
C
15
4
3
14
2
1
13
47
5

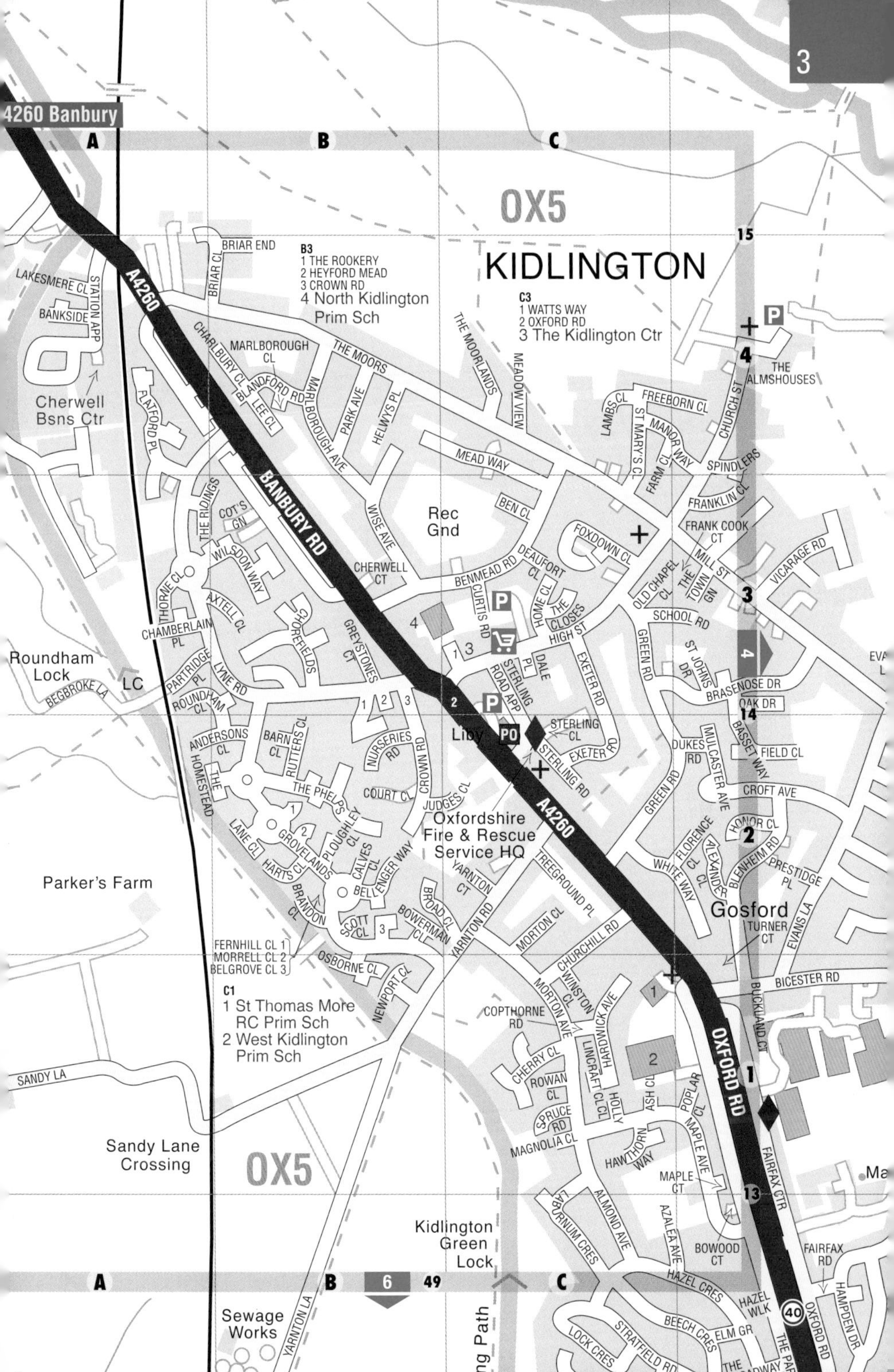

4260 Banbury
OX5
KIDLINGTON
B3
1 THE ROOKERY
2 HEYFORD MEAD
3 CROWN RD
4 North Kidlington Prim Sch
C3
1 WATTS WAY
2 OXFORD RD
3 The Kidlington Ctr
A4260
BANBURY RD
OXFORD RD
Cherwell Bsns Ctr
Roundham Lock
Rec Gnd
Oxfordshire Fire & Rescue Service HQ
Parker's Farm
Gosford
THE ALMSHOUSES
FERNHILL CL 1
MORRELL CL 2
BELGROVE CL 3
C1
1 St Thomas More RC Prim Sch
2 West Kidlington Prim Sch
Sandy Lane Crossing
Kidlington Green Lock
Sewage Works
BRIAR END
BRIAR CL
LAKESMERE CL
STATION APP
BANKSIDE
CHARLBURY CL
MARLBOROUGH CL
BLANDFORD RD
LEE CL
FLATFORD PL
THE MOORS
MARLBOROUGH AVE
PARK AVE
HELWYS PL
THE MOORLANDS
MEADOW VIEW
MEAD WAY
LAMBS CL
FREEBORN CL
ST MARY'S CL
MANOR WAY
FARM CL
CHURCH ST
SPINDLERS
FRANKLIN CL
FRANK COOK CT
MILL ST
VICARAGE RD
THE RIDINGS
COT'S GN
WILSDON WAY
WISE AVE
BEN CL
FOXDOWN CL
BENMEAD RD
DEAUFORT CL
CHERWELL CT
CURTIS RD
HOME CL
THE CLOSES
OLD CHAPEL CL
THE TOWN GN
THORNE CL
AXTELL CL
CHAMBERLAIN PL
CHOREFIELDS
GREYSTONES CT
HIGH ST
SCHOOL RD
GREEN RD
ST JOHNS DR
BRASENOSE DR
OAK DR
PARTRIDGE PL
LYNE RD
ROUNDHAM CL
BEGBROKE LA
LC
STERLING ROAD APP
DALE PL
EXETER RD
STERLING CL
STERLING RD
Liby
PO
ANDERSONS CL
BARN CL
RUTTERS CL
NURSERIES RD
CROWN RD
DUKES RD
MULCASTER AVE
BASSET WAY
FIELD CL
THE HOMESTEAD
THE PHELPS
COURT CL
JUDGES CL
CROFT AVE
HONOR CL
LANE CL
GROVELANDS
PLOUGHLEY CL
CALVES CL
BELLENGER WAY
FLORENCE CL
ALEXANDER CL
BLENHEIM RD
PRESTIDGE PL
HARTS CL
WHITE WAY
YARNTON CT
TREEGROUND PL
BRANDON CL
SCOTT CL
BROAD CL
BOWERMAN CL
YARNTON RD
MORTON CL
CHURCHILL RD
TURNER CT
EVANS LA
OSBORNE CL
NEWPORT CL
WINSTON CL
MORTON AVE
HARDWICK AVE
BICESTER RD
BUCKLAND CT
COPTHORNE RD
CHERRY CL
ROWAN CL
LINCRAFT CL
HOLLY CL
ASH CL
POPLAR CL
SPRUCE RD
MAGNOLIA CL
HAWTHORN WAY
MAPLE AVE
MAPLE CT
FAIRFAX CTR
SANDY LA
LABURNUM CRES
ALMOND AVE
AZALEA AVE
BOWOOD CT
FAIRFAX RD
HAZEL CRES
HAZEL WLK
BEECH CRES
ELM GR
LOCK CRES
STRATFIELD RD
HAMPDEN DR
YARNTON LA

4
6
49

OX5
KIDLINGTON
River Cherwell
Weir
Weir
Hampden Farm
Gosford
Gosford Bridge
Gosford Farm
Gosford Hill Sch
Edward Feild Prim Sch
Kidlington & Gosford Sports Ctr
Mast
Thames Valley Police HQ
THE ALMSHOUSES
A2
1 ANDOVER CT
2 BLENHEIM CT
3 CLEVEDON CT
4 DORCHESTER CT
5 EXETER CT
6 FARNHAM CT
7 GUILDFORD CT
8 HERTFORD CT
1 LOVELACE DR
2 WOODLANDS
OXFORD RD
BICESTER RD
MILL END
WATERMEAD
CHERWELL AVE
QUEENS AVE
WAVERLEY AVE
KINGSWAY DR
EDINBURGH DR
SPRINGFIELD RD
ORCHARD WAY
EVANS CT
EVANS LA
PRESTIDGE PL
BLENHEIM RD
HONOR CL
ALEXANDER CL
FLORENCE CL
WHITE WAY
CROFT AVE
MULCASTER AVE
DUKES RD
BASSET WAY
FIELD CL
OAK DR
BRASENOSE DR
ST JOHNS DR
GREEN RD
SCHOOL RD
OLD CHAPEL CL
THE TOWN GN
MILL ST
VICARAGE RD
PETRE PL
WEBB'S WAY
FRANK COOK CT
FRANKLIN CL
SPINDLERS
CHURCH ST
MANOR WAY
FARM CL
ST MARY'S CL
LAMBS CL
FREEBORN CL
FOXDOWN CL
THE MOORLANDS
MEADOW VIEW
MEAD WAY
BEN CL
BEAUFORT CL
CURTIS RD
HOME CL
THE CLOSES
HIGH ST
DALE PL
STERLING ROAD APP
STERLING CL
EXETER RD
STERLING RD
A4260
TREEGROUND PL
MORTON CL
CHURCHILL RD
WINSTON CL
MORTON AVE
CHERRY CL
ROWAN CL
SPRUCE RD
MAGNOLIA CL
HARDWICK AVE
LINCRAFT CL
HOLLY CL
ASH CL
POPLAR CL
MAPLE AVE
MAPLE CT
HAWTHORN WAY
LABURNUM CRES
AZALEA AVE
BOWOOD CT
HAZEL CRES
HAZEL WLK
BEECH CRES
ELM GR
LOCK CRES
STRATFIELD RD
THE BROADWAY
THE PAR
TURNER CT
GOSFORD HILL CT
BUCKLAND CT
CLEVELAND CL
CROMWELL WAY
CROMWELL WY
FAIRFAX CTR
FAIRFAX RD
HAMPDEN DR
GOSFORD CL
BEAGLES CL
WATER EATON LA
A34
OX2
Water Eato
Crossing
A
B
C
15
14
13
50
7
40
PH

A44
A
B
2
C
POPPY CL
LIVINGSTONE CL
SANDY LA
Begbroke Wood
STANLEY CL
BROAD FIELD RD
RYDER CL
13
WOODSTOCK ROAD
GRAVEL PITS LA
THE SPEARS
College Farm
Yarnton
WILLOW CL
AYSGARTH RD
FIELD CL
4
OX5
WOODSTOCK ROAD
RUTTEN LA
THE GARTH
FLETCHER CL
PO
MEADOW WAY
Yarnton House
William Fletcher Prim Sch
BARTHOLOMEW AVE
SPENCER AVE
DASHWOOD AVE
FOLLETS CL
Frogwelldown Lane
STOUTSFIELD CL
MERTON WAY
GREAT CLOSE RD
MARSH CL
PH
Little Blenheim
3
LITTLE BLENHEIM
BERNARD CL
Hill Farm
THE PADDOCKS
6
POUND CL
STOCKS TREE CL
CASSINGTON RD
12
PARK CL
Ind Est
The Red Lion (PH)
CHURCH LA
CASSINGTON RD
2
Manor House
Mead Farm
1
OX29
11
Oxey Mead
47
48
OX2
A40

KIDLINGTON
Sandy Lane Crossing
SANDY LA
A
3
B
C
COPTHORNE RD
CHERRY CL
ROWAN
SPRUCE RD
MAGNOLIA CL
LINCRAFT CL
HARDWICK AVE
HAWTHORN WAY
HOLLY
LABURNUM CRES
ALMOND AVE
STANLEY CL
BROAD FIELD RD
RYDER CL
13
WOODSTOCK ROAD
GRAVEL PITS LA
College Farm
4
AYSGARTH RD
FIELD CL
WOODSTOCK ROAD
Sewage Works
YARNTON LA
Kidlington Green Lock
Towing Path
LOCK CRES
STRATFIELD
CROXFORD GDNS
Garden City
THE GARTH
FLETCHER CL
PO
MEADOW WAY
SPENCER AVE
DASHWOOD AVE
FOLLETS CL
A44
OX5
MERTON WAY
GREAT CLOSE RD
MARSH CL
PH
LC
Oxford Canal Walk
Oxford Canal
3
BERNARD CL
THE PADDOCK
5
STOCKS TREE CL
12
CASSINGTON RD
MEAD RD
PARK CL
Ind Est
WOODSTOCK RD
Ickworth
CHURCH LA
Stonehouse Farm
2
Kingsbridge Brook
Mead Farm
Frieze Farm
1
Loop Farm
A44
A4260
11
Peartree Hill
A44
Oxey Mead
PEARTREE INTERCHANGE
48
A
8
B
49
C
OX2
A40
Duke's Lock
A34
A44
Red Barn

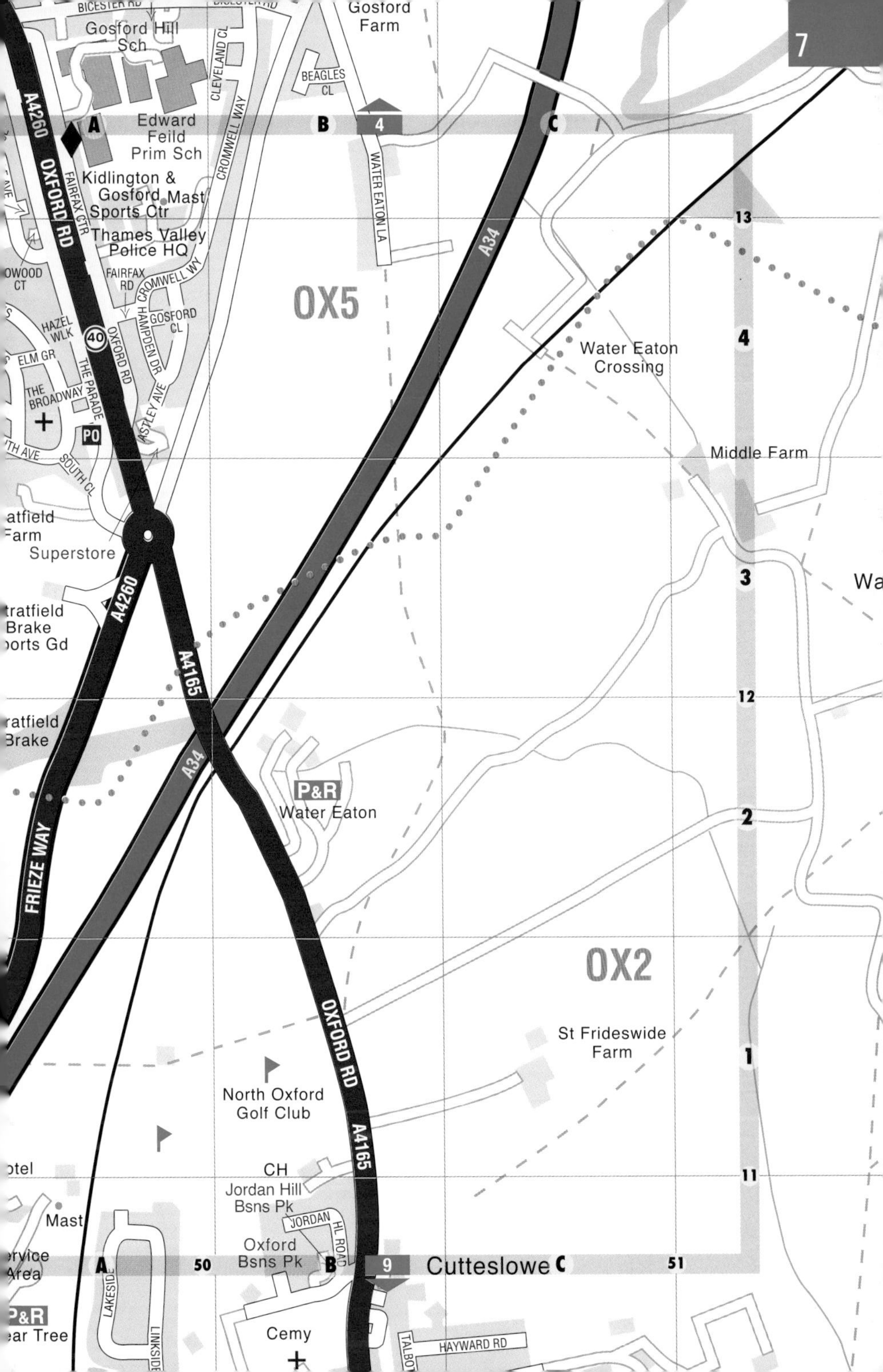

BICESTER RD
Gosford Farm
Gosford Hill Sch
CLEVELAND CL
BEAGLES CL
A
B
4
C
Edward Feild Prim Sch
CROMWELL WAY
WATER EATON LA
A4260
OXFORD RD
FAIRFAX CTR
Kidlington & Gosford Sports Ctr
Mast
Thames Valley Police HQ
13
A34
OWOOD CT
FAIRFAX RD
CROMWELL WY
OX5
HAZEL WLK
40
HAMPDEN DR
GOSFORD CL
4
Water Eaton Crossing
ELM GR
OXFORD RD
THE PARADE
THE BROADWAY
ASTLEY AVE
PO
TH AVE
SOUTH CL
Middle Farm
atfield Farm
Superstore
A4260
3
Wa
tratfield Brake
ports Gd
A4165
12
ratfield Brake
A34
P&R
Water Eaton
2
FRIEZE WAY
OX2
OXFORD RD
St Frideswide Farm
1
North Oxford Golf Club
A4165
otel
CH
11
Jordan Hill Bsns Pk
Mast
JORDAN HL ROAD
ervice Area
A
50
Oxford Bsns Pk
B
9
Cutteslowe
C
51
LAKESIDE
P&R
ear Tree
LINKSIDE
Cemy
TALBOT
HAYWARD RD

Frieze Farm
Kingsbr
Loop Farm
A
6
B
C
A44
A4260
OX5
Peartree Hill
A34
11
A40 Witney, Cheltenham
PEARTREE INTERCHANGE
Oxey Mead
OX2
4
Duke's Lock
A44
Red Barn Farm Cottage
River Thames or Isis
A40
WESTERN BY-PASS RD
NORTHERN BY- PASS R
King's Weir
Pixey Mead
King's Lock
3
Hotel
Manor Farm
A34
10
GOOSE GREEN CL
Weir
CLIFFORD PL
HOME CL
ROSAMUND RD
ELMTHORPE RD
Wolvercote
Pixey Mead
Paper Mill
2
MILL RD
GODSTOW RD
MILLSTREAM CT
PH
MEADOW PROSPECT
ROWLAND CL
DREWETT CT
WEBB'S CL
CHURCHILL PL 1
FAIRLAWN FLATS 2
SHERIFF'S DR 3
BLANDFORD AVE 4
THE QUADRANGLE 5
CYPRUS TERR 6
CHURCH LA 7
DOVE HO CL 8
Wolvercote Prim Sch 9
P
Thames Bridge
Lower Wolvercote
Trout Inn (PH)
Wolvercote Common
1
OX2
Woodview
Weir
A34
Godstow Abbey
(remains of)
09
Godstow Lock
48
A
12
B
49
C
Wytham
Linch Farm
Godstow Holt
Port Meadow

St Frideswide Farm
North Oxford Golf Club
OXFORD RD
A4165
7
A
B
C
CH
Jordan Hill Bsns Pk
JORDAN HL ROAD
Oxford Bsns Pk
OX2
Cutteslowe
C3
1 MILLER'S ACRE
2 SUNNYMEADE CT
3 WYATT RD
HASLEMERE GDNS
Mast
LAKESIDE
LINKSIDE AVE
Cemy
TALBOT RD
HAYWARD RD
HARBORD RD
PARK CL
PENNYWELL DR
Sports Gd
SOLLERSHOTT
LOVELACE SQ
BANBURY RD
LOVELACE RD
TEMPLAR RD
FOXTON CL
CAREY CL
FIVE MILE DR
ROTHAFIELD RD
KIRK CL
MARRIOTT CL
BOURNE CL
KENDALL CRES
PO
RIDDELL PL
HAREFIELDS
DAVID WALTER CL
SPARSEY PL
PRIOR'S FORGE
HOLT WEER CL
Cutteslowe Park
Cutteslowe Prim Sch
11
4
3
A44
SUNDERLAND AVE
A40
NORTH WAY
ELSFIELD WAY
HAWKSMOOR RD
JACKSON RD
PRIORY CT
10
WOLVERCOTE RDBT
Oxford Study Centre
BLANDFORD AVE
BANBURY RD RDBT
DAVENANT CT
CARLTON RD
WOLSEY RD
WREN RD
A4144
WOODSTOCK RD
DAVENANT RD
UPLAND PARK RD
SOUTHDALE RD
CAVENDISH RD
BODLEY PL
BUCKLER RD
SCOTT RD
ALDRICH RD
Recn Gd
FAIRLAWN END
MERE RD
FIRST TURN
ST PETER'S RD
PIXEY PL
PLOUGH CL
ULFGAR RD
BLADON CL
WOODSTOCK CL
SUMMERTOWN HO
WENTWORTH RD
SALISBURY CRES
GRIMBLY PL
ISLIP RD
MEADOW VIEW
EATON CT
WATER EATON RD
CHERWELL LODGE
BLENHEIM DR
WOODSTOCK CL FLATS
APSLEY RD
HERONS PL
HERNES CL
HARPES RD
2
Upper Wolvercote
WYNDHAM WAY
BLENHEIM CT
WOODSTOCK RD
FIELD HOUSE DR
MULBERRY CT
THE PADDOX
PADDOX CL
HERNES CRES
HERNES RD
THE FIRS
WEST GR
AVERY CT
Sunnymead
SQUITCHEY LA
CAPEL CL
VICTORIA GATE
VICTORIA RD
KING'S CROSS RD
LUCERNE RD
HAWKSWELL HO
HAWKSWELL GDNS
Oxford Canal
RICHARDS LA
SUMMERHILL RD
HAMILTON RD
Lynams Sch
HYDE PL
MARTIN CT
HOBSON RD
DUDLEY CT
PORTLAND RD
WOODSTOCK CT 1
RIDGEMONT CL 2
SUMMERTOWN CT 3
BISHOP KIRK PL
NEWCOMBE CT
MIDDLE WAY
GROVE ST
LONSDALE RD
OSBERTON RD
CENTURY ROW
ROGERS ST
1
Playing Field
PARMA HO
Liby
ST EDWARD'S AVE
MAYFIELD RD
Summer Fields Sch
SOUTH PAR
STRATFIELD RD
SUMMERFIELD RD
Summertown
St Edwards Sch
Northern House Sch
EWERT PL
Ferry Sports Ctr
The Cherwell Sch
09
Oxford Canal Walk
OAKTHORPE RD
DIAMOND PL
DORCHESTER CT
FERRY POOL RD
50
13
51
B4495
Sports Ctr
THORNCLIFFE RD
RADLEY HO
LARK HILL
BEECH CROFT RD
MARSTON FERRY CT
Oxford Hi
P&R
Mast
30

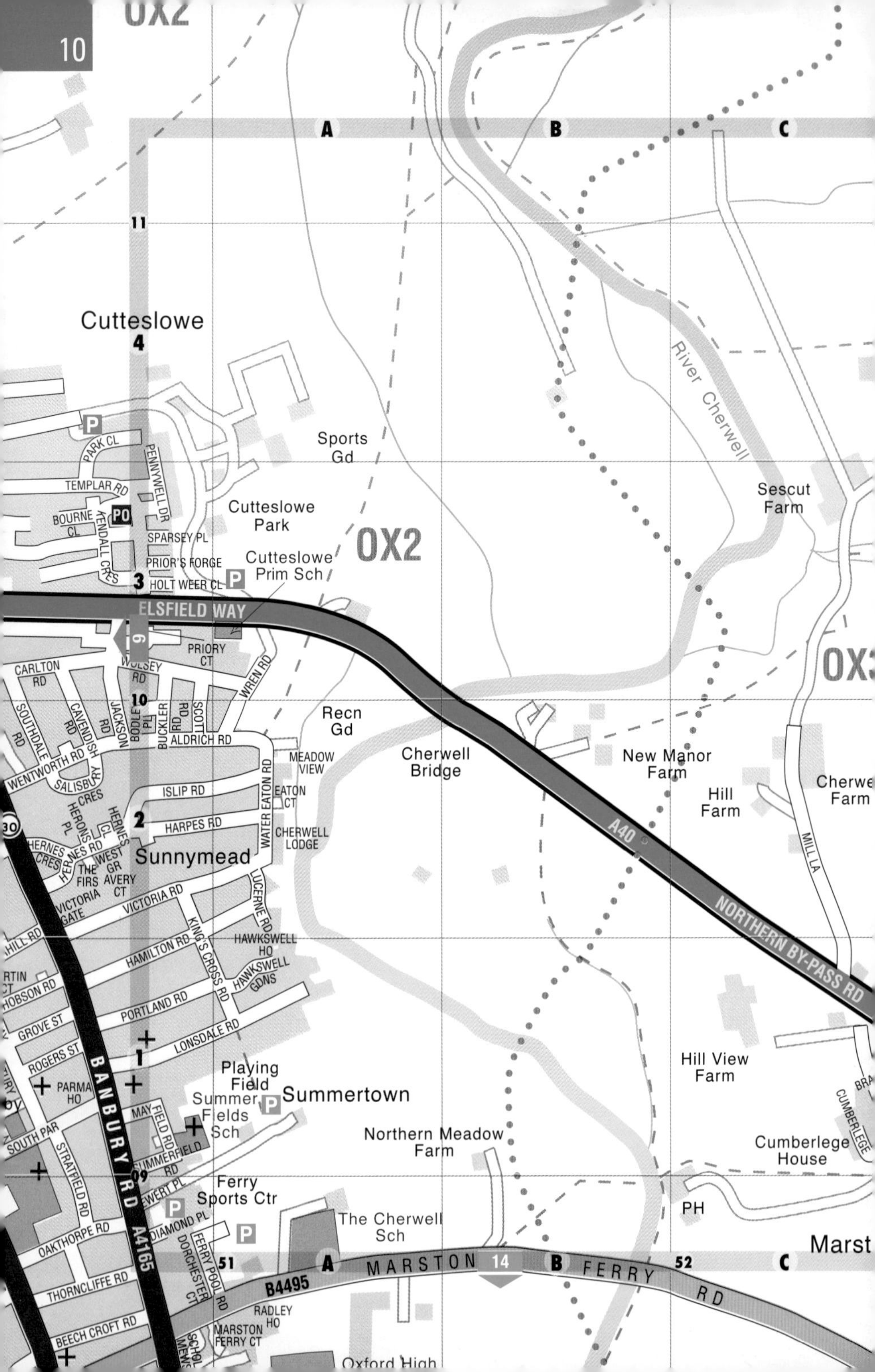
OX2
A
B
C
11
Cutteslowe
4
River Cherwell
Sports Gd
Cutteslowe Park
OX2
Cutteslowe Prim Sch
Sescut Farm
PARK CL
TEMPLAR RD
PENNYWELL DR
BOURNE CL
KENDALL CRES
PO
SPARSEY PL
PRIOR'S FORGE
HOLT WEER CL
3
ELSFIELD WAY
9
PRIORY CT
WOLSEY RD
CARLTON RD
CAVENDISH RD
JACKSON RD
SOUTHDALE RD
10
BODLEY PL
BUCKLER RD
SCOTT RD
WREN RD
ALDRICH RD
Recn Gd
Cherwell Bridge
New Manor Farm
Hill Farm
Cherwell Farm
WENTWORTH RD
SALISBURY CRES
MEADOW VIEW
EATON CT
WATER EATON RD
ISLIP RD
HARPES RD
2
HERONS PL
HERNES CL
HERNES RD
HERNES CRES
WEST GR
THE FIRS
AVERY CT
Sunnymead
CHERWELL LODGE
A40
MILL LA
VICTORIA GATE
VICTORIA RD
LUCERNE RD
NORTHERN BY-PASS RD
HAWKSWELL HO
HAWKSWELL GDNS
KING'S CROSS RD
HAMILTON RD
HOBSON RD
PORTLAND RD
GROVE ST
LONSDALE RD
ROGERS ST
1
Playing Field
PARMA HO
BANBURY RD
A4165
Summer Fields Sch
Summertown
Hill View Farm
MAYFIELD RD
SOUTH PAR
STRATFIELD RD
SUMMERFIELD RD
Northern Meadow Farm
Cumberlege House
CUMBERLEGE
09
EWERT PL
Ferry Sports Ctr
PH
DIAMOND PL
OAKTHORPE RD
DORCHESTER CT
FERRY POOL RD
The Cherwell Sch
Marst
51
A
MARSTON
14
B
FERRY
52
C
RD
B4495
THORNCLIFFE RD
RADLEY HO
BEECH CROFT RD
MARSTON FERRY CT
SCHOOL MEWS
Oxford High

Woodeaton Wood
Forest Farm
Long Wood
Sewage Works
Little Wood
Home Farm
Manor House
Elsfield
Church Farm
Pennywell Wood
Hill Farm
OX3
Marston Common
St Nicholas Pk (Caravan Pk)
B4150
A40
15
Cemy
LODGE CL
CHURCH LA
BUTTS LA
PONDS LA
LITTLE ACREAGE
ELSFIELD RD
CANNONS FIELD
WHITE HART
SOUTHCROFT
A
B
C
11
4
3
10
2
1
09
53
54

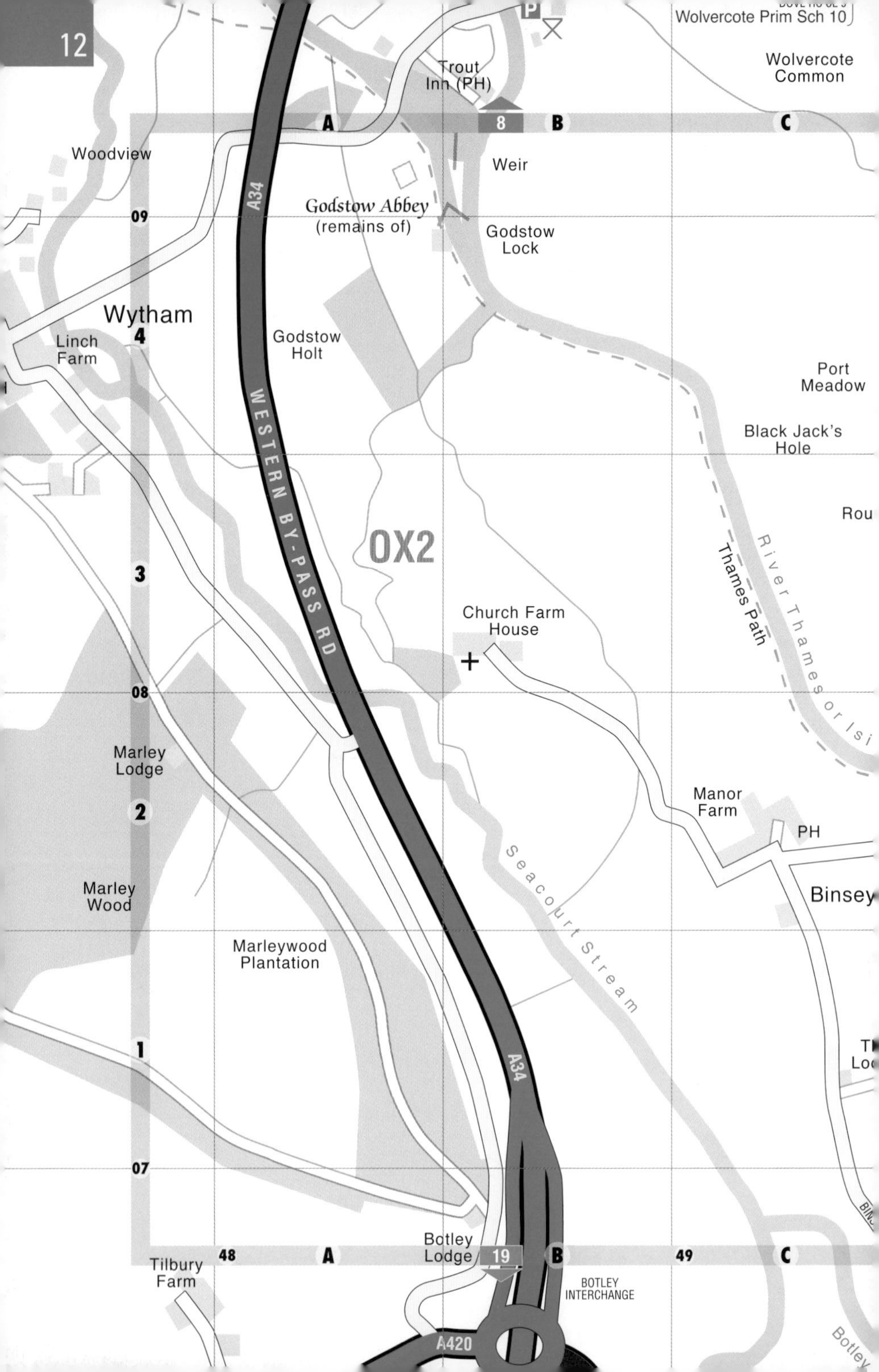

Wolvercote Prim Sch 10

Wolvercote
Common

Trout
Inn (PH)

Woodview

A | **8** | **B** | **C**

Weir

Godstow Abbey
(remains of)

Godstow
Lock

09

Wytham **4**

Linch
Farm

Godstow
Holt

Port
Meadow

Black Jack's
Hole

Rou

OX2

River Thames or Isi

Thames Path

3

Church Farm
House

WESTERN BY-PASS RD

A34

08

Marley
Lodge

Manor
Farm

PH

2

Binsey

Marley
Wood

Seacourt Stream

Marleywood
Plantation

1

T
Loc

A34

07

Bin

Tilbury
Farm

48 | **A** | Botley
Lodge **19** | **B** | **49** | **C**

BOTLEY
INTERCHANGE

A420

Botley

Summertown
North Oxford
Walton Manor
Jericho
OX2
OX1
Oxford Canal
Oxford Canal Walk
Castle Mill Stream
Fiddler's Island
Medley Manor Farm
Willow Walk
Isis Lock
A4144
A4165
B4495
WOODSTOCK RD
BANBURY RD
MORETON RD
ST GILES'
St Edwards Sch
Northern House Sch
Sports Ctr
Playing Field
Summer Fields Sch
Ferry Sports Ctr
The Cherwell Sch
Oxford High Sch
St Clares Oxford
Univ Coll Oxford (Annexe)
Swan Sch of Eng
Regent Sch
D'Overbroecks Coll
St Aloysius RC Prim Sch
SS Philip & James CE Prim Sch
St Hugh's Coll
Kellogg Coll
St Annes Coll
Somerville Coll
Keble Coll
St Johns Coll
Balliol Coll
Ruskin Coll
Walton Manor Cemy
Liby
PARK TOWN

Summertown
Playing Field
Summer Fields Sch
Northern Meadow Farm
Hill View Farm
Cumberlege House
Ferry Sports Ctr
The Cherwell Sch
PH
Marston
MARSTON FERRY RD
OX2
OX3
OX1
Oxford High Sch
St Clares Oxford
Wolfson Coll
River Cherwell
St Nicholas Prim Sch
Marston Brook
A2
1 Greycotes Oxford High Sch
2 St Clares Bardwell Road Centre
3 Wychwood Sch
4 The Oxford English Ctr
Swan Sch of Eng
Regent Sch
Dragon Sch
Boat Houses
Park Town
Lady Margaret Hall Coll
St Hugh's Coll
Kellogg Coll
Sports Grounds
Norham Manor
University Parks
Park Farm
St Annes Coll
University Mus & Pitt Rivers Mus
Mesopotamia Walk
Weir
Somerville Coll
Keble Coll
Linacre Coll
Great Meadow
Jericho
St Johns Coll
Balliol Coll
Trinity
Ruskin Coll
St Edwards Sch
WOODSTOCK RD
BANBURY RD
A4165
A4144
ST GILES'
B4495
MORETON RD
LONSDALE RD
SOUTH PARADE
STRATFIELD RD
OAKTHORPE RD
THORNCLIFFE RD
BEECH CROFT RD
LATHBURY RD
STAVERTON RD
CHALFONT RD
POLSTEAD RD
ST MARGARET'S RD
FARNDON RD
WARNBOROUGH RD
LECKFORD RD
PLANTATION RD
ST BERNARD'S RD
OBSERVATORY ST
ADELAIDE ST
WALTON CRES
NELSON ST
RICHMOND RD
BELBROUGHTON RD
CHARLBURY RD
GARFORD RD
NORTHMOOR PL
NORTH MOOR RD
LINTON RD
CHADLINGTON RD
BARDWELL RD
NORHAM RD
FYFIELD RD
CRICK RD
BRADMORE RD
NORHAM GDNS
CANTERBURY RD
WINCHESTER RD
BEVINGTON RD
KEBLE RD
BLACKHALL RD
PARKS RD
SOUTH PARKS RD
MANSFIELD RD
ST CROSS RD
MANOR RD
A
B
C
10
13
58
21
51
52

NORTHERN BY-PASS RD
A40
B4150
11
OX3
Court Place Farm
(Oxford City FC)
Bayswater Brook
Cemy
Back Lane
Liby
MARSH LA
CHERWELL DR
B4495
New Marston Prim Sch
New Marston
Headington
Ruskin Coll
John Radcliffe
John Radcliffe Hospl Sch
St Josephs RC Prim Sch
Oxford Brookes Univ
HEADLEY WAY
Rye St Antony Sch
Headington Hill
St Michaels CE First Sch
EF Int Lang Sch
Cuckoo La
Headington Sch
A420
HEADINGTON RD
MARSTON RD
The Manor
JACK STRAW'S LA
OXFORD RD
ELSFIELD RD
PONDS LA
DENTS CL
ELMS DR
COPSE LA
DERWENT AVE
CONISTON AVE
BOWNESS AVE
AMBLESIDE DR
EDEN DR
SAXON WAY
DUNSTAN RD
OSLER RD
STAUNTON RD
SANDFIELD RD
WILLIAM ST
1 HASTOE GRANGE
2 HEADLEY HO
3 RAYSON HO
ALESWORTH GR 1
BROADHEAD PL 2
22
16
A
B
C
09
08
07
53
54

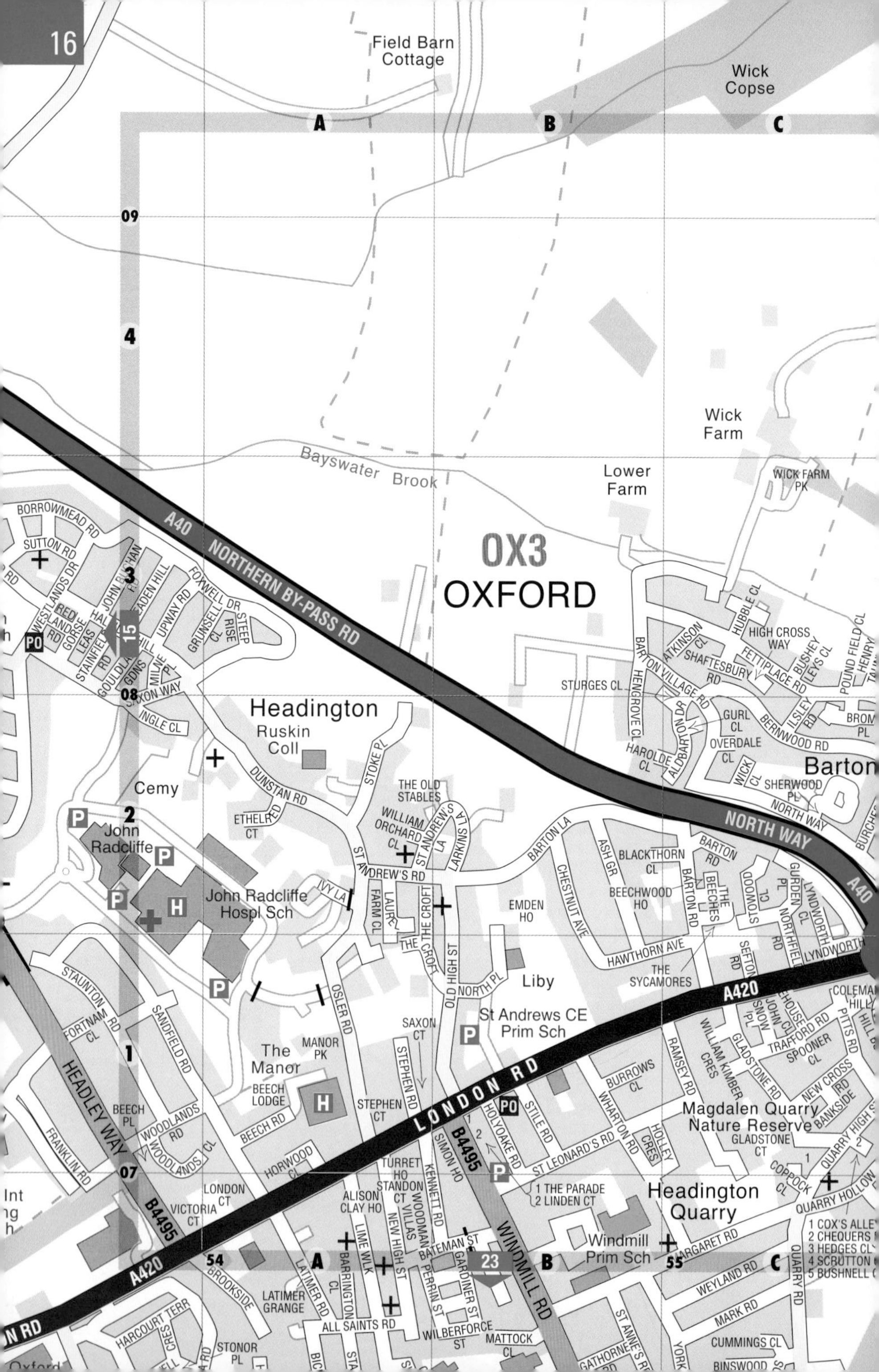
Field Barn Cottage
Wick Copse
A
B
C
09
4
Bayswater Brook
Wick Farm
Lower Farm
WICK FARM PK
OX3
OXFORD
A40 NORTHERN BY-PASS RD
BORROWMEAD RD
SUTTON RD
WESTLANDS DR
JOHN BUCHAN RD
EDEN HILL
UPWAY RD
FOXWELL DR
GRUNSELL CL
RISE
STEEP
3
15
PO
GOULDLAND GDNS
MILNE PL
SAXON WAY
08
INGLE CL
Headington
Ruskin Coll
STOKE PL
Cemy
DUNSTAN RD
ETHELRED CT
2
John Radcliffe
John Radcliffe Hospl Sch
THE OLD STABLES
WILLIAM ORCHARD CL
ST ANDREW'S LA
LARKINS LA
ST ANDREW'S RD
IVY LA
FARM CL
THE CROFT
OLD HIGH ST
NORTH PL
Liby
EMDEN HO
BARTON LA
ASH GR
CHESTNUT AVE
BLACKTHORN CL
BEECHWOOD HO
BARTON RD
THE BEECHES
HAWTHORN AVE
THE SYCAMORES
STURGES CL
HENGROVE CL
BARTON VILLAGE RD
ATKINSON CL
HUBBLE CL
HIGH CROSS WAY
SHAFTESBURY
FETTIPLACE RD
BUSHEY LEYS CL
POUND FIELD CL
HAROLDE CL
ALDBARTON DR
GURL CL
OVERDALE CL
BERNWOOD RD
ILSLEY RD
WICK CL
SHERWOOD PL
NORTH WAY
Barton
A40
STOWOOD CL
GURDEN PL
NORTHFIELD RD
LYNDWORTH CL
SEFTON RD
SNOW PL
JOHN CL
A420
STAUNTON RD
FORTNAM CL
SANDFIELD RD
1
HEADLEY WAY
FRANKLIN RD
BEECH PL
WOODLANDS RD
WOODLANDS CL
07
OSLER RD
MANOR PK
The Manor
BEECH LODGE
BEECH RD
SAXON CT
STEPHEN RD
STEPHEN CT
St Andrews CE Prim Sch
LONDON RD
HOLYOAKE RD
STILE RD
B4495
BURROWS CL
RAMSEY RD
WILLIAM KIMBER CRES
GLADSTONE RD
TRAFFORD RD
PITTS RD
SPOONER CL
NEW CROSS RD
BANKSIDE
Magdalen Quarry Nature Reserve
GLADSTONE CT
WHARTON RD
HOLLEY CRES
ST LEONARD'S RD
COPPOCK CL
QUARRY HIGH ST
QUARRY HOLLOW
1 THE PARADE
2 LINDEN CT
Headington Quarry
HORWOOD CL
TURRET HO
STANDON CT
KENNETT RD
SIMON HO
ALISON CLAY HO
WOODMAN VILLAS
LONDON CT
VICTORIA CT
LIME WLK
NEW HIGH ST
BATEMAN ST
GARDINER ST
PERRIN ST
WINDMILL RD
23
Windmill Prim Sch
MARGARET RD
55
WEYLAND RD
QUARRY RD
1 COX'S ALLE
2 CHEQUERS
3 HEDGES CL
4 SCRUTTON
5 BUSHNELL
54
BROOKSIDE
BARRINGTON CL
LATIMER GRANGE
LATIMER RD
ALL SAINTS RD
WILBERFORCE ST
MATTOCK CL
MARK RD
CUMMINGS CL
BINSWOOD
ST ANNE'S RD
GATHORNE RD
YORK
HARCOURT TERR
STONOR PL
A420
COLEMAN HILL
HILL RD
LYNDWORTH
BROM PL
BURCHES
HENRY TAUNT

A
B
C
BAYSWATER RD
Shepherd's Pit
OX33
09
4
Crem
Ashen Copse
3
STOWFORD CT
Baynards Hill Prim Sch
Stowford Farm
Bayswater Mill
TAGGS GATE
08
STOWFORD RD
WAYNFLETE RD
ROUTH RD
MATHER RD
HANDLO PL
BASSETT RD
BASSETT RD
HUMFREY RD
WATERMILL WAY
BAYSWATER FARM RD
BAYSWATER FARM
WILCOTE RD
BAYSWATER ROAD
CRANLEY RD
WAYNFLETE RD
ROBERTS CL
Sandhills
HILL VIEW
2
AMPTON RD
MALFORD RD
THE DALE
COLWELL DR
BURDELL AVE
DELBUSH AVE
Sandhills Prim Sch
CLAYMOND RD
MEREWOOD AVE
TERRETT AVE
CRESS HILL PL
GREEN RIDGES
ELTON CL
SWEETGREEN CL
Pool
WAYNFLETE RD
HOSKER CL
BURSILL CL
LYDIA CL
HEADINGTON RDBT
THE ROUNDWAY
BURLINGTON CRES
A40
LONDON RD
A40 M40 Juncs 8a,8
OX3
A4142
FOREST RD
GREEN RD
THE LARCHES
DOWNSIDE END
ROWLANDS HO
P&R
Thornhill
RIDGEWAY RD
THE LINK
STANWAY RD
1
COLLINWOOD RD
DOWNSIDE RD
POND CL
Swilly
Thornhill Farm
COLLINWOOD CL
RINGWOOD RD
EASTERN BY-PASS RD
DOWNSIDE RD
PO
STANWAY RD
Risinghurst
GROVELANDS RD
07
KILN LA
SHELLEY CL
COLLINWOOD RD
BAKER CL
RICHARDS WAY
NETHERWOODS RD
KILN LA
SPRING LA
NACRE CT
A
56
B
24
C
57
WYCHWOOD LA
Monk's Wood
SLAYMAKER CL

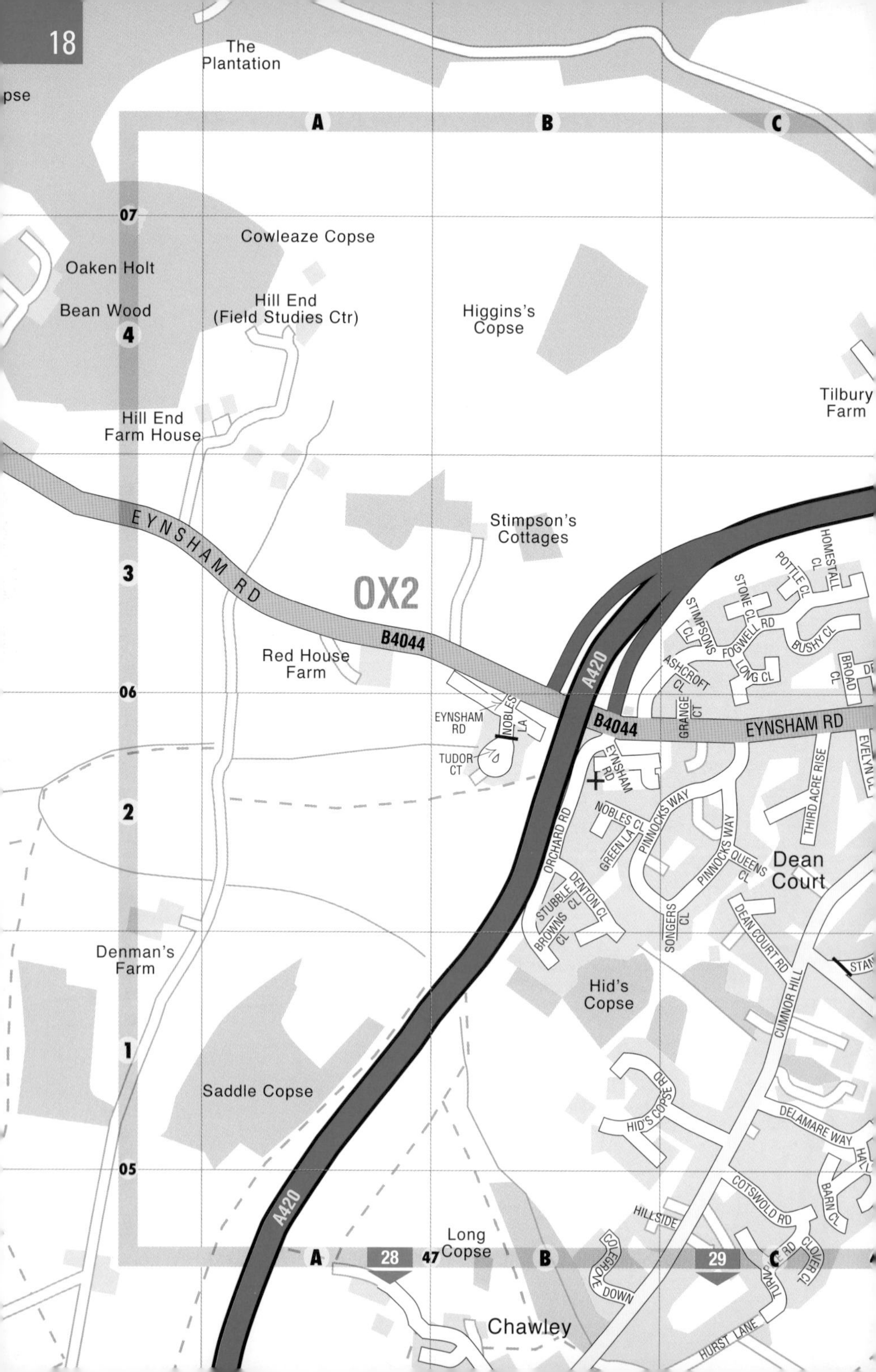
The Plantation
pse
A
B
C
07
Cowleaze Copse
Oaken Holt
Bean Wood
Hill End (Field Studies Ctr)
Higgins's Copse
4
Tilbury Farm
Hill End Farm House
EYNSHAM RD
Stimpson's Cottages
3
OX2
B4044
Red House Farm
06
EYNSHAM RD
NOBLES LA
TUDOR CT
A420
B4044
EYNSHAM RD
GRANGE CT
ASHCROFT CL
STIMPSONS CL
STONE CL
FOGWELL RD
LONG CL
POTTLE CL
HOMESTALL CL
BUSHY CL
BROAD CL
EVELYN CL
THIRD ACRE RISE
2
ORCHARD RD
NOBLES CL
GREEN LA
PINNOCKS WAY
QUEENS CL
Dean Court
STUBBLE CL
DENTON CL
BROWNS CL
SONGERS CL
DEAN COURT RD
STAN
Denman's Farm
Hid's Copse
CUMNOR HILL
1
Saddle Copse
HID'S COPSE RD
DELAMARE WAY
05
COTSWOLD RD
BARN CL
HILLSIDE
A420
Long Copse
A
28
47
B
29
C
COLEGROVE DOWN
TURNS RD
CLOVER CL
Chawley
HURST LANE

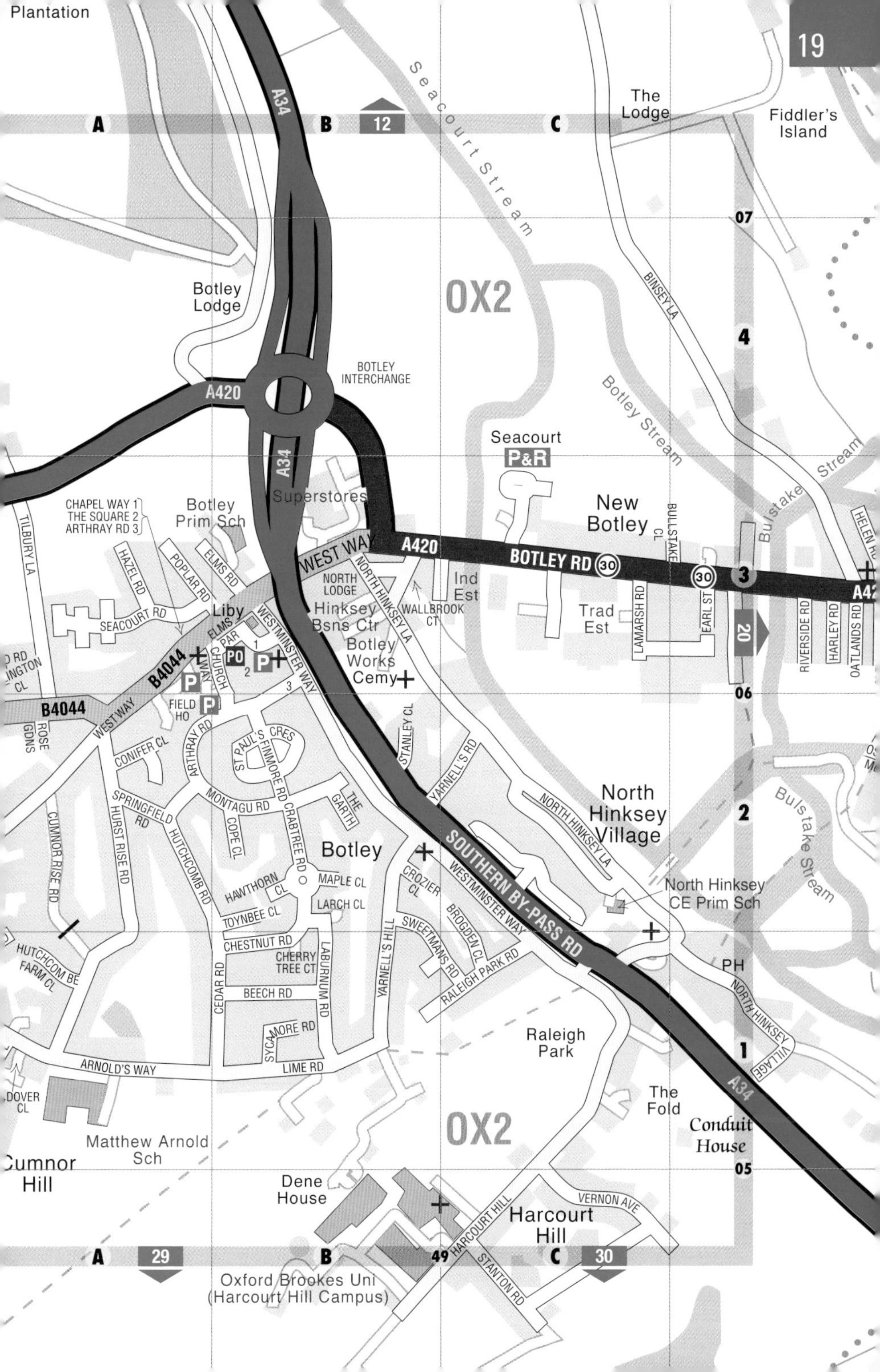

Plantation
The Lodge
Fiddler's Island
A
B
12
C
Seacourt Stream
07
Botley Lodge
OX2
BINSEY LA
4
BOTLEY INTERCHANGE
A420
A34
Botley Stream
Seacourt
P&R
Bulstake Stream
Superstores
New Botley
CHAPEL WAY 1
THE SQUARE 2
ARTHRAY RD 3
Botley Prim Sch
BULLSTAKE CL
HELEN RD
TILBURY LA
HAZEL RD
POPLAR RD
ELMS RD
WEST WAY
NORTH LODGE
NORTH HINKSEY LA
A420
BOTLEY RD
30
Ind Est
3
SEACOURT RD
Liby
ELMS PAR
WESTMINSTER WAY
Hinksey Bsns Ctr
WALLBROOK CT
Trad Est
LAMARSH RD
EARL ST
20
RIVERSIDE RD
HARLEY RD
OATLANDS RD
B4044
CHURCH WAY
PO
P
Botley Works Cemy
FIELD HO
06
B4044
ROSE GDNS
WEST WAY
ARTHRAY RD
ST PAUL'S CRES
STANLEY CL
CONIFER CL
FINMORE RD
YARNELL'S RD
MONTAGU RD
THE GARTH
NORTH HINKSEY LA
North Hinksey Village
2
Bulstake Stream
SPRINGFIELD RD
HURST RISE RD
HUTCHCOMB RD
CUMNOR RISE RD
COPE CL
CRABTREE RD
Botley
SOUTHERN BY-PASS RD
HAWTHORN CL
MAPLE CL
LARCH CL
CROZIER CL
WESTMINSTER WAY
North Hinksey CE Prim Sch
TOYNBEE CL
BROGDEN CL
SWEETMANS RD
HUTCHCOMBE FARM CL
CHESTNUT RD
CHERRY TREE CT
LABURNUM RD
YARNELL'S HILL
RALEIGH PARK RD
PH
CEDAR RD
BEECH RD
NORTH HINKSEY VILLAGE
SYCAMORE RD
Raleigh Park
1
ARNOLD'S WAY
LIME RD
The Fold
A34
Conduit House
OX2
Matthew Arnold Sch
Cumnor Hill
05
Dene House
VERNON AVE
HARCOURT HILL
Harcourt Hill
A
29
B
49
C
30
STANTON RD
Oxford Brookes Uni (Harcourt Hill Campus)

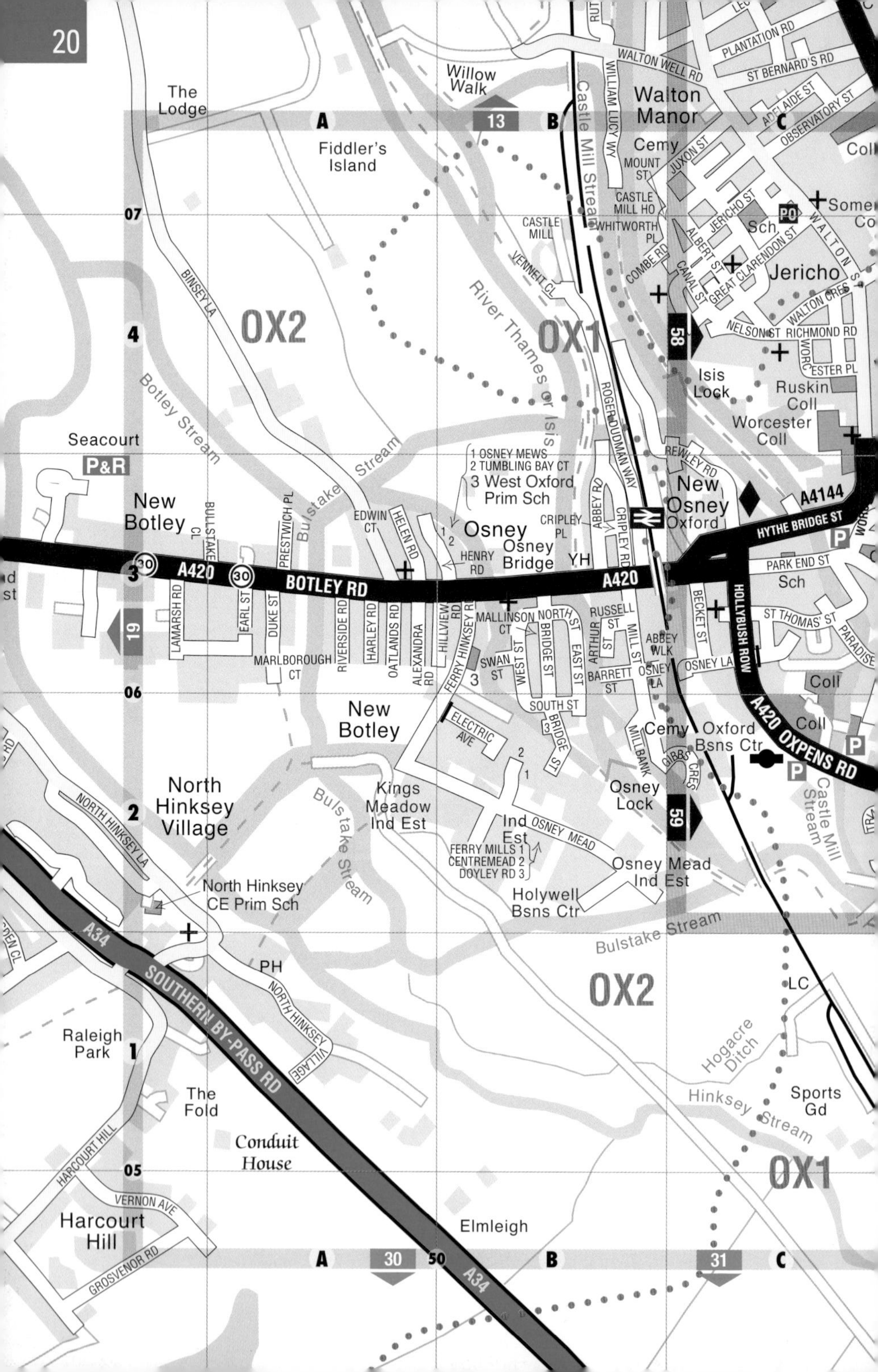

The Lodge
Willow Walk
Fiddler's Island
Walton Manor
Cemy
Jericho
OX2
OX1
Botley Stream
Bulstake Stream
River Thames or Isis
Castle Mill Stream
Seacourt
P&R
New Botley
Osney
Osney Bridge
New Osney
Oxford
A420
BOTLEY RD
A4144
HYTHE BRIDGE ST
A420 OXPENS RD
HOLLYBUSH ROW
Isis Lock
Ruskin Coll
Worcester Coll
Oxford Bsns Ctr
Osney Lock
Kings Meadow Ind Est
Ind Est
Osney Mead Ind Est
Holywell Bsns Ctr
North Hinksey Village
North Hinksey CE Prim Sch
PH
A34
SOUTHERN BY-PASS RD
Raleigh Park
The Fold
Conduit House
Harcourt Hill
Elmleigh
Hogacre Ditch
Hinksey Stream
Sports Gd
LC
1 OSNEY MEWS
2 TUMBLING BAY CT
3 West Oxford Prim Sch
FERRY MILLS 1
CENTREMEAD 2
DOYLEY RD 3
13
19
30
31
58
59

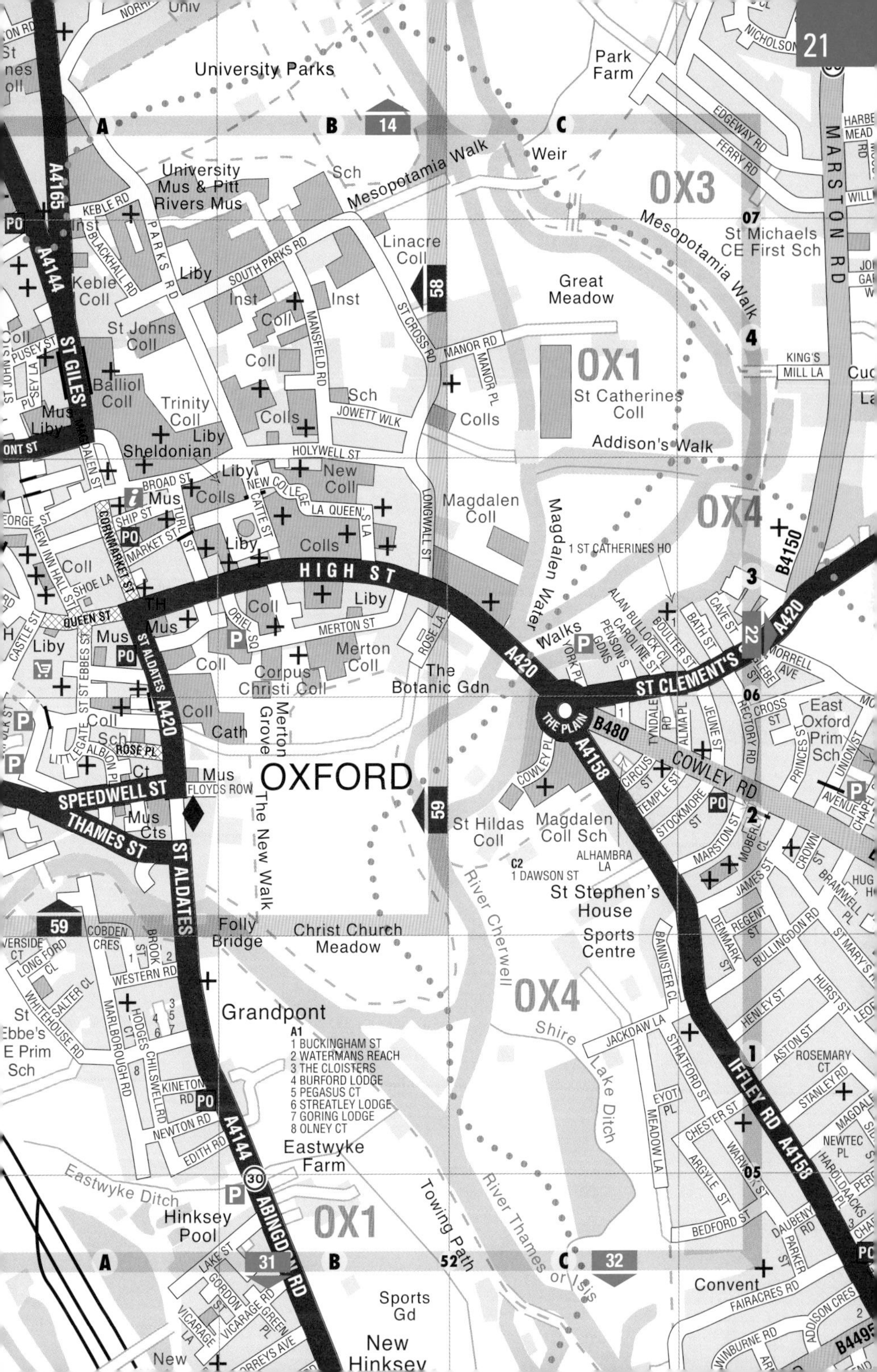

University Parks
Park Farm
A
B
14
C
Weir
OX3
University Mus & Pitt Rivers Mus
Sch
Mesopotamia Walk
Linacre Coll
58
St Michaels CE First Sch
Keble Coll
Liby
Inst
Great Meadow
St Johns Coll
Coll
Mansfield Rd
St Cross Rd
Manor Rd
OX1
St Catherines Coll
Balliol Coll
Trinity Coll
Sch
Colls
Sheldonian
Liby
Addison's Walk
Holywell St
New Coll
Magdalen Coll
OX4
Magdalen Water
1 St Catherines Ho
High St
Mus
Coll
Liby
Merton St
Merton Coll
Walks
St Clement's
22
A420
Corpus Christi Coll
The Botanic Gdn
The Plain
B480
Cowley Rd
East Oxford Prim Sch
Cath
Merton Grove
Speedwell St
Thames St
St Aldates
OXFORD
59
The New Walk
St Hildas Coll
Magdalen Coll Sch
Alhambra La
C2
1 Dawson St
St Stephen's House
River Cherwell
Folly Bridge
Christ Church Meadow
Sports Centre
OX4
Grandpont
Shire Lake Ditch
A1
1 Buckingham St
2 Watermans Reach
3 The Cloisters
4 Burford Lodge
5 Pegasus Ct
6 Streatley Lodge
7 Goring Lodge
8 Olney Ct
Eastwyke Farm
Iffley Rd
A4158
Eastwyke Ditch
Hinksey Pool
OX1
Towing Path
River Thames or Isis
A
31
B
52
C
32
Convent
Sports Gd
New Hinksey
Abingdon Rd
A4144
Marston Rd
B4150

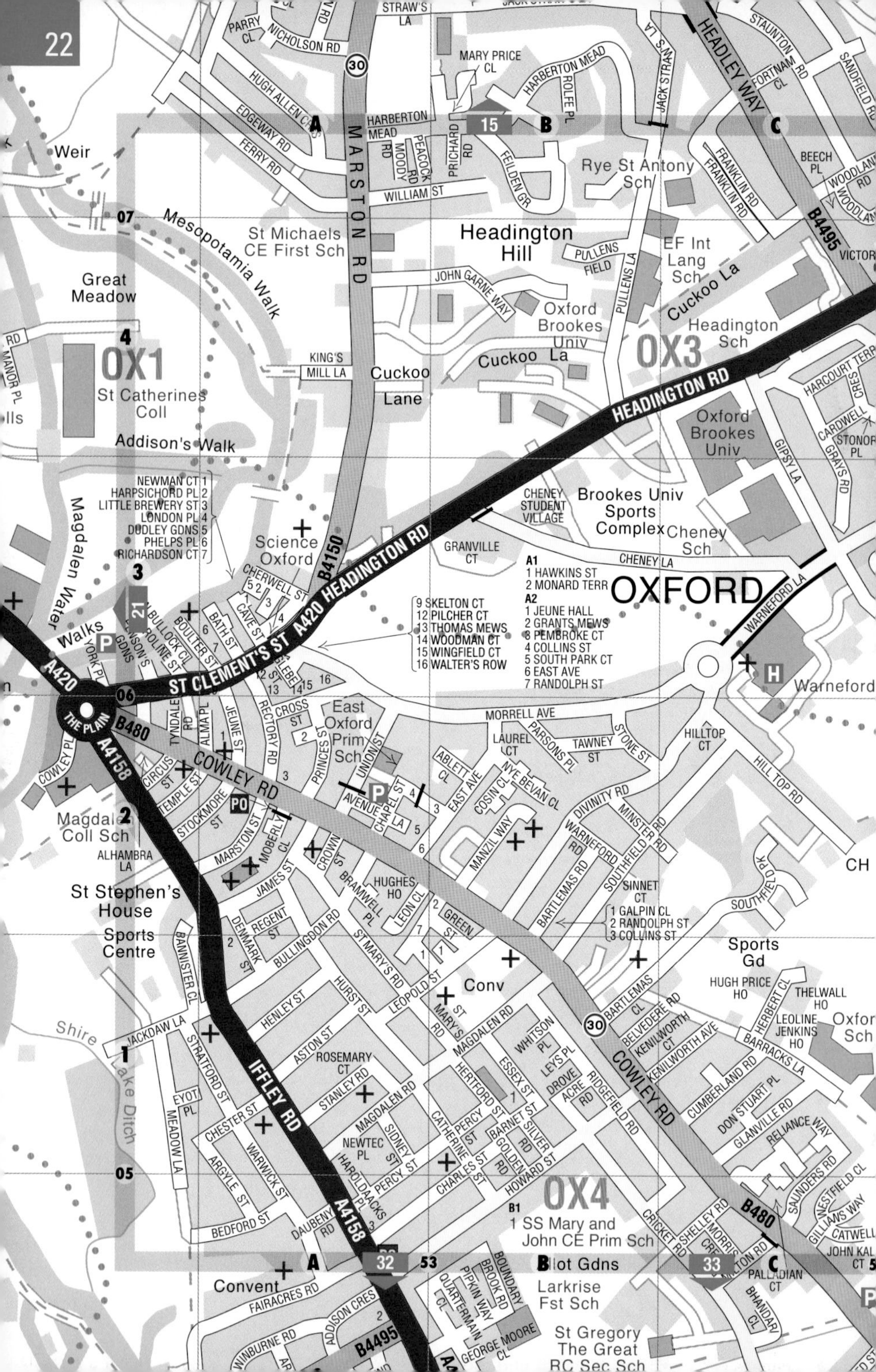

MARSTON RD
HEADLEY WAY
HEADINGTON RD
A420 HEADINGTON RD
ST CLEMENT'S ST
COWLEY RD
IFFLEY RD
THE PLAIN
OX1
OX3
OX4
OXFORD
Headington Hill
Weir
Great Meadow
Mesopotamia Walk
St Catherines Coll
Addison's Walk
Magdalen Water Walks
St Michaels CE First Sch
Rye St Antony Sch
EF Int Lang Sch
Oxford Brookes Univ
Headington Sch
Cuckoo Lane
Cuckoo La
Science Oxford
Brookes Univ Sports Complex
Cheney Sch
CHENEY STUDENT VILLAGE
GRANVILLE CT
CHENEY LA
Warneford
East Oxford Prim Sch
Magdalen Coll Sch
St Stephen's House
Sports Centre
Shire Lake Ditch
Conv
Sports Gd
Convent
Larkrise Fst Sch
St Gregory The Great RC Sec Sch
Oxford Sch
NEWMAN CT 1
HARPSICHORD PL 2
LITTLE BREWERY ST 3
LONDON PL 4
DUDLEY GDNS 5
PHELPS PL 6
RICHARDSON CT 7
9 SKELTON CT
12 PILCHER CT
13 THOMAS MEWS
14 WOODMAN CT
15 WINGFIELD CT
16 WALTER'S ROW
A1
1 HAWKINS ST
2 MONARD TERR
A2
1 JEUNE HALL
2 GRANTS MEWS
3 PEMBROKE CT
4 COLLINS ST
5 SOUTH PARK CT
6 EAST AVE
7 RANDOLPH ST
1 GALPIN CL
2 RANDOLPH ST
3 COLLINS ST
B1
1 SS Mary and John CE Prim Sch
Iffley Gdns
A B C
15 21 32 33 53
07 06 05

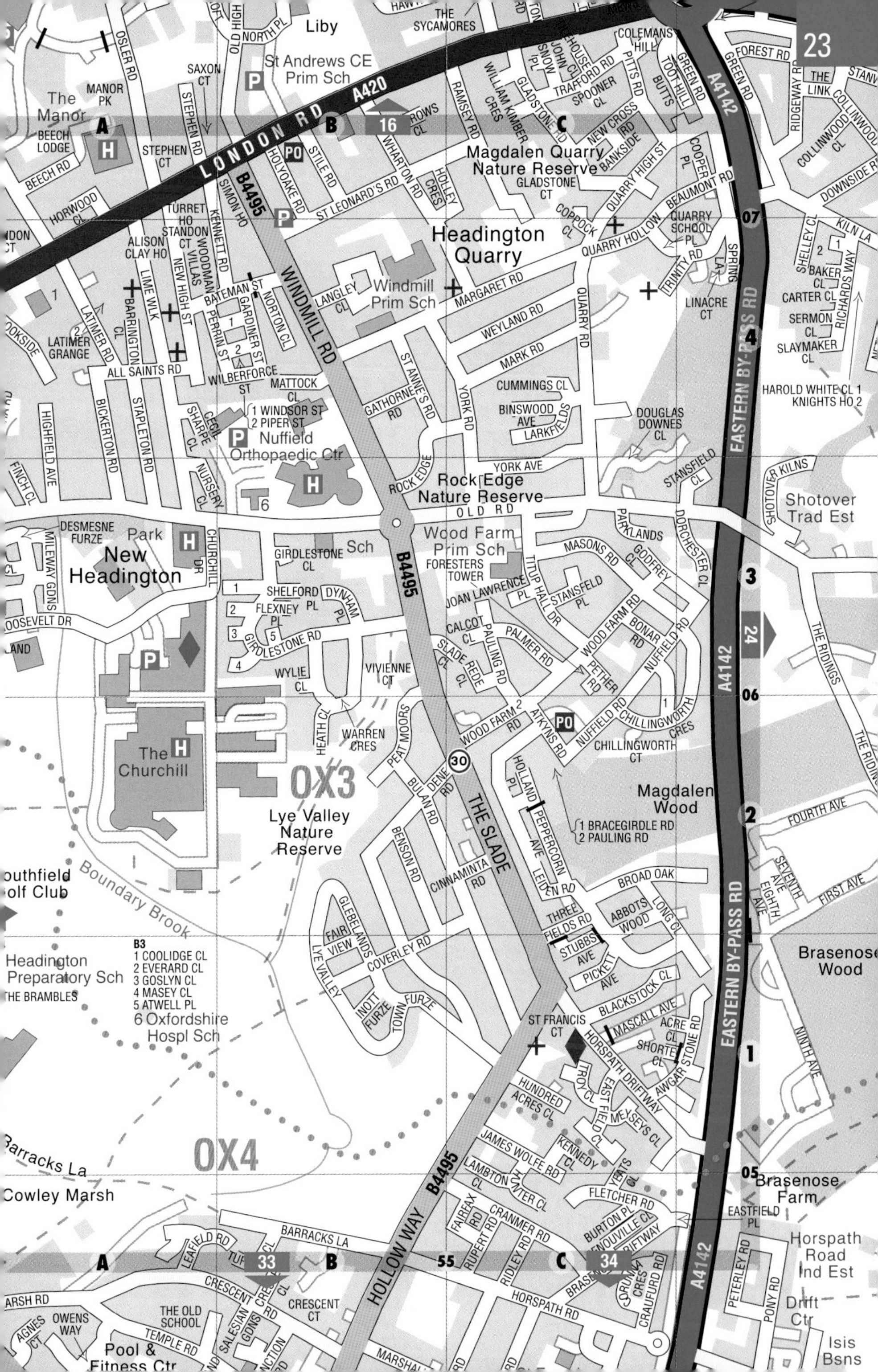

Headington Quarry
Magdalen Quarry Nature Reserve
Windmill Prim Sch
St Andrews CE Prim Sch
LONDON RD
A420
WINDMILL RD
B4495
The Manor
New Headington
Nuffield Orthopaedic Ctr
Rock Edge Nature Reserve
Wood Farm Prim Sch
The Churchill
OX3
Lye Valley Nature Reserve
Magdalen Wood
EASTERN BY-PASS RD
A4142
Shotover Trad Est
Brasenose Wood
Brasenose Farm
Horspath Road Ind Est
THE SLADE
HOLLOW WAY
OX4
Cowley Marsh
Barracks La
Boundary Brook
Headington Preparatory Sch
Southfield Golf Club
Pool & Fitness Ctr
B3
1 COOLIDGE CL
2 EVERARD CL
3 GOSLYN CL
4 MASEY CL
5 ATWELL PL
6 Oxfordshire Hospl Sch
1 WINDSOR ST
2 PIPER ST
1 BRACEGIRDLE RD
2 PAULING RD
HAROLD WHITE CL 1
KNIGHTS HO 2
16
24
33
34

A40
LONDON RD
P&R
Thornhill
Swilly
Risinghurst
OX3
Monk's Wood
Monk's Farm
Shotover Hill
Forest Farm
Shotover Plain
Shotover Trad Est
OLD RD
Shotover Cleve
Shotover Country Park
OX3
Westhill Farm
Brasenose Wood
Open Brasnose
OX33
OX4
Brasenose Farm
Horspath Road Ind Est
Drift Ctr
Isis Bsns
Athletics & Sports Ground
Magdalen Wood
EASTERN BY-PASS RD
A4142
dington
uarry
Edge
Reserve
FOREST RD
GREEN RD
THE LINK
STANWAY RD
THE LARCHES
DOWNSIDE END
ROWLANDS HO
COLLINWOOD CL
COLLINWOOD RD
DOWNSIDE RD
ST ANWAYRD
GROVELANDS RD
KILN LA
SHELLEY CL
BAKER CL
CARTER CL
SERMON CL
SLAYMAKER CL
RICHARDS WAY
NETHERWOODS RD
LEWIS CL
WYCHWOOD LA
HAROLD WHITE CL 1
KNIGHTS HO 2
BAYSWATER RD
SHOTOVER KILNS
THE RIDINGS
FOURTH AVE
SEVENTH AVE
EIGHTH AVE
FIRST AVE
NINTH AVE
1 OLD BARN GROUND
2 NETHER DURNFORD CL
COLEMANS HILL
TRAFFORD RD
PITTS RD
SPOONER CL
BUTTS
TOOT HILL
NEW CROSS RD
BANKSIDE
QUARRY HIGH ST
COOPER PL
BEAUMONT RD
GLADSTONE CT
COPPOCK CL
QUARRY HOLLOW
QUARRY SCHOOL PL
TRINITY RD
SPRING LA
MARGARET RD
WEYLAND RD
QUARRY RD
MARK RD
LINACRE CT
CUMMINGS CL
BINSWOOD AVE
LARKFIELDS
DOUGLAS DOWNES CL
YORK AVE
STANSFIELD CL
PARKLANDS
DORCHESTER CL
MASONS RD
GODFREY CL
TITUP HALL DR
STANSFIELD PL
LAWRENCE
PL
PAULING RD
PALMER RD
BONAR RD
NUFFIELD RD
CHILLINGWORTH CRES
CHILLINGWORTH CT
ATKYNS RD
PO
HOLLAND PL
THE SLADE
PEPPERCORN AVE
LEIDEN RD
BROAD OAK
ABBOTS WOOD
LONG CL
THREE FIELDS RD
STUBBS AVE
PICKETT AVE
BLACKSTOCK CL
MASCALL AVE
ACRE CL
STONE RD
SHORTE CL
AWGAR
ST FRANCIS CT
HORSPATH DRIFTWAY
TROY CL
EAST FIELD CL
MEYSEYS CL
HUNDRED ACRES CL
JAMES WOLFE RD
KENNEDY CL
HUNTER CL
YEATS CL
FLETCHER RD
BURTON PL
BENOUVILLE CL
BRASENOSE DRIFTWAY
CRANMER RD
RIDLEY RD
CORUNNA CRES
CRAUFURD RD
HORSPATH RD
EASTFIELD PL
PETERLEY RD
PONY RD
17
23
34
35
56
07
06
05

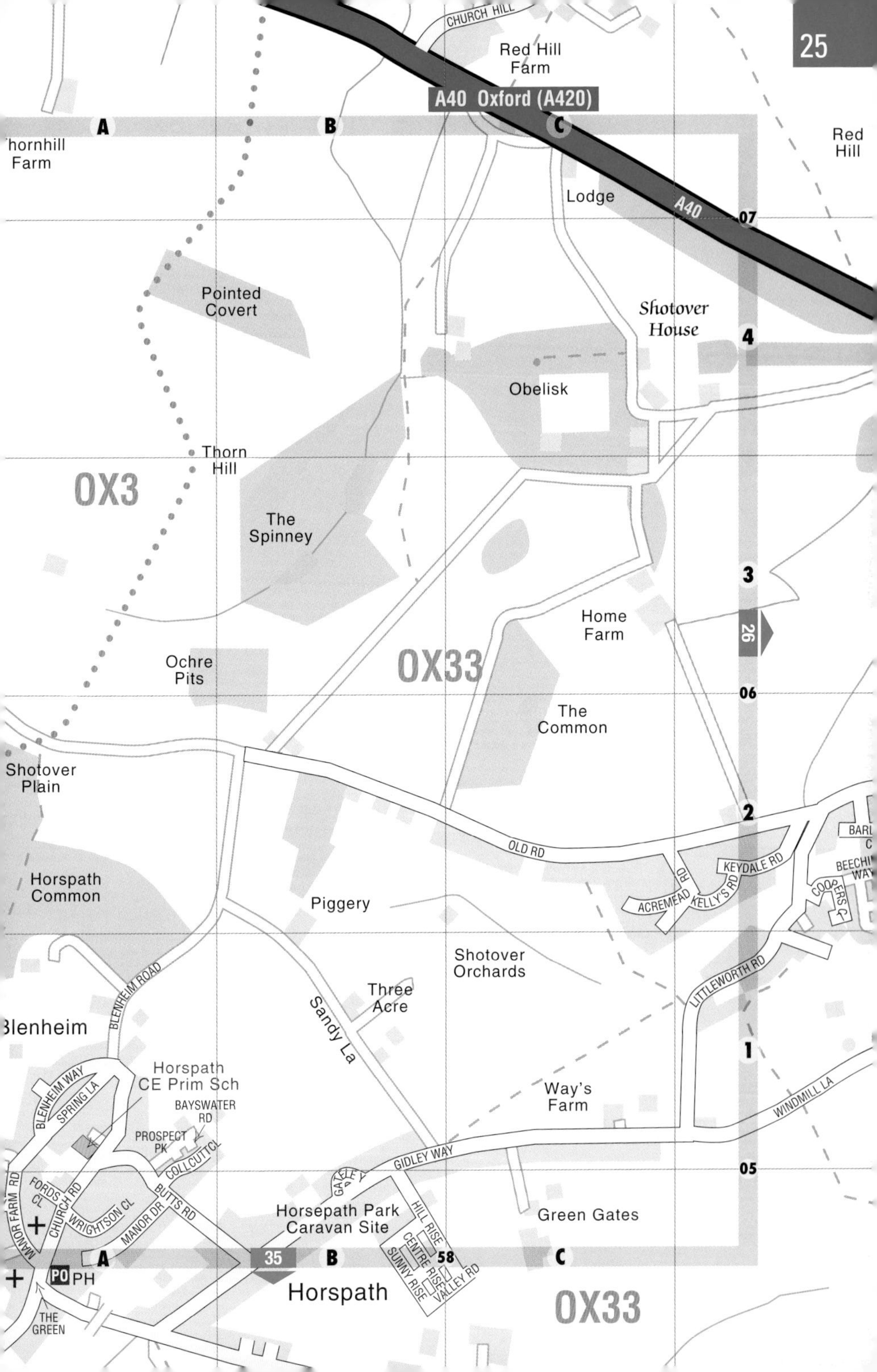
CHURCH HILL
Red Hill Farm
A40 Oxford (A420)
A
B
C
Thornhill Farm
Red Hill
Lodge
A40
07
Pointed Covert
Shotover House
4
Obelisk
Thorn Hill
OX3
The Spinney
3
Home Farm
26
Ochre Pits
OX33
06
The Common
Shotover Plain
2
OLD RD
KEYDALE RD
Horspath Common
ACREMEAD RD
KELLY'S RD
BEECH WAY
COOPERS C
Piggery
Shotover Orchards
LITTLEWORTH RD
BLENHEIM ROAD
Three Acre
Sandy La
Blenheim
1
Horspath CE Prim Sch
Way's Farm
WINDMILL LA
BLENHEIM WAY
SPRING LA
BAYSWATER RD
PROSPECT PK
COLLCUTT CL
GIDLEY WAY
GAWLEY
05
FORDS CL
CHURCH RD
MANOR FARM RD
WRIGHTSON CL
MANOR DR
BUTTS RD
Horsepath Park Caravan Site
HILL RISE
Green Gates
CENTRE RISE
SUNNY RISE
VALLEY RD
35
58
PO PH
Horspath
OX33
THE GREEN

Farm

Keeper's
Cottage

Warren
Farm **C**

A Red
Hill **B**

Lodge
07

Warren
Wood

A40

B4027

WHEATLEY RD

Shotover
House

B4027

Lyehill Quarries
(dis)

4

Wheatley
Park Sch

Recn
Gd

The Park
Sports Ctr

BAF

3 Home
Farm

25

PARK HILL

WESTFIELD RD

WESTFIELD RD

LONDON RD

A40

06 The
Common

KILN LA

TEMPLARS CLT

MORLAND
CL

GARDINER
CL

OX33

John
Watson
Sch

BLENHEIM LA

STATION RD

WAY

ST MARY'S CL

ST MARY'S
HO

THE GLEBE

Oxford House
Sch of English

P

Liby

CHURCH RD

2 LITTLEWORTH RD

LITTLEWORTH PK

BARLOW
CL

Wheatley
CE Prim Sch

Wheatley

HIGH
ST

BELL LA

WREN
CL & RD

PO

FRIDAY LA

HIGH
ST

CROW

OLD RD

KEYDALE RD

BEECHING
WAY

COOPERS CL

HATHAWAYS

FARM CL

SIMON'S CL

FARM CLOSE

CROWN
LA

MALBERRY LA

ORCHARD
CL

ACREMEAD

KELLY'S RD

RD

LITTLEWORTH
IND EST

LITTLEWORTH
PK

HOWE CL

KIMBER CL

BEECH RD

Littleworth
Bsns Ctr

KELHAM HALL DR

Littleworth

Windmill
(disused)

1 Way's
Farm

WINDMILL LA

WINDMILL LA

WINDMILL LA

LADDER HILL

05

Coombe House

A 59 **B** **C**

Pond
Farm
A
B
C
Old Park
Farm
07
BURYHOOK
CNR
Cottage
Copse
Warwick Close
Farm
4
The
Rectory
Holton
Place
Holton
M40
Church Farm
3
Garden
Copse
Brookes Univ
(Wheatley
Campus)
COLLEGE CL
06
OX33
Bsns
Ctr
FAIRFAX GATE
BISCOE CT
SUNNYSIDE
TYNDALE
PL
2
ANSON CL
30
AMBROSE RISE
OLD LONDON RD
Holton Mill
House
CULLUM
HO
CULLUM
RD
A40
LEYSHON RD
THE AVENUE
LONDON RD
SACKIES LA
HILLARY WAY
MILLER RD
ELM CL
WINDOWS
CT
ELTON CRES
ROMAN RD
Wheatley
Bridge
1
A40
M40 juncs 8a,8
A418
Sewage
Works
Hotel
Superstore
ASHHURST
CT
05
A
B
61
C
Castle Hill
Farm
River Th

Farm
Denman's Copse
Hid's Copse
A
B
18
C
A420
Saddle Copse
05
4
Long Copse
CHAWLEY LA
COLEGROVE DOWN
Chawley
TUMBLEDOWN HILL
HIGH ST
College Farm
Cumnor CE Prim Sch
DENMAN'S LA
A420
NORREYS RD
BERTIE RD
Cumnor
3
SANDS CL
OXFORD RD
CUMNOR HILL
PO
PH
PH
OX2
GLEBE RD
THE GLEBE
04
APPLETON RD
B4017
THE WINNYARDS
THE PARK
KENILWORTH RD
FORSTER LA
ABINGDON RD
ROBSART PL
2
Cross Roads Farm
1
Bradley Cottages
Spring Farm
OX13
Bradley Farm
OX1
FARINGDON RD
es
03
B4017
Henwood Farm
46
A
B
36
47
C
A420 Swindon

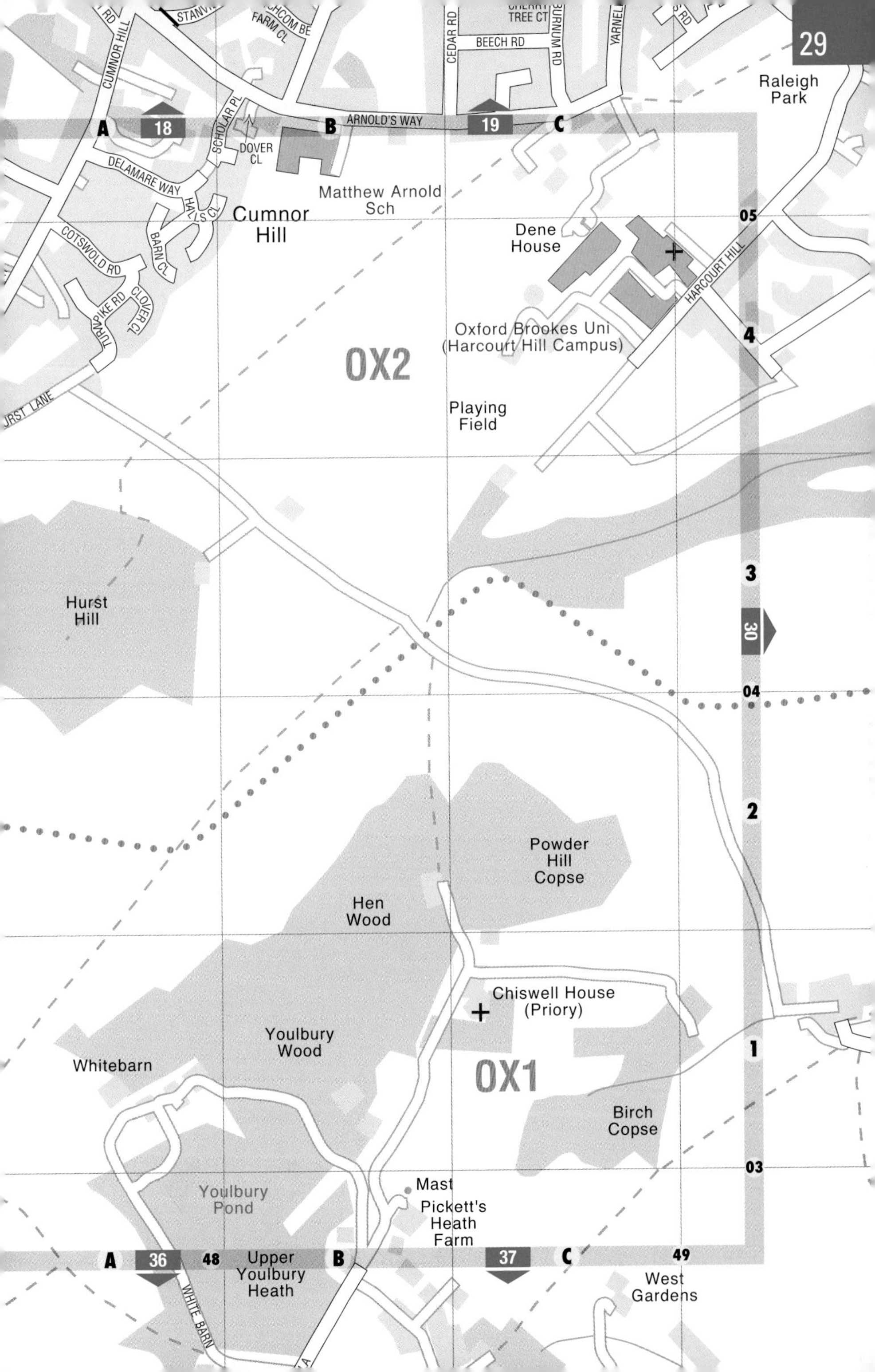

CUMNOR HILL
FARM CL
CEDAR RD
BEECH RD
CHERRY TREE CT
BURNUM RD
YARNELL
Raleigh Park
A
18
B
ARNOLD'S WAY
19
C
SCHOLAR PL
DOVER CL
DELAMARE WAY
HALLS CL
Matthew Arnold Sch
Cumnor Hill
COTSWOLD RD
BARN CL
TURNPIKE RD
CLOVER CL
Dene House
HARCOURT HILL
Oxford Brookes Uni (Harcourt Hill Campus)
05
4
OX2
Playing Field
Hurst Hill
3
30
04
2
Powder Hill Copse
Hen Wood
Chiswell House (Priory)
Youlbury Wood
Whitebarn
OX1
1
Birch Copse
03
Youlbury Pond
Mast
Pickett's Heath Farm
A
36
48
Upper Youlbury Heath
B
37
C
49
West Gardens
WHITE BARN

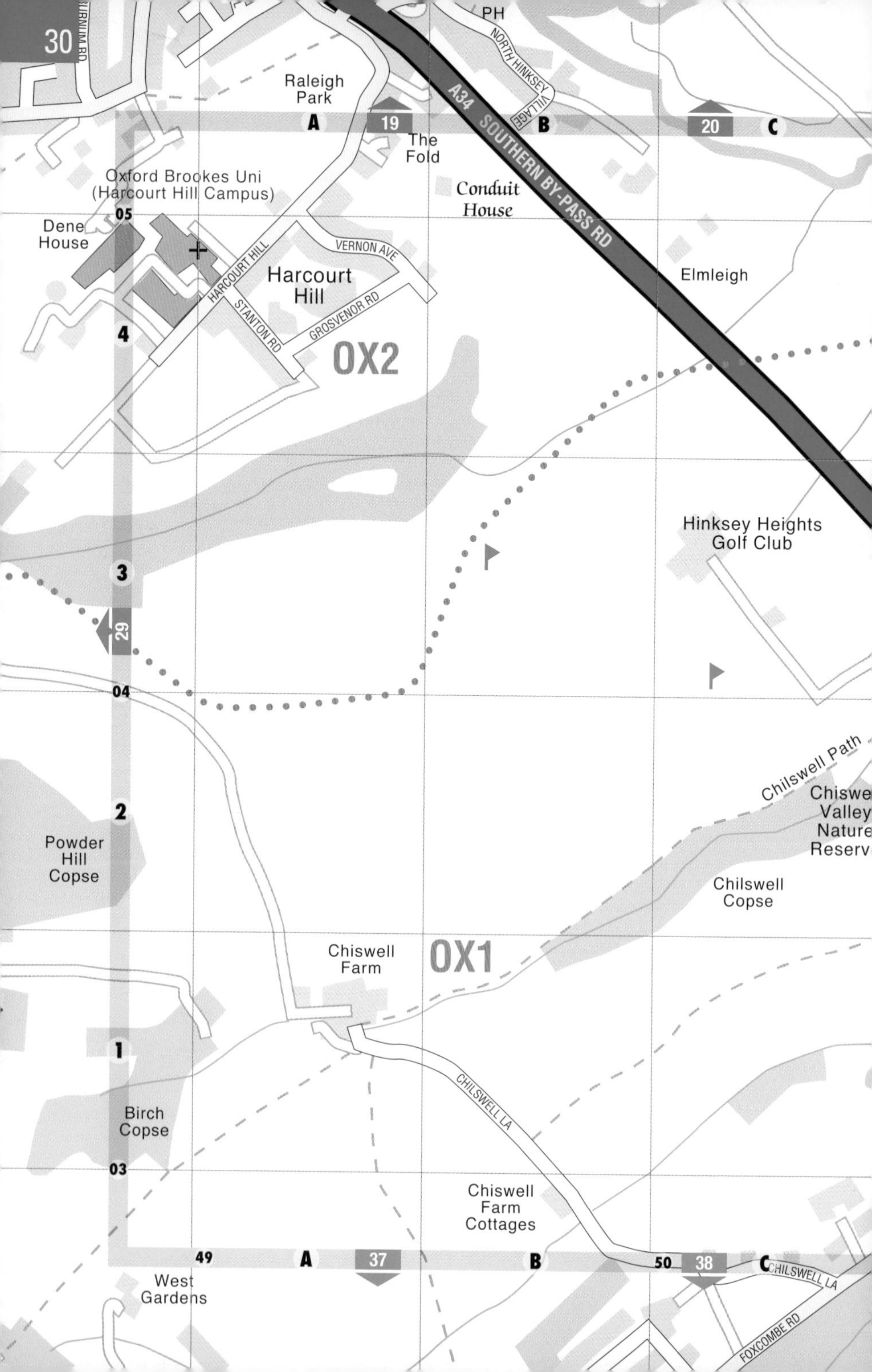

Raleigh Park

A 19 **B** 20 **C**

The Fold

North Hinksey

Conduit House

A34 SOUTHERN BY-PASS RD

Oxford Brookes Uni (Harcourt Hill Campus)

Elmleigh

Dene House 05

Harcourt Hill

Vernon Ave

Harcourt Hill

Stanton Rd

Grosvenor Rd

4

OX2

Hinksey Heights Golf Club

3

29

04

Chilswell Path

Chiswe Valley Nature Reserv

2

Powder Hill Copse

Chilswell Copse

Chiswell Farm

OX1

1

Birch Copse

03

Chiswell Farm Cottages

49 **A** 37 **B** 50 38 **C** Chilswell La

West Gardens

Chilswell La

Foxcombe Rd

OX2
LC
St Ebbe's CE Prim Sch
Grandpont
WESTERN RD
MARLBOROUGH RD
WHITEHOUSE RD
SALTER CL
HODGES CT
CHILSWELL RD
KINETON RD
NEWTON RD
EDITH RD
A 20 B 21 C
Hogacre Ditch
Hinksey Stream
Sports Gd
A4144
Eastwyke Farm
Eastwyke Ditch
Shire Lake Ditch
JACKDAW
River Thames or Isis
Towing Path
05
Hinksey Pool
SCHOOL PL 1
STEWART ST 2
SUMMERFIELD 3
VICARAGE CT 4
LAKE ST
GORDON ST
VICARAGE RD
VICARAGE LA
GREEN PL
ABINGDON RD
Sports Gd
New Hinksey
4
NORREYS AVE
New Hinksey CE Prim Sch
SUNNINGWELL RD
LINCOLN RD
MONMOUTH RD
NORTHAMPTON RD
WYTHAM ST
OSWESTRY RD
CHATHAM RD
FOX CRES
Weir
Donnington Bridge
WEIRS LA B4495
3
Thames
The Devil's Backbone
PH
MANOR RD
South Hinksey
JOHN TOWLE CL
PEEL PL
CANNING CRES
Iffley Meadow Nature Reserve
32
Cold Harbour
PH
CHURCH CL
ST LAWRENCE RD
JOHN PIERS LA
Pin Farm
BARLEYCOTT LA
GORDON WOODWARD WAY
ISIS CL
04
LEANDER WY
EGROVE CL
BERTIE PL
Weirs Mill Stream
SOUTHERN BY-PASS RD
A34
Oxfordshire Circular Walks
ABINGDON RD
Nursery
OX1
Redbridge
P&R
2
RED BRIDGE HOLLOW
KENNINGTON RD
A423
SOUTHERN BY-PASS RD
HINKSEY HILL INTERCHANGE
KENNINGTON RDBT
BETTY LA
Egrove Cottage
1
Bagley Croft
SPRING COPSE
HINKSEY HILL
OLD NURSERY VIEW
BADGER LA
FORESTSIDE
03
JACKSON DR
PERKINS
Spring Copse
KENVILLE RD
COLLEY WOOD
HUNDER CT
A 38 51 B 39 C 52
OXFORD RD
KENNINGTON RD
Hotel
Hangman's Bottom
BAGLEY CL
BLACKMAN

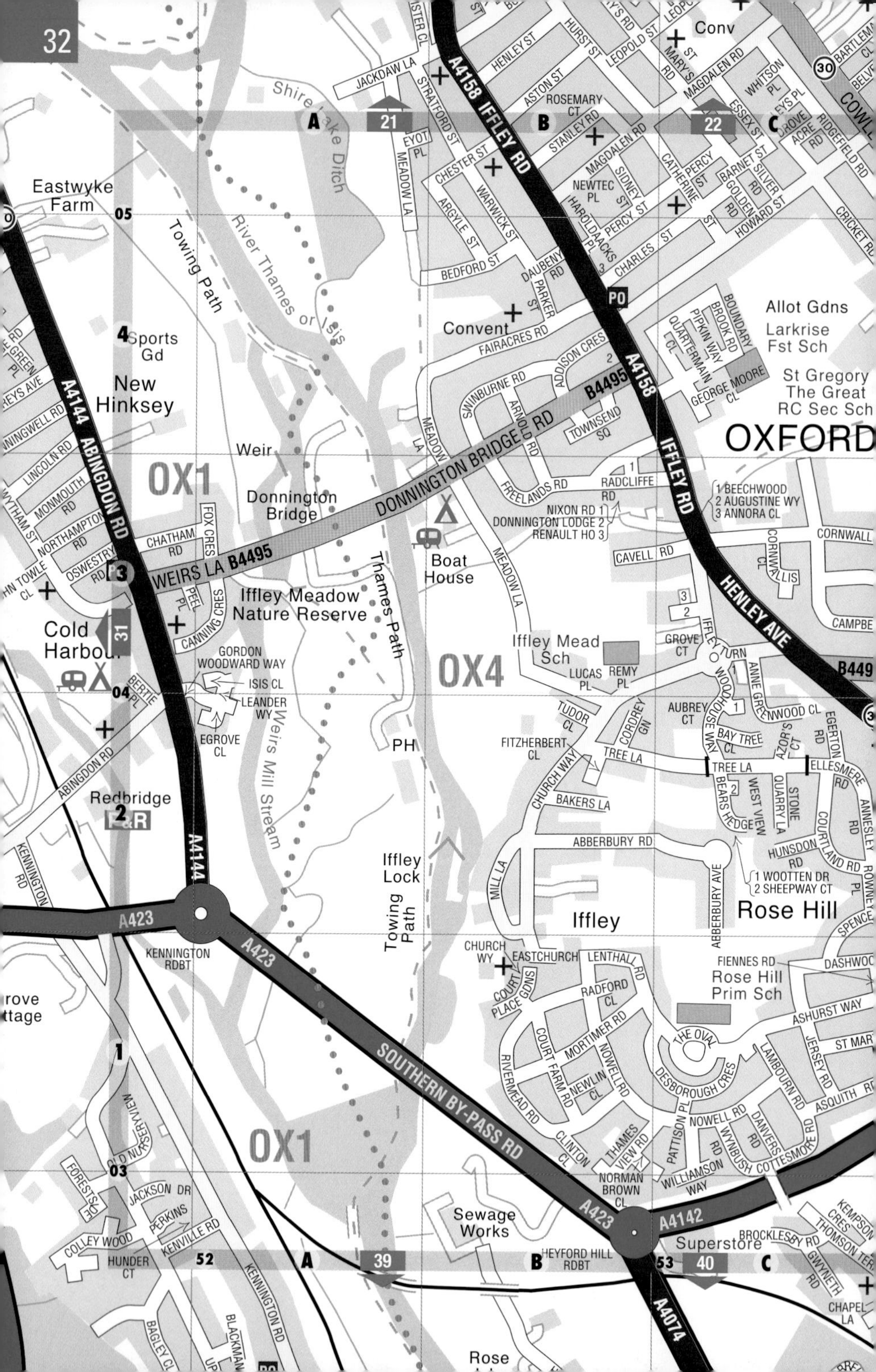

Conv
Shire Lake Ditch
Eastwyke Farm
Towing Path
River Thames or Isis
Convent
Allot Gdns
Larkrise Fst Sch
St Gregory The Great RC Sec Sch
OXFORD
Sports Gd
New Hinksey
OX1
Weir
Donnington Bridge
DONNINGTON BRIDGE RD
WEIRS LA B4495
IFFLEY RD
A4158
ABINGDON RD
A4144
Iffley Meadow Nature Reserve
Thames Path
Boat House
Cold Harbour
Iffley Mead Sch
OX4
HENLEY AVE
Weirs Mill Stream
PH
Redbridge
Iffley Lock
Towing Path
Iffley
Rose Hill
Rose Hill Prim Sch
A423
KENNINGTON RDBT
SOUTHERN BY-PASS RD
OX1
Sewage Works
A4142
Superstore
HEYFORD HILL RDBT
A4074

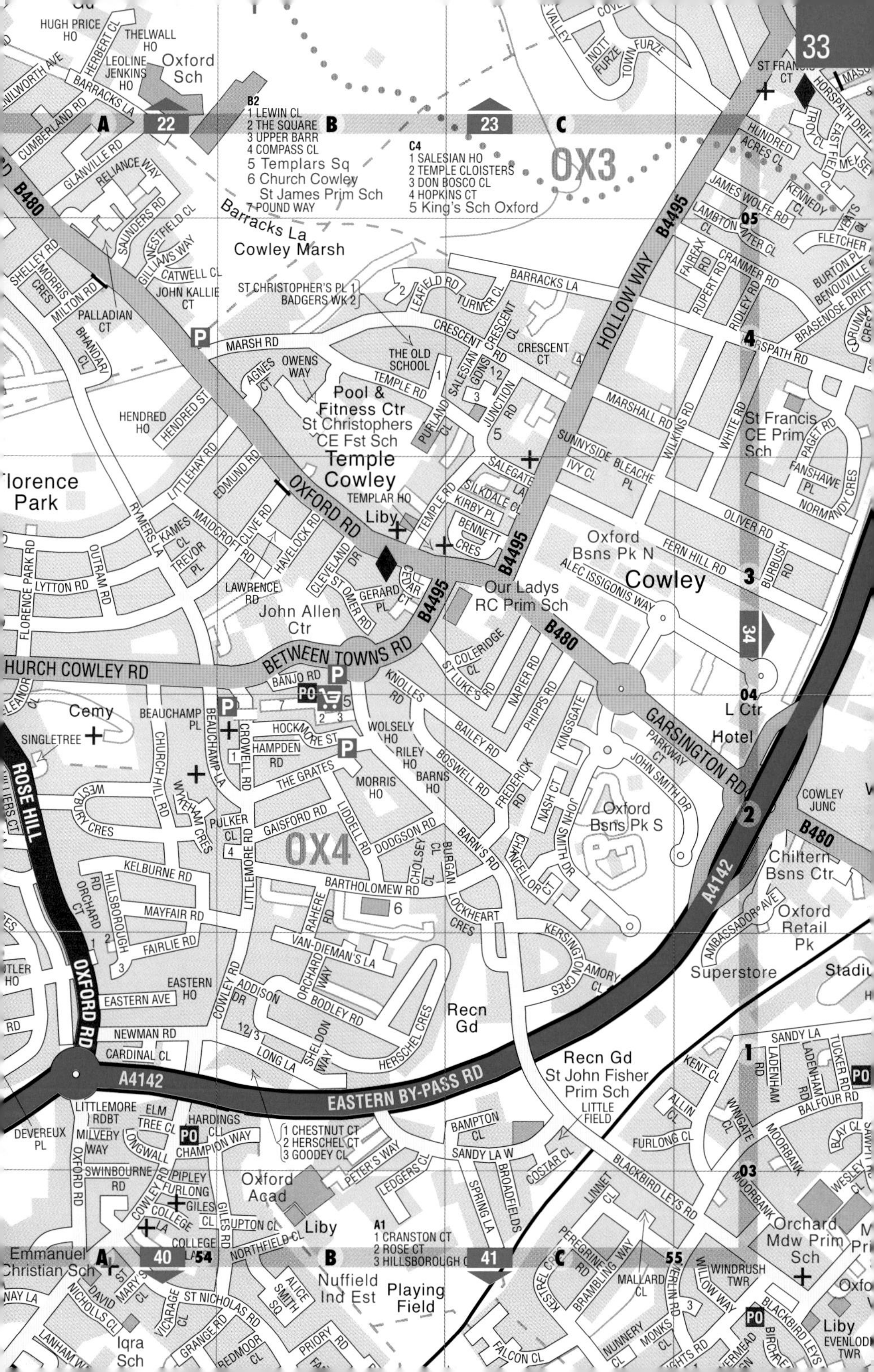
HUGH PRICE HO
THELWALL HO
HERBERT CL
LEOLINE JENKINS HO
Oxford Sch
KENILWORTH AVE
BARRACKS LA
CUMBERLAND RD
A
22
B
23
C
B2
1 LEWIN CL
2 THE SQUARE
3 UPPER BARR
4 COMPASS CL
5 Templars Sq
6 Church Cowley St James Prim Sch
7 POUND WAY
C4
1 SALESIAN HO
2 TEMPLE CLOISTERS
3 DON BOSCO CL
4 HOPKINS CT
5 King's Sch Oxford
OX3
GLANVILLE RD
RELIANCE WAY
SAUNDERS RD
WESTFIELD CL
GILLIANS WAY
CATWELL CL
JOHN KALLIE CT
Barracks La
Cowley Marsh
ST CHRISTOPHER'S PL 1
BADGERS WK 2
B480
SHELLEY RD
MORRIS CRES
MILTON RD
PALLADIAN CT
BHANDARI CL
MARSH RD
AGNES CT
OWENS WAY
LEAFIELD RD
TURNER CL
BARRACKS LA
CRESCENT RD
CRESCENT CL
CRESCENT CT
THE OLD SCHOOL
TEMPLE RD
SALESIAN GDNS
JUNCTION RD
Pool & Fitness Ctr
St Christophers CE Fst Sch
Temple Cowley
PURLAND CL
HOLLOW WAY
B4495
HUNDRED ACRES CL
ST FRANCIS CT
TROY CL
EAST FIELD CL
HORSPATH DRIFT
MEYSEY
JAMES WOLFE RD
KENNEDY CL
LAMBTON CL
VIXTER CL
YEATS CL
FLETCHER
FAIRFAX RD
CRANMER RD
BURTON PL
BENOUVILLE
RUPERT RD
RIDLEY RD
BRASENOSE DRIFT
HORSPATH RD
MARSHALL RD
WILKINS RD
WHITE RD
St Francis CE Prim Sch
PAGET RD
FANSHAWE PL
NORMANDY CRES
SUNNYSIDE
IVY CL
BLEACHE PL
OLIVER RD
FERN HILL RD
BURBUSH RD
HENDRED HO
HENDRED ST
LITTLEHAY RD
EDMUND RD
Florence Park
RYMERS LA
KAMES CL
TREVOR PL
MAIDCROFT RD
CLIVE RD
HAVELOCK RD
OXFORD RD
TEMPLAR HO
Liby
SALEGATE LA
SILKDALE CL
KIRBY PL
BENNETT CRES
Oxford Bsns Pk N
Cowley
ALEC ISSIGONIS WAY
FLORENCE PARK RD
OUTRAM RD
LYTTON RD
LAWRENCE RD
CLEVELAND DR
ST OMER RD
GERARD PL
CEDAR CT
John Allen Ctr
Our Ladys RC Prim Sch
34
CHURCH COWLEY RD
BETWEEN TOWNS RD
BANJO RD
PO
COLERIDGE CL
ST LUKE'S RD
NAPIER RD
PHIPPS RD
KNOLLES RD
GARSINGTON RD
PARKWAY CT
L Ctr
Hotel
Cemy
BEAUCHAMP PL
BEAUCHAMP LA
CROWELL RD
HOCKMORE ST
WOLSELY HO
BAILEY RD
KINGSGATE
SINGLETREE
HAMPDEN RD
RILEY HO
BOSWELL RD
JOHN SMITH DR
ROSE HILL
CHURCH HILL RD
THE GRATES
MORRIS HO
BARNS HO
FREDERICK RD
NASH CT
Oxford Bsns Pk S
COWLEY JUNC
WESTBURY CRES
WYKEHAM CRES
PULKER CL
GAISFORD RD
LIDDELL RD
DODGSON RD
OX4
CHOLSEY CL
BURGAN CL
BARN'S RD
CHANCELLOR CT
B480
Chiltern Bsns Ctr
A4142
KELBURNE RD
HILLSBOROUGH RD
ORCHARD RD
LITTLEMORE RD
BARTHOLOMEW RD
RAHERE RD
LOCKHEART CRES
AMBASSADOR AVE
Oxford Retail Pk
MAYFAIR RD
FAIRLIE RD
VAN-DIEMAN'S LA
KERSINGTON CRES
AMORY CL
Superstore
EASTERN HO
EASTERN AVE
COWLEY RD
ADDISON DR
ORCHARD WAY
BODLEY RD
SHELDON WAY
HERSCHEL CRES
Recn Gd
NEWMAN RD
CARDINAL CL
LONG LA
A4142
EASTERN BY-PASS RD
Recn Gd
St John Fisher Prim Sch
SANDY LA
LADENHAM RD
TUCKER RD
KENT CL
BALFOUR RD
LITTLEMORE RDBT
ELM TREE CL
HARDINGS CL
DEVEREUX PL
MILVERY WAY
LONGWALL
CHAMPION WAY
1 CHESTNUT CT
2 HERSCHEL CT
3 GOODEY CL
BAMPTON CL
LITTLE FIELD
ALLIN CL
WINGATE CL
MOORBANK
BLAY CL
SWINBOURNE RD
PIPLEY FURLONG
PETER'S WAY
SANDY LA W
FURLONG CL
BROADFIELDS
COSTAR CL
BLACKBIRD LEYS RD
LINNET CL
WESLEY CL
OXFORD RD
COWLEY RD
COLLEGE LA
GILES CL
GILES RD
UPTON CL
Oxford Acad
LEDGERS CL
SPRING LA
Liby
COLLEGE LA
NORTHFIELD CL
A1
1 CRANSTON CT
2 ROSE CT
3 HILLSBOROUGH CL
PEREGRINE RD
BRAMBLING WAY
Orchard Mdw Prim Sch
Emmanuel Christian Sch
40
54
41
55
ST MARY'S CL
DAVID NICHOLLS CL
ST NICHOLAS RD
Nuffield Ind Est
Playing Field
KESTREL CRES
MALLARD CL
MERLIN RD
WILLOW WAY
WINDRUSH TWR
VICARAGE CL
GRANGE RD
ALICE SMITH SQ
PRIORY RD
NUNNERY CL
MONKS CL
BLACKBIRD LEYS RD
Liby
EVENLODE TWR
LANHAM WAY
Iqra Sch
REDMOOR CL
FALCON CL
Stadium

OX3
OX4
OX44
Cowley
Blackbird Leys
Wood
Open Brasnose
Brasenose Farm
Horspath Road Ind Est
Drift Ctr
Isis Bsns Ctr
Athletics & Sports Ground
Works
Depot
County Trad Est
Northfie Far
Guydens Farm
Oxford Bsns Pk N
Oxford Bsns Pk S
St Francis CE Prim Sch
L Ctr
Hotel
Chiltern Bsns Ctr
Oxford Retail Pk
Superstore
Stadium
Cowley Bsns Ctr
Recn Gd
St John Fisher Prim Sch
Orchard Mdw Prim Sch
Mabel Prichard Sch
Park
Pegasus Fst Sch
Oxford & Cherwell Valley Coll
Liby
HOLLOW WAY
B4495
B480
A4142
EASTERN BY-PASS RD
GARSINGTON RD
WATLINGTON RD
HORSPATH RD
BARRACKS LA
MARSHALL RD
OLIVER RD
FERN HILL RD
CRANMER RD
BRASENOSE DRIFTWAY
FLETCHER RD
ROMAN WAY
OXFORD RD
BLACKBIRD LEYS RD
CUDDESDON WAY
BALFOUR RD
SANDY LA
JUNIPER DR
FIELD AVE
A 23 B 24 C
A 41 B 42 C
33
30
05
04
03
55
56

Farm
OX3
Blenheim
BLENHEIM ROAD
Three Acre
Sandy La
A
24
B
25
C
Way's Farm
BLENHEIM WAY
SPRING LA
BAYSWATER RD
Horspath CE Prim Sch
PROSPECT PK
COLLCUTT CL
GIDLEY WAY
05
COLLEGE WAY
MANOR FARM RD
FORDS CL
CHURCH RD
WRIGHTSON CL
BUTTS RD
GATELEY
HILL RISE
Horsepath Park Caravan Site
Green Gates
MANOR DR
CENTRE RISE
SUNNY RISE
VALLEY RD
PO
PH
Horspath
4
THE GREEN
BUTLER CL
COPCOT CL
OXFORD RD
Brookside
CUDDESDON RD
OX33
Hollow Brook
3
04
Warehouse
Works
2
City Farm
OX44
WHEATLEY RD
1
Northfield Brook
03
OXFORD RD
JOHNSON CL
PINE CL
POPLAR CL
BIRCH RD
Sc
OX4
Blenheim
Upper Farm
A
42
57
B
ELM
43
C
58
WILLOW CL
HAZEL END
Kiln Farm
COMBEWELL

Bradley Cottages
28
Whitebarn
29
A
B
C
Bradley Farm
A420
03
OX2
Henwood Farm
Youlbur Pon
4
WHITE BARN
FARINGDON RD
HENWOOD COTTS
HENWOOD DR
ROCKLEY COTTS
50
Wootton Close
3
WHITE HILL LA
Mayo's Farm
Henwood
B4017
White Hill Farm
OX1
02
HILL VIEW LA
Wootton CE Prim Sch
2
Depot
CUMNOR RD
BESSELSLEIGH RD
Sandford Brook
Middle Farm
Wootton Village
Wootton Bsns Pk
ROBINSON RD
P
WERRELL DR
LEIGH CROFT
MANOR RD
1
BEECH CL
Manor Farm
THE WILLOWS
OX13
BESSELSLEIGH RD
PH
Tommy's Farm
SANDLEIGH RD
WATSON CRES
MITCHELL CL
HOME CL
BERRYMERE RD
LASHFORD LA
01
Community Ctr
B4017 LAMBOROUGH HILL
COUPLAND RD
CANDY WAY
LANSDOWNE ROAD
30
47
44
Wootton
ARTHUR EVANS CL
THE FIELD
LASHFORD LA
ST PETER'S CL

Farm
Youlbury Wood
Chiswell House (Priory)
A
29
B
C
30
CHILSWELL LA
Birch Copse
03
Chiswell Farm Cottages
Mast
Pickett's Heath Farm
OX1
Upper Youlbury Heath
West Gardens
4
SANDY LA
RIDGEWAY
Jarn Mound
BEDWELLS HEATH
Yatscombe Copse
Boars Hill
3
FOXCOMBE RD
Old Boars Hill
JARN WAY
38
BAYWORTH LA
Foxcombe Hall
BERKELEY RD
WOODLAND WLK
ORCHARD LA
02
JARN WY
JARN WY
FOXCOMBE RD
Foxcombe Hill
Old Boars Hill
Blackthorn
2
Duckling's Copse
OLD BOARS HILL
PH
Hotel
OX1
1
LINCOMBE LA
THE QUARRY
FOX LA
Broom Hill Copse
01
QUARRY RD
Copse View
Blagrove Copse
A
44
B
49
C
45
OX13
Sunningwell
PH

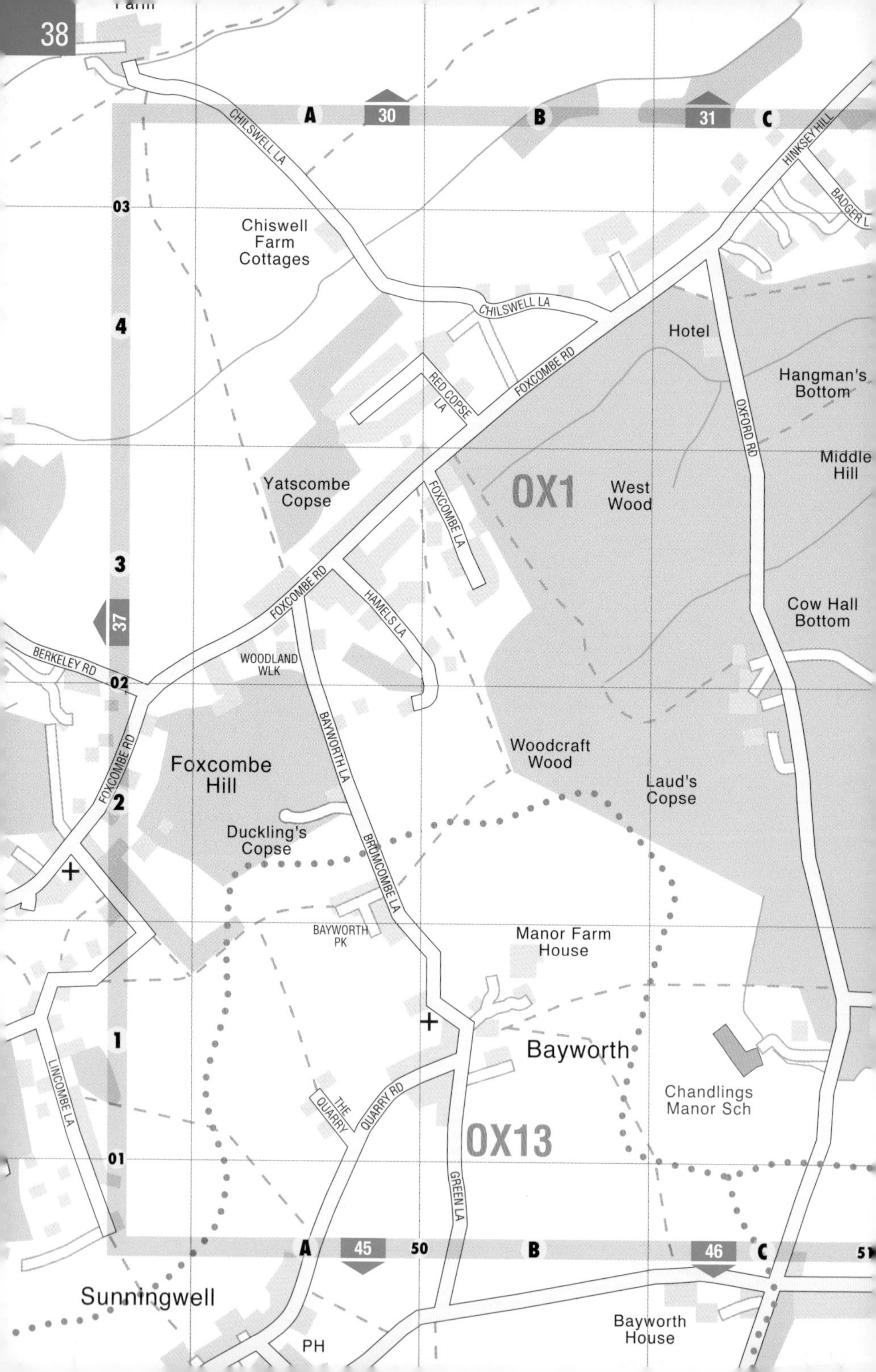

A
30
B
31
C
CHILSWELL LA
HINKSEY HILL
BADGER L
03
Chiswell Farm Cottages
CHILSWELL LA
4
Hotel
FOXCOMBE RD
RED COPSE LA
Hangman's Bottom
OXFORD RD
Middle Hill
OX1
West Wood
Yatscombe Copse
FOXCOMBE LA
3
Cow Hall Bottom
FOXCOMBE RD
HAMELS LA
37
BERKELEY RD
WOODLAND WLK
02
FOXCOMBE RD
BAYWORTH LA
Woodcraft Wood
Foxcombe Hill
Laud's Copse
2
Duckling's Copse
BRUMCOMBE LA
BAYWORTH PK
Manor Farm House
1
Bayworth
LINCOMBE LA
Chandlings Manor Sch
THE QUARRY
QUARRY RD
OX13
01
GREEN LA
A
45
50
B
46
C
51
Sunningwell
Bayworth House
PH

Egrove Cottage
Bagley Croft
SPRING COPSE
A
31
B
C
32
SOUTHERN BY-PASS RD
A423
COURT PLACE GDNS
MORTIMER
NOWELL
CLINTON CL
03
Sewage Works
A34
OLD NURSERY VIEW
FORESTERS
JACKSON DR
PERKINS
KENVILLE RD
COLLEY WOOD
HUNDER CT
Spring Copse
KENNINGTON RD
BAGLEY CL
BLACKMAN CL
UPPER RD
PO
4
OX4
Rose Isle
HEYFORD HILL LA
Colley's Ladder East
EDWARD RD
Liby
EDITH CT
ROWLES CL
WOODCROFT
Bagley Wood
OX1
COW LA
3
ROSS CT
RIVER VIEW
OTTERS REACH
BAGLEY WOOD RD
BEAUMONT CT
THE AVENUE
Under Woods
GRUNDY CRES
POPLAR GR
40
02
Little London
St Swithuns CE Prim Sch
KIRK CL
ST SWITHUN'S RD
MEADOW VIEW RD
Bagley Wood
2
SIMPSONS WAY
THE AVENUE
POPLAR GR
Old Peg Brake
LIDDIARD CL
Milestone Piece
LINKS RD
BAGLEY WOOD RD
PLAYFIELD RD
MANOR GR
POPLAR GR
Kennington
Lower Sugworth Copse
FAIRWAYS
CRANBROOK DR
Upper Sugworth Copse
1
THE PADDOCK
HAZELNUT PATH
The Woodland Pk Caravan Site
BLUEBELL RIDE
SYCAMORE CRES
FIR TREES
WILLOW WAY
SANDFORD
LA
Ind
01
OAK AVE
BLOSSOMS GLADE
Radley Large Wood
A
46
OX14
B
52
C
47
KENNINGTON RD
SUGWORTH LA

40
Rose Hill Prim Sch
BUTLER HO
EASTERN AVE
EASTERN HO
RADFORD CL
MORTIMER RD
COURT FARM RD
RIVERMEAD RD
THE OVAL
ASHURST WAY
FIENNES RD
ST MARTIN'S RD
DEVEREUX PL
NEWMAN RD
CARDINAL CL
SOUTHERN BY-PASS RD
A
32
DESBOROUGH CRES
B
LAMBOURN RD
JERSEY RD
ASQUITH RD
33
C
CLINTON CL
THAMES VIEW RD
PATTISON PL
NOWELL RD
WYNBUSH RD
DANVERS RD
COTTESMORE RD
LITTLEMORE RDBT
ELM TREE CL
MILVERY WAY
LONGWALL
PO
NORMAN BROWN CL
WILLIAMSON WAY
MARLBOROUGH CL 1
BLEWITT CT 2
MEDHURST WY 3
DUDGEON DR 4
OXFORD RD
SWINBOURNE RD
COWLEY RD
COLLEGE LA
03
Sewage Works
A423
A4142
HEYFORD HILL RDBT
Superstore
BROCKLESBY RD
THOMSON TERR
KEMPSON CRES
GWYNETH RD
Emmanuel Christian Sch
ST MARY'S CL
DAVID NICHOLLS CL
VICARAGE CL
KENNINGTON RD
4
A4074
CHAPEL LA
RAILWAY LA
BLACKMAN CL
PO
Rose Isle
LANHAM WAY
Iqra Sch
MORRELL CRES
EDWARD RD
HEYFORD HILL LA
John Henry Newman Prim Sch
Liby
ROWLES CL
PHEASANT WLK
MANDLEBROTE DR
Littlemore
SANDFORD RD
COW LA
YEFTLY DR
3
OTTERS REACH
BROADHURST GDNS
ARMSTRONG RD
Littlemore Brook
BEAUMONT CT
THE AVENUE
39
BATTEN PL
EDMUND HALLEY
Kennington
JANAWAY 1
BUCKLER PL 2
FOX FURLONG 3
GRUNDY CRES
02
St Swithuns CE Prim Sch
OX4
Orchard House
SANDFORD RD
A4074
OX1
River Thames or Isis
Hotel
MEADOW VIEW RD
POPLAR GR
ROCK FARM LA
KEENE CL
GRENOBLE
2
Fiddler's Elbow
SIMPSONS WAY
CHURCH RD
LINKS RD
PH
HENLEY RD
Sandford Pool
RIVER VIEW
PLAYFIELD RD
MANOR GR
BURRA CL
PH
Sandford-on-Thames
CRANBROOK DR
Lock
1
THE PADDOCK
SANDFORD LA
SYCAMORE CRES
FIR TREES
Ind Est
WILLOW WAY
SANDFORD LA
OAK AVE
01
LOWER FARM LA
Peeble Hill Mobile Home Pk
A
47
53
B
C
KENNINGTON RD
OX14
Lower Farm

Recn Gd
Recn Gd
St John Fisher Prim Sch
Oxford Acad
Liby
Nuffield Ind Est
OX4
Playing Field
Orchard Mdw Prim Sch
Mabel Prichard Sch
Blackbird Leys
Park
Oxford & Cherwell Valley Coll
Liby
L Ctr
Pegasus Fst Sch
Northfield Sch
Windale Prim Sch
Northfield Brook
The Oxford Science Pk
Ozone Leisure Pk
Kassam Stad (Oxford Utd FC)
Sewage Works
Caravan Site
Sandfordbrake Farm
Bushy Copse
OX4
OX44
A4074 Reading
A4142
WATLINGTON RD
C3
1 NUTHATCH CL
2 VERBENA WAY
3 BROOKLIME WLK
4 CLEAVERS SQ
5 SAXIFRAGE SQ
6 BERGAMONT PL
7 FOXGLOVE CL
8 CRANESBILL WAY
C4
1 NORTHBROOK HO
2 WINDALE HO
3 WHITETHORN WY
FIELDFARE RD 1
WAYFARING CL 2
ANEMONE CL 3
THISTLE DOWN CL 4
ACACIA AVE 5
OXEYE CT 6
HYACINTH WLK 7
SPRUCE GDNS 8
FIRS MDW 9
APPLETREE CL 10

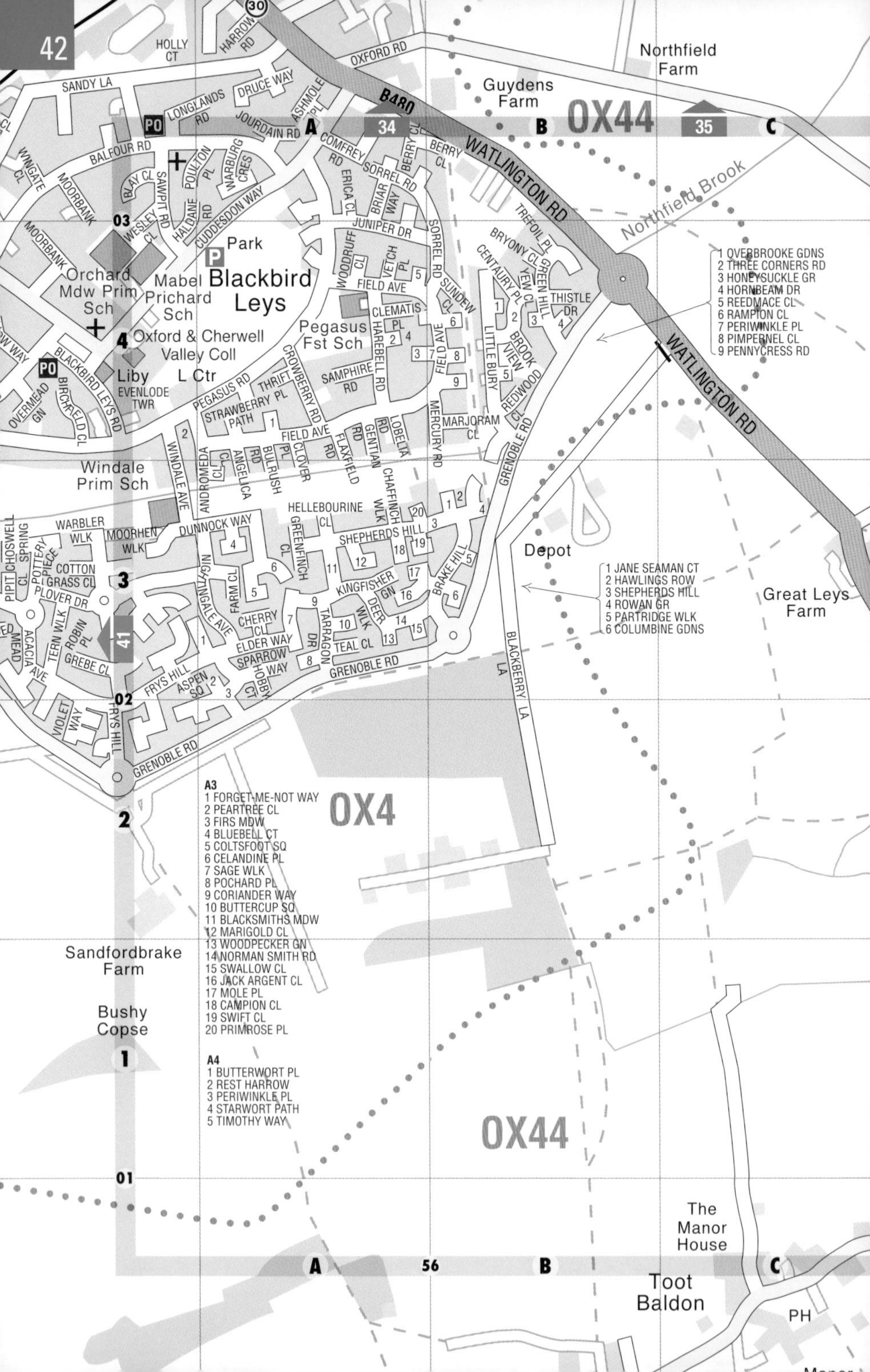
Northfield Farm
Guydens Farm
OX44
Blackbird Leys
Park
Orchard Mdw Prim Sch
Mabel Prichard Sch
Pegasus Fst Sch
Oxford & Cherwell Valley Coll
L Ctr
Liby
EVENLODE TWR
Windale Prim Sch
Depot
Great Leys Farm
OX4
Sandfordbrake Farm
Bushy Copse
The Manor House
Toot Baldon
PH
WATLINGTON RD
OXFORD RD
B480
Northfield Brook
GRENOBLE RD
BLACKBERRY LA
1 OVERBROOKE GDNS
2 THREE CORNERS RD
3 HONEYSUCKLE GR
4 HORNBEAM DR
5 REEDMACE CL
6 RAMPION CL
7 PERIWINKLE PL
8 PIMPERNEL CL
9 PENNYCRESS RD
1 JANE SEAMAN CT
2 HAWLINGS ROW
3 SHEPHERDS HILL
4 ROWAN GR
5 PARTRIDGE WLK
6 COLUMBINE GDNS
A3
1 FORGET-ME-NOT WAY
2 PEARTREE CL
3 FIRS MDW
4 BLUEBELL CT
5 COLTSFOOT SQ
6 CELANDINE PL
7 SAGE WLK
8 POCHARD PL
9 CORIANDER WAY
10 BUTTERCUP SQ
11 BLACKSMITHS MDW
12 MARIGOLD CL
13 WOODPECKER GN
14 NORMAN SMITH RD
15 SWALLOW CL
16 JACK ARGENT CL
17 MOLE PL
18 CAMPION CL
19 SWIFT CL
20 PRIMROSE PL
A4
1 BUTTERWORT PL
2 REST HARROW
3 PERIWINKLE PL
4 STARWORT PATH
5 TIMOTHY WAY
34
35
41
56

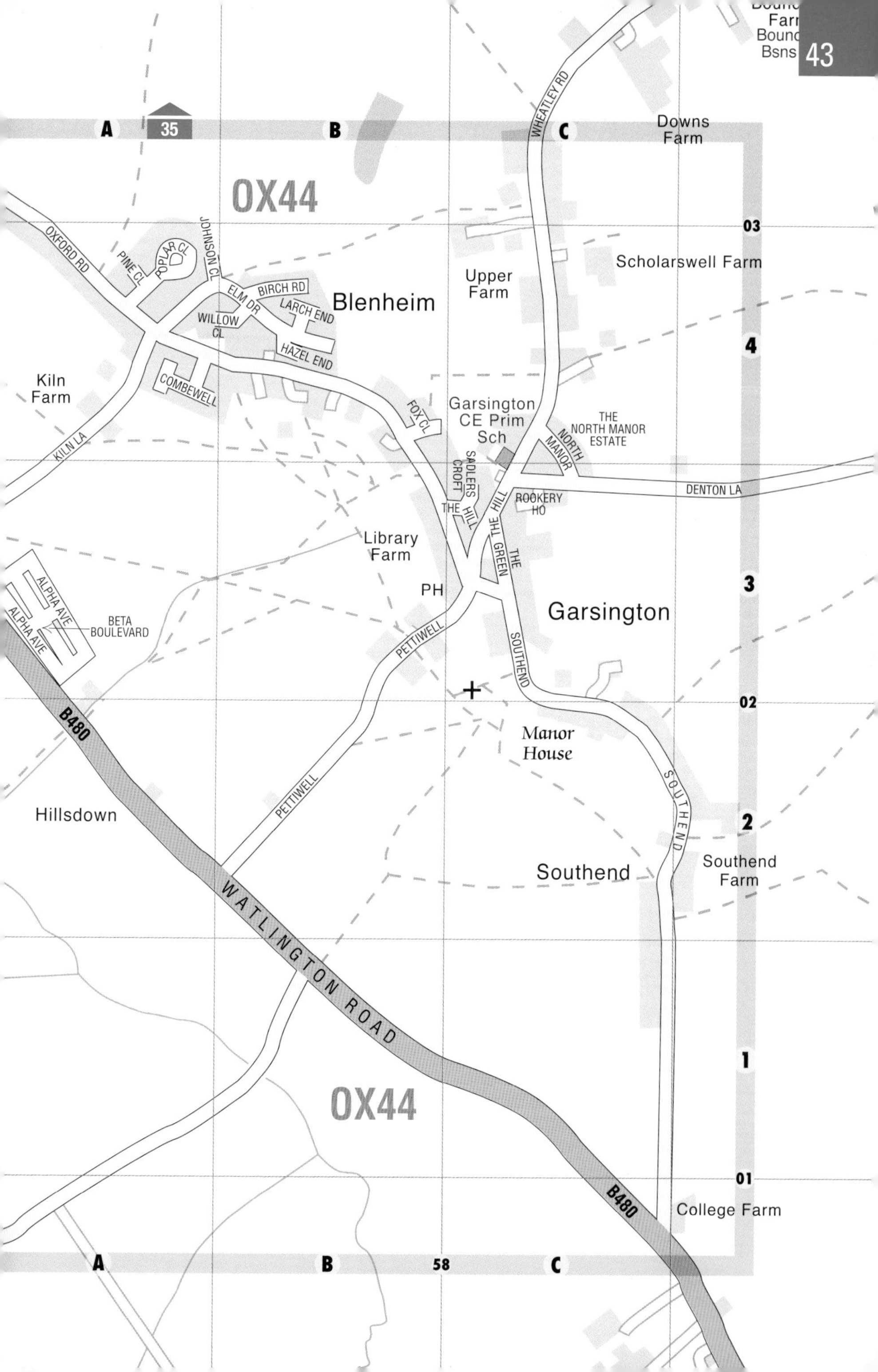
Bound
Farm
Bound
Bsns
A
35
B
C
Downs Farm
WHEATLEY RD
OX44
03
Scholarswell Farm
OXFORD RD
PINE CL
POPLAR CL
JOHNSON CL
BIRCH RD
ELM DR
LARCH END
WILLOW CL
HAZEL END
Blenheim
Upper Farm
4
Kiln Farm
COMBEWELL
FOX CL
Garsington CE Prim Sch
THE NORTH MANOR ESTATE
NORTH MANOR
KILN LA
SADLERS CROFT
THE HILL
THE HILL
ROOKERY HO
DENTON LA
Library Farm
THE GREEN
THE GREEN
PH
3
ALPHA AVE
ALPHA AVE
BETA BOULEVARD
Garsington
PETTIWELL
SOUTHEND
02
B480
Manor House
PETTIWELL
SOUTHEND
Hillsdown
2
Southend
Southend Farm
WATLINGTON ROAD
1
OX44
01
B480
College Farm
A
B
58
C

LEIGH CROFT
BEECH CL
PH
BESSELSLEIGH RD
SANDLEIGH RD
WATSON CRES
BERRYMERE RD
MITCHELL CL
COUPLAND RD
SDOWNE ROAD
01
Community Ctr
CANDY WAY
Wootton
THE WILLOWS
Manor Farm
A
36
B
37
C
Tommy's Farm
HOME CL
OX1
FOX LA
Broom H Copse
Copse View
Blagrove Copse
B4017 LAMBOROUGH HILL
30
MATHEWS WAY
HUXLEY CL
ARTHUR EVANS CL
ST PETER'S CL
HAWKINS WAY
THE OLD POUND
4
Blagrove Farm
3
HONEYBOTTOM LA
GREEN LA
Starveall Farm
00
OX13
WHITECROSS
2
LONG FURLONG RD
Airfield
SPEY RD
MEDWAY RD
MEDWAY CL
1
CHOLSWELL CT
DART RD
Dalton Barracks
Dunmore Farm
B4017
99
CHOLSWELL RD
WELLAND CL
AVON RD
TYNE RD
CONWAY RD
SEVERN RD
DERWENT CL
NENE RD
LONG TOW
48

37
38
Bayworth
Chandlings Manor Sch
OX1
01
LINCOMBE LA
THE QUARRY
QUARRY RD
GREEN LA
OX1
4
Bayworth House
Sunningwell
Sunningwell CE Prim Sch
PH
DARK LA
PO
PEN LA
BEAULIEU CT
BULLSMEAD
OX13
LODGE HILL INTERCHANGE
3
A34
46
00
Sugnell Copse
Nursery
PEN LA
Depot
SUNNINGWELL RD
A4183
LODGE HILL
2
OX14
OXFORD RD
1 PRINCE GR
2 BALLARD CHASE
3 CULLERNE CL
DUNMORE RD
Long Furlong Farm
LOVELACE CL
KNOLLYS CL
ALEXANDER CL
Tilsley Park
ROSE AVE
HANSON RD
BOULTER DR
GIBSON CL
1
MATTOCK WAY
RAINBOW WAY
HUNTER CL
PYTENRY CL
A34
FOSTER RD
WOODLEY CL
LOYD CL
NORTHFIELD RD
SUMMER FIELDS
LYFORD WAY
CARSE CL
THISTLECROFT CL
KYSBIE CL
Long Furlong Prim Sch
EDEN CROFT
THE GROVE
COMPTON DR
99
BOREFORD CL
OTWELL CL
LYNGES CL
LANGLEY RD
FRANKLYN CL
NORTH AVE
ABINGDON
DUNMORE RD
SPENLOVE CL
ALLDER CL
SOUTH AVE
WEST AVE
30
MANDEVILLE CL
CHILDREY WAY
LUMBERD RD
BRODE CL
PYKES CL
HEAN CL
49
50
SOUTH AVE
WHEATCROFT CL
HILLVIEW RD
HOLLAND RD
WELFORD GDNS
GARFORD CL
APPLEFORD
P
FARM RD
AUSTIN PL
LINDSAY DR
BEECH
SELLWOOD RD

Bayworth
A
38
Upper Sugworth Copse
B
Lower Sugworth Copse
39
C
Chandlings Manor Sch
OX1
A34
01
GREEN LA
OX13
4
SUGWORTH LA
Bayworth House
3
A4183
45
A34
LODGE HILL INTERCHANGE
OX14
Sugnell Copse
00
Nursery
OXFORD RD
Depot
LODGE HILL
Radley Park
2
Radley Coll
ABINGDON
DUNMORE RD
LOVELACE CL
KNOLLYS CL
ALEXANDER CL
1
1 SADLERS CT
2 BUCKLERS BURY RD
3 SHRIEVES CL
4 BARFLEUR CL
Peach Croft Farm
GIBSON CL
MATTOCK WAY
RAINBOW WAY
HUNTER CL
PYTENRY CL
COVENT CL
LOYD CL
SUMMER FIELDS
LYFORD WAY
CARSE CL
ETHELHELM CL
TWELVE ACRE DR
NORTHFIELD RD
EDEN CROFT
99
A4183
THE GROVE
COMPTON DR
THISTLECROFT CL
BOREFORD RD
AMYCE CL
WHITE
NORTH AVE
SOUTH AVE
WEST AVE
30
OTWELL CL
LYNGES CL
ELIZABETH AVE
PENN CL
RUSHMEAD COPSE
MANDEVILLE
CHILDREY WAY
BEAGLE CL
SOUTH AVE
A
PYKES CL
HEAN CL
51
50
B
WICK CL
C
WHEATCR CL
GINGE CL
CHARNEY AVE
WELFORD GDNS
GARFORD CL
APPLEFOR
P
LINDSAY DR
PEACHCROFT RD
ENEY CL
PAGISTERS RD
HOUND CL
WOOD RD
BUS
NORRIS
CHAMPS
BARROW

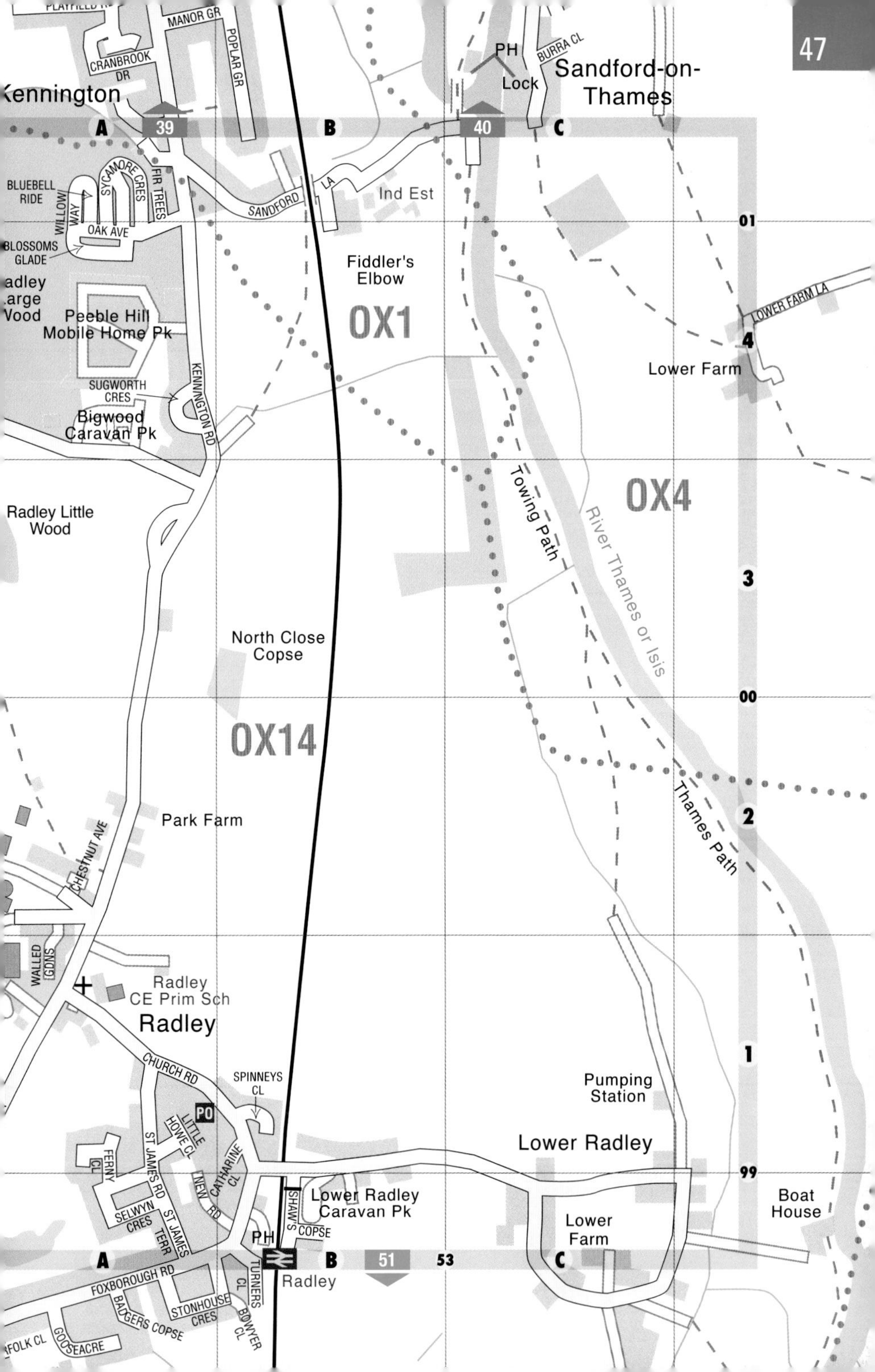

Kennington
Sandford-on-Thames
PH
Lock
BURRA CL
MANOR GR
POPLAR GR
CRANBROOK DR
A
39
B
40
C
BLUEBELL RIDE
WILLOW WAY
SYCAMORE CRES
FIR TREES
OAK AVE
BLOSSOMS GLADE
SANDFORD LA
Ind Est
01
Fiddler's Elbow
Radley Large Wood
Peeble Hill Mobile Home Pk
OX1
LOWER FARM LA
4
Lower Farm
SUGWORTH CRES
KENNINGTON RD
Bigwood Caravan Pk
Towing Path
OX4
River Thames or Isis
Radley Little Wood
3
North Close Copse
00
OX14
Thames Path
2
Park Farm
CHESTNUT AVE
WALLED GDNS
Radley CE Prim Sch
Radley
1
CHURCH RD
SPINNEYS CL
Pumping Station
PO
LITTLE HOWE CL
Lower Radley
FERNY CL
ST JAMES RD
CATHARINE CL
NEW RD
99
SHAW'S COPSE
Lower Radley Caravan Pk
Boat House
SELWYN CRES
ST JAMES TERR
Lower Farm
PH
A
B
51
53
C
FOXBOROUGH RD
TURNERS CL
Radley
BADGERS COPSE
STONHOUSE CRES
BOWYER CL
GOOSEACRE

44
A
B
C
99
4
3
98
2
1
97
Dalton Barracks
Airfield
Dunmore Farm
Stowford House
Shippon
Manor Prep Sch
Manor Farm
Church Farm
OX13
OX14
Sch of St Helen & St Katharine
Larkmead Sch
New Cemy
Old Cemy
Abingdon Bsns Pk
Abingdon Community
Fairacres Sh & Trad Est
Supermarket
Ock Bridge
Weir
River Ock
Wildmoor Brook
Larkhill Stream
SPEY RD
MEDWAY RD
MEDWAY CL
CHOLSWELL CT
DART RD
WELLAND CL
DERWENT CL
AVON RD
TYNE RD
CONWAY RD
SEVERN RD
NENE RD
LONG TOW
CHOLSWELL RD
CHERRY TREE DR
LABURNUM AVE
MERLIN RD
HAWTHORNE AVE
SYCAMORE CL
CHESTNUT TREE CL
WILLOW TREE CL
ROOKERY CL
ELM TREE WLK
WHITEHOUSE CL
FARINGDON RD
BARROW RD
THE SPINNEY 1
LARKHILL RD 2
LARKHILL PL 3
COPENHAGEN DR
YPRES WAY
MONS WAY
INKERMAN CL
STEVENSON DR
RAWLINGS GR
HARDING RD
KNAPP CL
CURTYN CL
FIELDSIDE
WYNDYKE FURLONG
FOXCOMBE CT
WINDRUSH CT
WESTFIELDS
SPRING GDNS
ANNA PAVLOVA CL
SPRING RD
HITCHINGS CT
BLACKLANDS WAY
NUFFIELD WAY
COLWELL DR
WILLOW BROOK
CEMETERY RD
EYSTON WAY
KIMBER RD
FAIRACRES
WINTERBORNE RD
EXBOURNE RD
VICTORIA RD
EDWARD ST
C1
1 BUCKLES CL
2 SPRING TERR
3 BUCKLAND MEWS
4 JUNIPER CT
5 The Unicorn Sch
A415 Witney
A415
MARCHAM RD
A34
B4017
OCK MILL CL
48
52
JENYNS CT
POTENGER WAY
CHAUNTERELL WAY
SHEPHERD GDNS
NASH DR
FRANCIS
SUFFOLK
RILEY CL
LADYGROVE PADDOCK
LADYGROVE

Long Furlong Farm
Tilsley Park
OX14
Long Furlong Prim Sch
A1
1 MAYOTT'S RD
2 CARSWELL CT
3 CROWN MEWS
4 TOMKIN'S ALMSHOUSES
5 OCK MEWS
A2
1 THORNHILL WLK
2 BOROUGH WLK
3 FINMORE CL
Dunmore Prim Sch
Wildmoor
Abingdon & Witney Coll
Fitzharrys Sch
Northcourt
Rush Common Prim Sch
Radley Road Ind Est
Thomas Reade Prim Sch
Wootton Rd Ind Est
John Mason Sch
St Nicolas CE Prim Sch
Recn Gd
Our Ladys Convent Jun & Sen Sch
Kingfisher Sch
St Edmunds RC Prim Sch
ABINGDON
Abingdon Sch
Carswell Prim Sch
Liby
County Hall Mus
Thames View Ind Pk
Thames View Bsns Ctr
Abbey Stream
B1
1 BANBURY CT
2 THE VINES
3 THE SQUARE
4 MARKET PL
5 LOMBARD ST
6 OLD STATION YD
7 BURGESS CL
8 THE CHARTER
9 VINTNER RD
10 QUAKERS CT
11 REGAL CL
Weir
Lock
Thames Path
OX14
Rye Farm
A34
A4183
OXFORD RD
VINEYARD A4183
STRATTON WAY
STERT ST
HIGH ST
A415
BRIDGE ST A415
B4017
WOOTTON RD
BATH ST
45
50
53

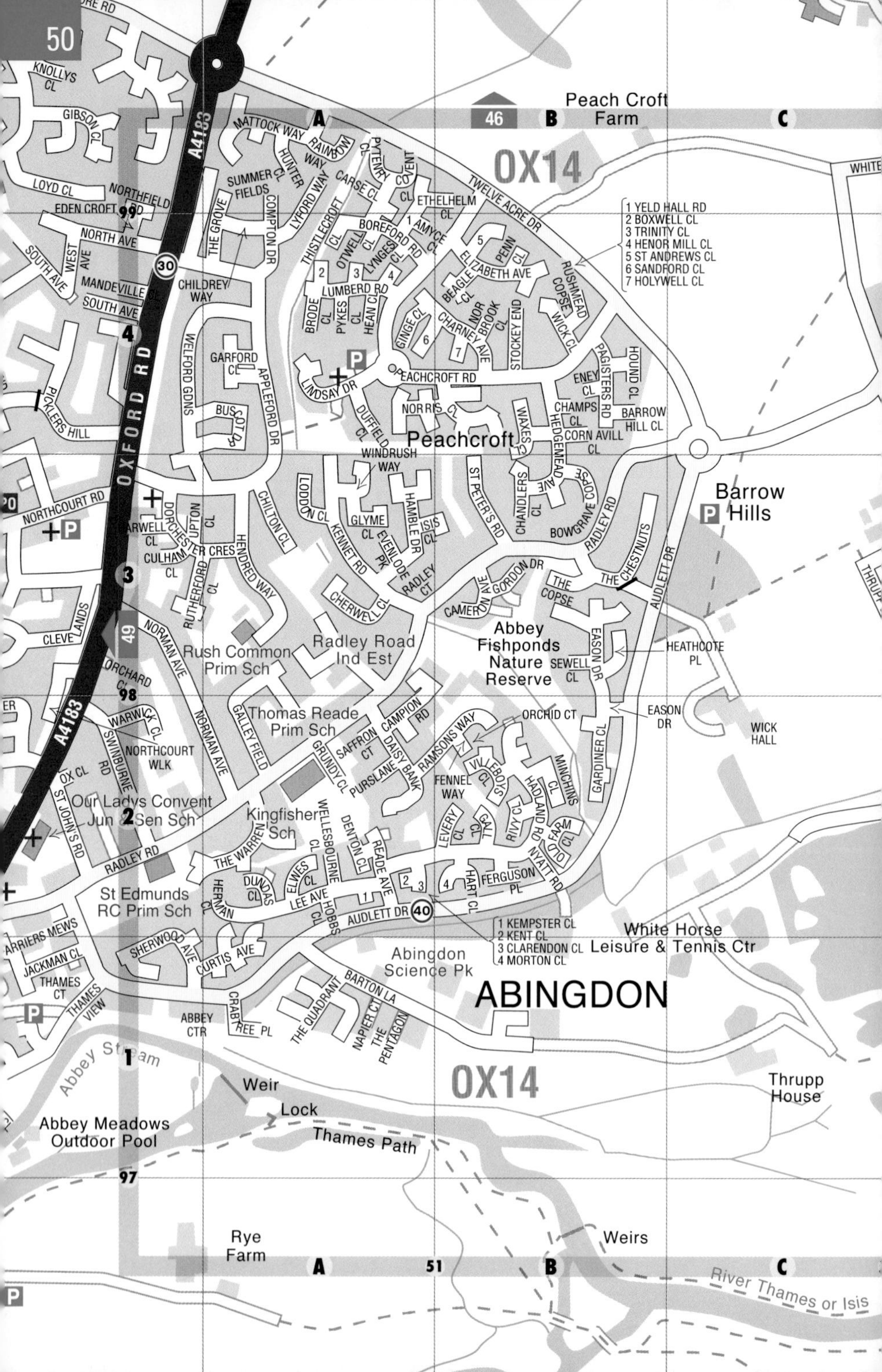
Peach Croft Farm
A
46
B
C
OX14
1 YELD HALL RD
2 BOXWELL CL
3 TRINITY CL
4 HENOR MILL CL
5 ST ANDREWS CL
6 SANDFORD CL
7 HOLYWELL CL
Peachcroft
Barrow Hills
Abbey Fishponds Nature Reserve
Radley Road Ind Est
Rush Common Prim Sch
Thomas Reade Prim Sch
Our Ladys Convent Jun & Sen Sch
Kingfisher Sch
St Edmunds RC Prim Sch
1 KEMPSTER CL
2 KENT CL
3 CLARENDON CL
4 MORTON CL
White Horse Leisure & Tennis Ctr
Abingdon Science Pk
ABINGDON
OX14
Abbey Meadows Outdoor Pool
Weir
Lock
Thames Path
Thrupp House
Weirs
Rye Farm
A
51
B
C
River Thames or Isis
Abbey Stream
WICK HALL
ABBEY CTR
OXFORD RD
A4183
99
98
97
4
3
2
1
49
30
40

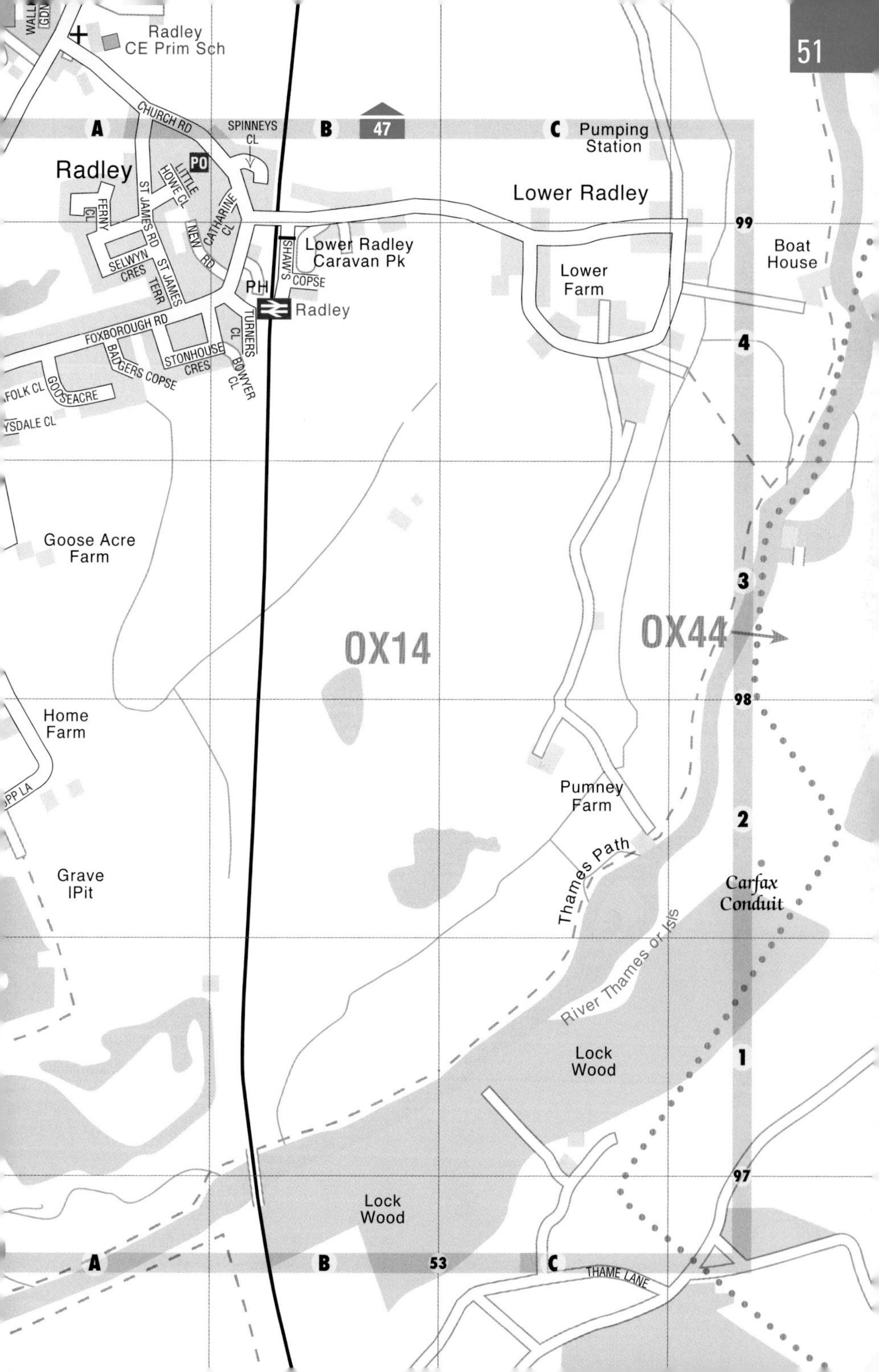
Radley CE Prim Sch
A
B
47
C
CHURCH RD
SPINNEYS CL
Pumping Station
Radley
PO
LITTLE HOWE CL
ST JAMES RD
FERNY CL
NEW RD
CATHARINE CL
Lower Radley
SELWYN CRES
ST JAMES TERR
SHAW'S COPSE
Lower Radley Caravan Pk
Lower Farm
99
Boat House
PH
Radley
FOXBOROUGH RD
TURNERS CL
STONHOUSE CRES
BADGERS COPSE
BOWYER CL
GOOSEACRE
FOLK CL
YSDALE CL
4
Goose Acre Farm
3
OX14
OX44
98
Home Farm
PP LA
Pumney Farm
2
Thames Path
Grave lPit
Carfax Conduit
River Thames or Isis
Lock Wood
1
97
Lock Wood
A
B
53
C
THAME LANE

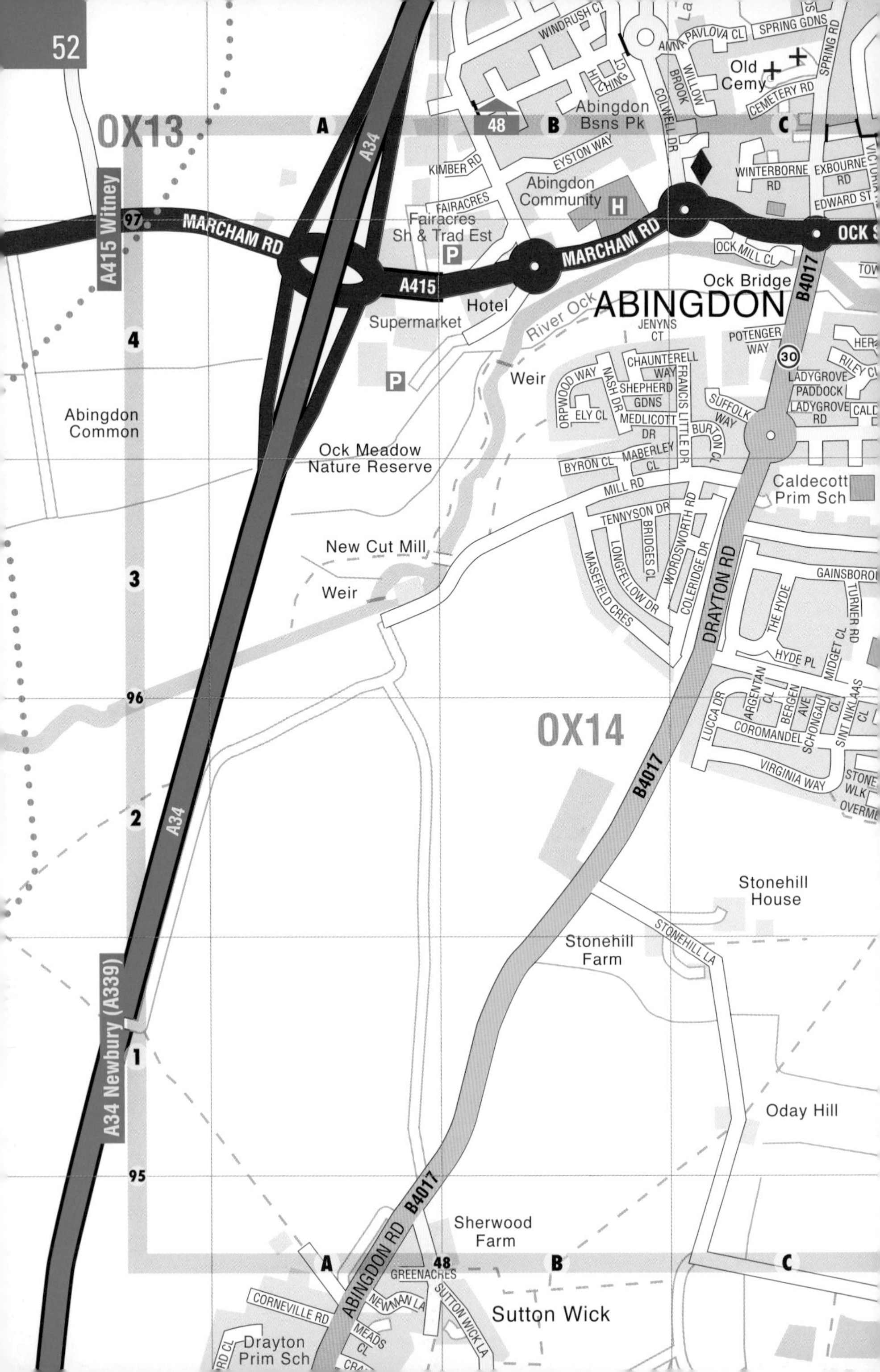
OX13
A
48
B
C
Abingdon Bsns Pk
WINDRUSH CL
ANNA PAVLOVA CL
SPRING GDNS
SPRING RD
Old Cemy
CEMETERY RD
HITCHING CT
BROOK
WILLOW
COLWELL DR
EYSTON WAY
KIMBER RD
WINTERBORNE RD
EXBOURNE RD
EDWARD ST
FAIRACRES
Fairacres Sh & Trad Est
Abingdon Community
A415 Witney
MARCHAM RD
A34
A415
OCK MILL CL
OCK ST
Ock Bridge
B4017
Hotel
Supermarket
River Ock
ABINGDON
JENYNS CT
POTENGER WAY
Weir
CHAUNTERELL WAY
NASH DR
SHEPHERD GDNS
ORPWOOD WAY
ELY CL
MEDLICOTT DR
FRANCIS LITTLE DR
SUFFOLK WAY
BURTON CL
LADYGROVE PADDOCK
LADYGROVE RD
RILEY CL
Abingdon Common
Ock Meadow Nature Reserve
BYRON CL
MABERLEY CL
MILL RD
Caldecott Prim Sch
TENNYSON DR
BRIDGES CL
WORDSWORTH RD
LONGFELLOW DR
MASEFIELD CRES
COLERIDGE DR
DRAYTON RD
New Cut Mill
Weir
THE HYDE
HYDE PL
TURNER RD
MIDGET CL
GAINSBOROUGH
LUCCA DR
ARGENTAN CL
BERGEN AVE
SCHONGAU CL
SINT NIKLAAS CL
COROMANDEL
VIRGINIA WAY
STONE WLK
OVERMEAD
OX14
4
3
96
2
1
95
97
30
A34 Newbury (A339)
Stonehill House
Stonehill Farm
STONEHILL LA
Oday Hill
ABINGDON RD
Sherwood Farm
GREENACRES
NEWMAN LA
SUTTON WICK LA
Sutton Wick
CORNEVILLE RD
MEADS CL
Drayton Prim Sch

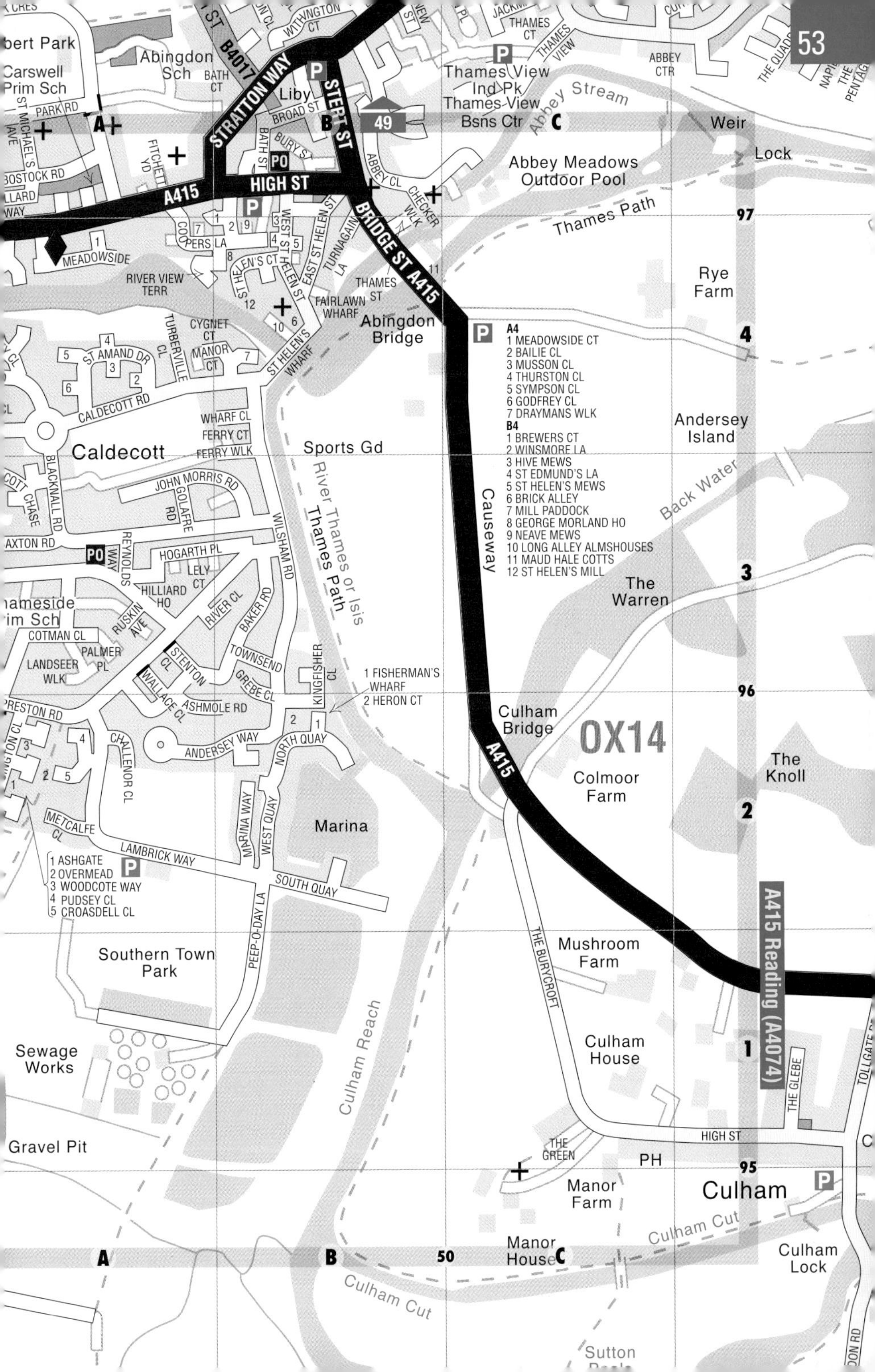

Carswell Prim Sch

Abingdon Sch

BATH CT

Liby

BROAD ST

THAMES CT

THAMES VIEW

ABBEY CTR

Thames View Ind Pk

Thames View Bsns Ctr

Abbey Stream

Weir

Lock

Abbey Meadows Outdoor Pool

97

B4017

STRATTON WAY

STERT ST

49

BURY'S ST

A415

HIGH ST

PO

BATH ST

FITCHETTS YD

River View Terr

MEADOWSIDE

ST HELEN'S ST

ST HELEN'S ST

COPERS LA

WEST ST HELEN'S ST

EAST ST HELEN'S ST

TURNAGAIN LA

ABBEY CL

CHECKER WLK

THAMES ST

11

BRIDGE ST A415

Thames Path

Rye Farm

97

FAIRLAWN WHARF

Abingdon Bridge

CYGNET

TURBERVILLE LA

ST AMAND DR

MANOR CT

CALDECOTT RD

ST HELEN'S WHARF

WHARF CL

FERRY CT

FERRY WLK

Sports Gd

A4
1 MEADOWSIDE CT
2 BAILIE CL
3 MUSSON CL
4 THURSTON CL
5 SYMPSON CL
6 GODFREY CL
7 DRAYMANS WLK

B4
1 BREWERS CT
2 WINSMORE LA
3 HIVE MEWS
4 ST EDMUND'S LA
5 ST HELEN'S MEWS
6 BRICK ALLEY
7 MILL PADDOCK
8 GEORGE MORLAND HO
9 NEAVE MEWS
10 LONG ALLEY ALMSHOUSES
11 MAUD HALE COTTS
12 ST HELEN'S MILL

4

Andersey Island

Back Water

Caldecott

BLACKNALL RD

COTT CHASE

JOHN MORRIS RD

GO-LAFRE RD

WILSHAM RD

River Thames or Isis

Thames Path

The Warren

3

AXTON RD

REYNOLDS WAY

PO

HOGARTH PL

HILLIARD HO

LELY CT

RUSKIN AVE

RIVER CL

BAKER RD

STENTON CL

TOWNSEND

GREBE CL

KINGFISHER

3

1 FISHERMAN'S WHARF
2 HERON CT

96

Thameside Prim Sch

COTMAN CL

PALMER PL

WALLACE CL

ASHMOLE RD

ANDERSEY WAY

NORTH QUAY

Culham Bridge

A415

Colmoor Farm

The Knoll

2

LANDSEER WLK

PRESTON RD

CHALLENOR CL

MARINA WAY

WEST QUAY

Marina

METCALFE CL

LAMBRICK WAY

PEEP-O-DAY LA

SOUTH QUAY

Mushroom Farm

THE BURYCROFT

A415 Reading (A4074)

1 ASHGATE
2 OVERMEAD
3 WOODCOTE WAY
4 PUDSEY CL
5 CROASDELL CL

Southern Town Park

Culham Reach

Culham House

THE GLEBE

TOLLGATE RD

1

Sewage Works

THE GREEN

HIGH ST

PH

95

Culham

Gravel Pit

Manor Farm

Culham Cut

Culham Lock

A

B

50

Manor House

C

Culham Cut

Sutton

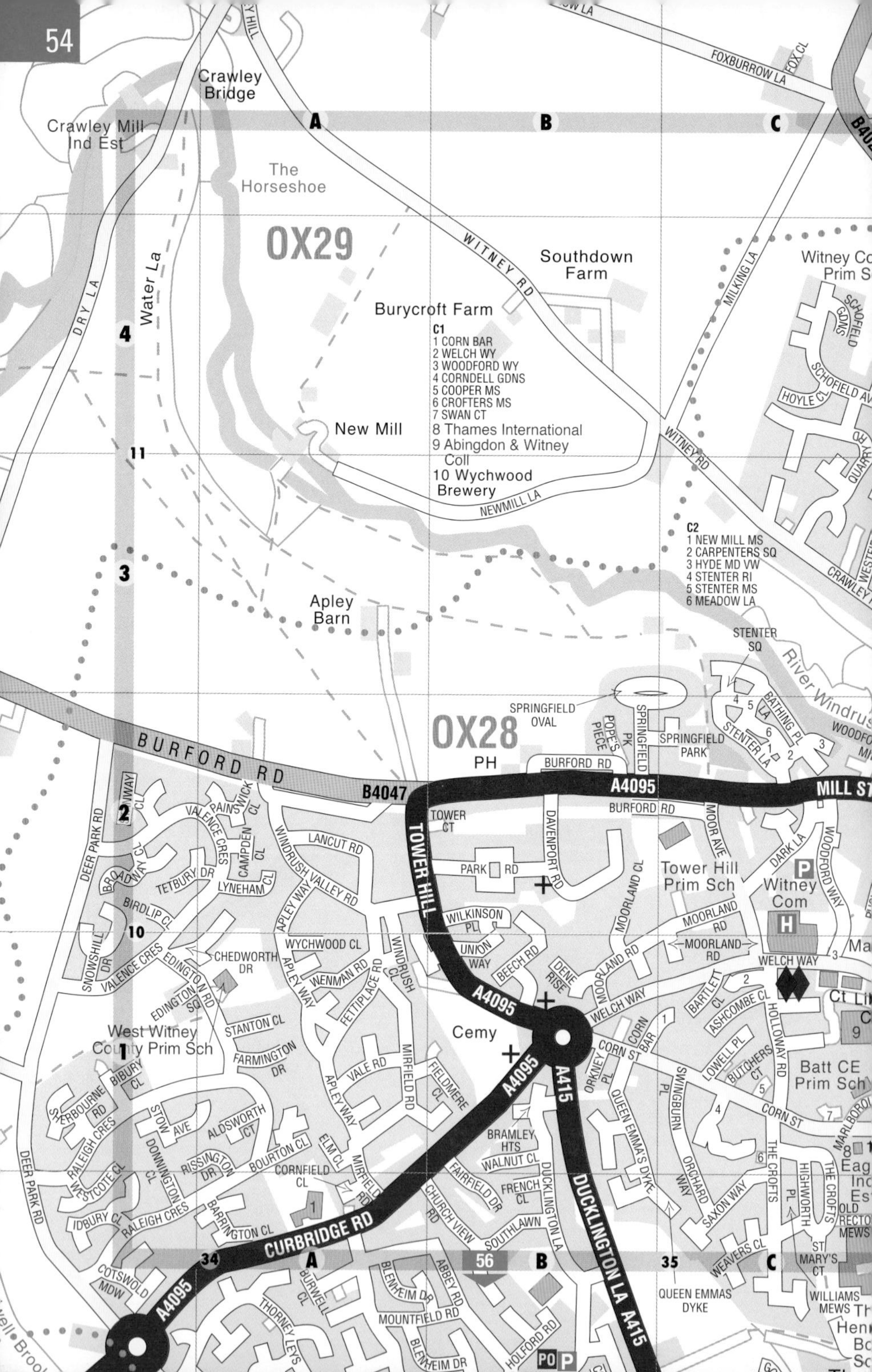
Crawley Bridge
Crawley Mill Ind Est
The Horseshoe
OX29
Water La
DRY LA
WITNEY RD
Southdown Farm
Burycroft Farm
C1
1 CORN BAR
2 WELCH WY
3 WOODFORD WY
4 CORNDELL GDNS
5 COOPER MS
6 CROFTERS MS
7 SWAN CT
8 Thames International
9 Abingdon & Witney Coll
10 Wychwood Brewery
New Mill
NEWMILL LA
FOXBURROW LA
FOX CL
MILKING LA
Witney Co Prim S
SCHOFIELD GDNS
SCHOFIELD AV
HOYLE CL
QUARRY RD
C2
1 NEW MILL MS
2 CARPENTERS SQ
3 HYDE MD VW
4 STENTER RI
5 STENTER MS
6 MEADOW LA
CRAWLEY
Apley Barn
STENTER SQ
River Windrus
SPRINGFIELD OVAL
OX28
POPE'S PIECE
SPRINGFIELD PK
SPRINGFIELD PARK
BATHING PL
STENTER LA
WOODFO
PH
BURFORD RD
BURFORD RD
B4047
A4095
MILL ST
TOWER CT
TOWER HILL
DAVENPORT RD
MOOR AVE
PARK RD
DARK LA
WOODFORD WAY
Tower Hill Prim Sch
Witney Com
MOORLAND CL
MOORLAND RD
WILKINSON PL
UNION WAY
BEECH RD
DENE RISE
WELCH WAY
DEER PARK RD
PAINSWICK CL
VALENCE CRES
CAMPDEN CL
LANCUT RD
WINDRUSH VALLEY RD
BROADWAY CL
TETBURY DR
LYNEHAM CL
BIRDLIP CL
SNOWSHILL DR
APLEY WAY
WYCHWOOD CL
WINDRUSH CL
CHEDWORTH DR
EDINGTON RD
EDINGTON SQ
WENMAN RD
FETTIPLACE RD
A4095
Cemy
BARTLETT CL
ASHCOMBE CL
HOLLOWAY RD
CORN BAR
CORN ST
ORKNEY PL
LOWELL PL
BUTCHERS CT
Batt CE Prim Sch
West Witney County Prim Sch
STANTON CL
FARMINGTON DR
VALE RD
MIRFIELD RD
FIELDMERE CL
A415
BIBURY CL
SHERBOURNE RD
RALEIGH CRES
STOW AVE
ALDSWORTH CT
BOURTON CL
DONNINGTON CL
RISSINGTON DR
WESTCOTE CL
ELM CL
CORNFIELD CL
BRAMLEY HTS
WALNUT CL
FRENCH CL
FAIRFIELD DR
DUCKLINGTON LA
QUEEN EMMA'S DYKE
SWINGBURN PL
ORCHARD WAY
SAXON WAY
THE CROFTS
HIGHWORTH PL
MARLBOROUGH
OLD RECTORY MEWS
IDBURY CL
BARRINGTON CL
CHURCH VIEW RD
SOUTHLAWN
CURBRIDGE RD
WEAVERS CL
ST MARY'S CT
34
A
56
B
35
C
COTSWOLD MDW
BURWELL CL
BLENHEIM DR
ABBEY RD
QUEEN EMMAS DYKE
THORNEY LEYS
MOUNTFIELD RD
HOLFORD RD
DUCKLINGTON LA A415
WILLIAMS MEWS
PO P

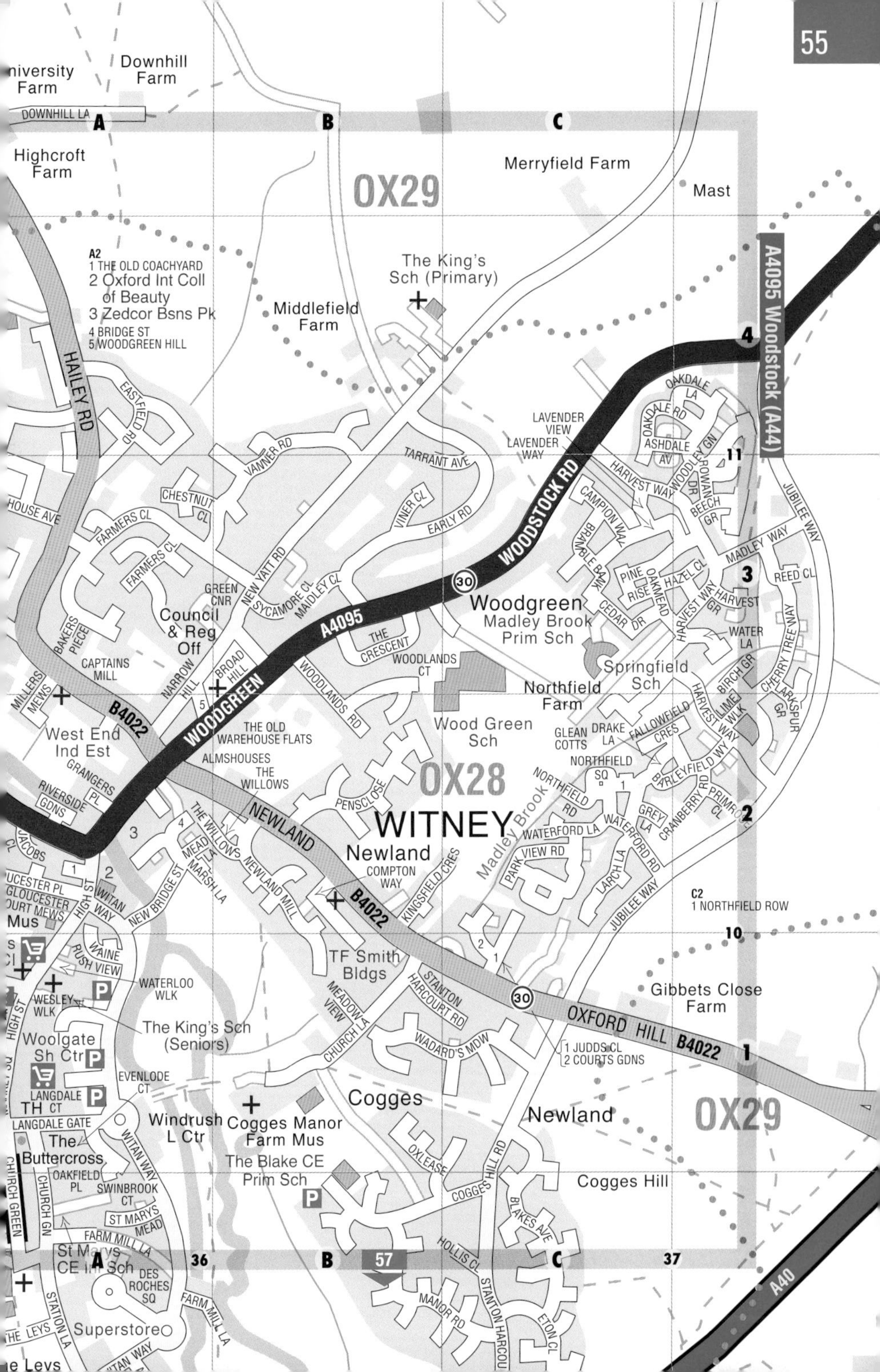

Downhill Farm
niversity Farm
DOWNHILL LA
Highcroft Farm
OX29
Merryfield Farm
Mast
A4095 Woodstock (A44)
A2
1 THE OLD COACHYARD
2 Oxford Int Coll of Beauty
3 Zedcor Bsns Pk
4 BRIDGE ST
5 WOODGREEN HILL
The King's Sch (Primary)
Middlefield Farm
HAILEY RD
EASTFIELD RD
VANNER RD
TARRANT AVE
CHESTNUT CL
FARMERS CL
VINER CL
EARLY RD
WOODSTOCK RD
GREEN CNR
NEW YATT RD
SYCAMORE CL
MAIDLEY CL
A4095
Council & Reg Off
BAKERS PIECE
CAPTAINS MILL
NARROW HILL
BROAD HILL
WOODGREEN
THE CRESCENT
WOODLANDS CT
WOODLANDS RD
Woodgreen
Madley Brook Prim Sch
Springfield Sch
Northfield Farm
Wood Green Sch
MILLERS MEWS
B4022
West End Ind Est
GRANGERS PL
RIVERSIDE GDNS
THE OLD WAREHOUSE FLATS
ALMSHOUSES
THE WILLOWS
PENSCLOSE
OX28
WITNEY
Newland
NEWLAND
MEAD LA
MARSH LA
NEW BRIDGE ST
NEWLAND MILL
COMPTON WAY
KINGSFIELD CRES
JACOBS
GLOUCESTER PL
COURT MEWS
HIGH ST
WITAN WAY
Mus
WAINE RUSH VIEW
WATERLOO WLK
WESLEY WLK
The King's Sch (Seniors)
Woolgate Sh Ctr
EVENLODE CT
LANGDALE CT
TH
LANGDALE GATE
The Buttercross
CHURCH GREEN
CHURCH GN
OAKFIELD PL
SWINBROOK CT
ST MARYS MEAD
FARM MILL LA
St Marys CE Inf Sch
DES ROCHES SQ
STATION LA
THE LEYS
Superstore
Leys
Windrush L Ctr
Cogges Manor Farm Mus
The Blake CE Prim Sch
TF Smith Bldgs
MEADOW VIEW
CHURCH LA
STANTON HARCOURT RD
WADARD'S MDW
Cogges
OXLEASE
COGGES HILL RD
BLAKES AVE
HOLLIS CL
MANOR RD
STANTON HARCOU
ETON CL
OXFORD HILL
1 JUDDS CL
2 COURTS GDNS
Newland
Cogges Hill
Gibbets Close Farm
OX29
A40
57
OAKDALE LA
OAKDALE RD
ASHDALE AV
LAVENDER VIEW
LAVENDER WAY
HARVEST WAY
WOODLEY GN
ROWAN DR
BEECH GR
CAMPION WAY
BRAMBLE BANK
PINE RISE
OAKMEAD
HAZEL CL
CEDAR DR
MADLEY WAY
REED CL
JUBILEE WAY
HARVEST GR
WATER LA
CHERRY TREE WAY
BIRCH GR
LIME WLK
LARKSPUR GR
GLEAN COTTS
DRAKE LA
FALLOWFIELD CRES
NORTHFIELD SQ
NORTHFIELD RD
BARLEYFIELD WY
CRANBERRY RD
PRIMROSE CL
GREY LA
WATERFORD LA
WATERFORD RD
PARK VIEW RD
LARCH LA
Madley Brook
C2
1 NORTHFIELD ROW
36
37

Cemy
54
A4095
A415
CURBRIDGE RD
DUCKLINGTON LA
A40 Cheltenham
A4095 Faringdon
A40
Queens Dyke
Prim Sch
Batt CE
Prim Sch
OX28
OX29
Thorney Leys
Ind Pk
THORNEY LEYS
A4
1 Our Lady of Lourdes
RC Prim Sch
Sewage
Works
NEW CLOSE LANE
Hotel
The Leys
Ducklington
Coursehill
Farm
Davis's
Copse
Moulden's
Wood
WELCH WAY
CORN ST
BURWELL DR
MOUNTFIELD RD
BLENHEIM DR
HOLFORD RD
COLWELL DR
FARMHOUSE MDW
BURWELL MDW
KINGFISHER DR
MALLARD DR
HENRY BOX CL
GORDON WAY
STONEGABLES
BEECHGATE
AVENUE ONE
LAKESIDE
DALE WLK
MOORS CL
BEAMHILL CL
BEANHILL RD
CURBRIDGE RD
CHALCROFT CL
WITNEY RD
PARK RD
RALEIGH CRES
DEER PARK RD
SHERBOURNE RD
BIBURY CL
STOW AVE
ALDSWORTH CT
DONNINGTON CL
RISSINGTON DR
BOURTON CL
BARRINGTON CL
IDBURY CL
WESTCOTE CL
FARMINGTON DR
STANTON CL
EDINGTON RD
EDINGTON SQ
VALENCE CL
APLEY WAY
VALE RD
MIRFIELD RD
FIELDMERE CL
WENMAN RD
FETTIPLACE RD
ELM CL
CORNFIELD CL
CHURCH VIEW
FAIRFIELD DR
SOUTHLAWN
FRENCH CL
WALNUT CL
BRAMLEY HTS
DUCKLINGTON LA
ORKNEY PL
QUEEN EMMA'S DYKE
SWINGBURN PL
ORCHARD WAY
SAXON WAY
WEAVERS CL
THESPRINGS
SPRING CL
THE CROFTS
HIGHWORTH PL
HOLLOWAY RD
BUTCHERS CT
LOWELL PL
ASHCOMBE CL
BARTLETT CL
ST MARY'S CT
WILLIAMS MEWS
BURWELL CL
THORNEY LEYS
ABBEY RD
BURWELL CT
WILMOT CL
PO P
09
08
4
3
2
1
A
B
C
34
35

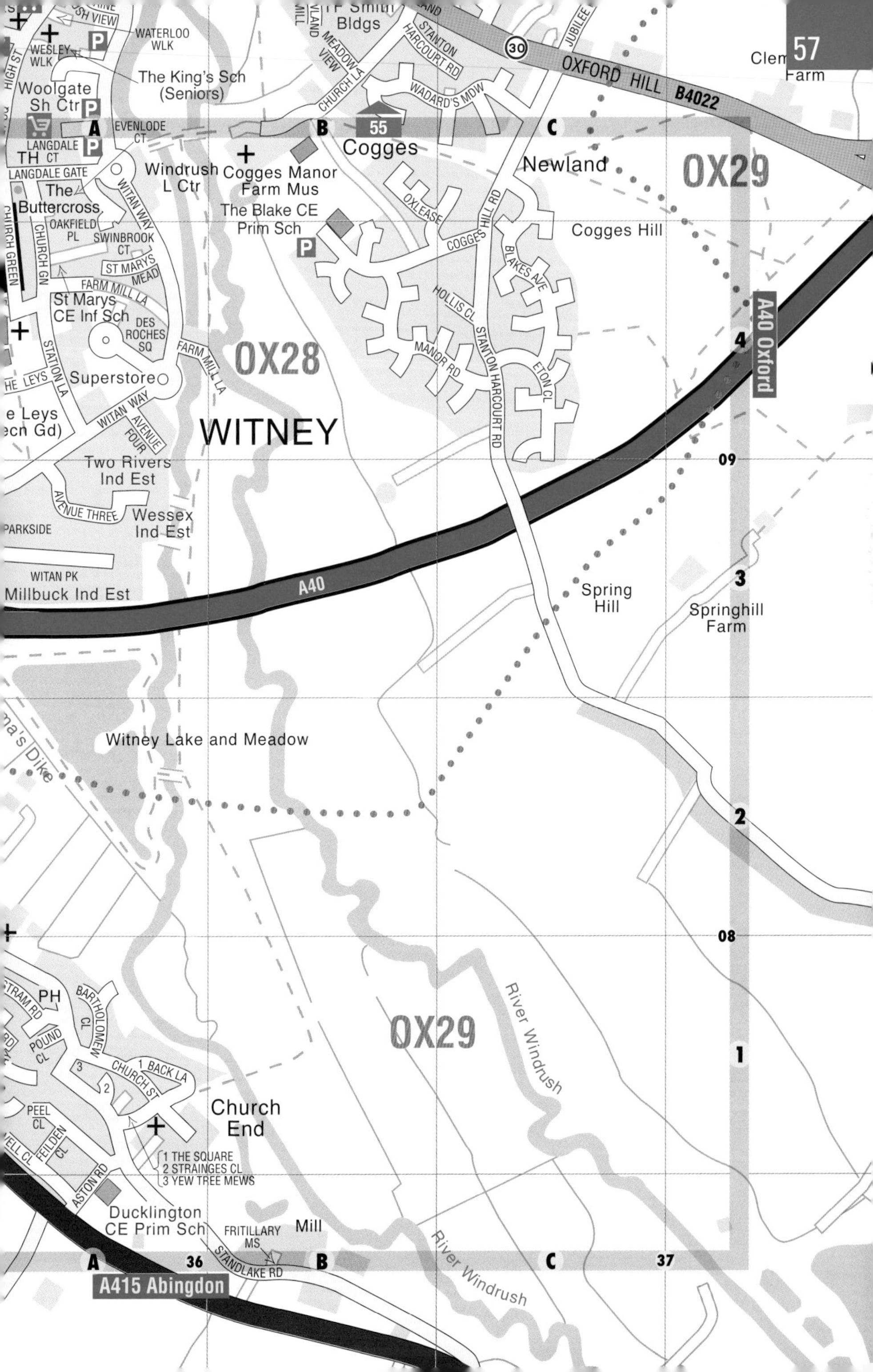

Bldgs
STANTON HARCOURT RD
JUBILEE
30
OXFORD HILL
B4022
Clem
Farm
SH VIEW
WATERLOO WLK
WESLEY WLK
HIGH ST
MEADOW VIEW
CHURCH LA
WADARD'S MDW
The King's Sch (Seniors)
Woolgate Sh Ctr
A
EVENLODE CT
B
55
C
LANGDALE CT
TH
Cogges
Newland
OX29
LANGDALE GATE
Windrush L Ctr
Cogges Manor Farm Mus
The Buttercross
WITAN WAY
OXLEASE
COGGES HILL RD
Cogges Hill
The Blake CE Prim Sch
OAKFIELD PL
SWINBROOK CT
CHURCH GREEN
CHURCH GN
COGGES
BLAKES AVE
ST MARYS MEAD
FARM MILL LA
HOLLIS CL
St Marys CE Inf Sch
DES ROCHES SQ
STANTON HARCOURT RD
A40 Oxford
4
STATION LA
OX28
MANOR RD
ETON CL
FARM MILL LA
THE LEYS
Superstore
WITAN WAY
Leys
Recn Gd)
AVENUE FOUR
WITNEY
Two Rivers Ind Est
09
AVENUE THREE
Wessex Ind Est
PARKSIDE
WITAN PK
3
Spring Hill
Millbuck Ind Est
A40
Springhill Farm
Witney Lake and Meadow
Dike
2
08
PH
BARTHOLOMEW CL
POUND CL
OX29
River Windrush
1
3
CHURCH ST
1 BACK LA
2
Church End
PEEL CL
FEILDEN CL
1 THE SQUARE
2 STRAINGES CL
3 YEW TREE MEWS
ASTON RD
Ducklington CE Prim Sch
FRITILLARY MS
Mill
A
36
STANDLAKE RD
B
C
37
River Windrush
A415 Abingdon

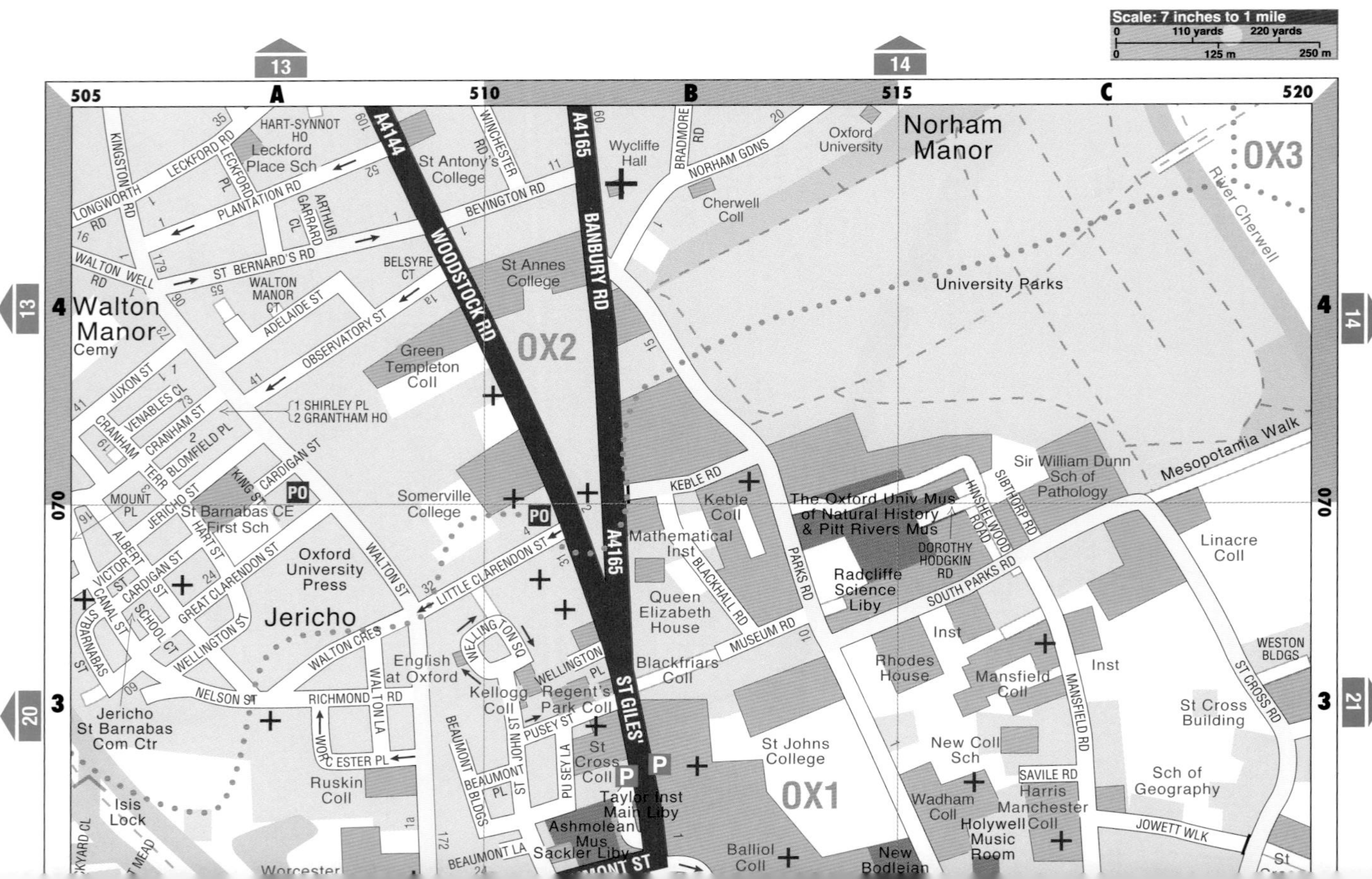
Scale: 7 inches to 1 mile
0
110 yards
220 yards
125 m
250 m
13
14
20
21
4
3
A
B
C
505
510
515
520
070
OX1
OX2
OX3
Norham Manor
Walton Manor
Cemy
Jericho
River Cherwell
Mesopotamia Walk
University Parks
Oxford University
Linacre Coll
Sir William Dunn Sch of Pathology
St Cross Building
Sch of Geography
Inst
Mansfield Coll
Harris Manchester Coll
Holywell Music Room
Wadham Coll
New Coll Sch
Rhodes House
New Bodleian
The Oxford Univ Mus of Natural History & Pitt Rivers Mus
Radcliffe Science Liby
St Johns College
Balliol Coll
Keble Coll
Mathematical Inst
Queen Elizabeth House
Blackfriars Coll
Cherwell Coll
Wycliffe Hall
St Annes College
St Antony's College
Green Templeton Coll
Somerville College
Regent's Park Coll
St Cross Coll
Taylor Inst Main Liby
Ashmolean Mus
Sackler Liby
Kellogg Coll
English at Oxford
Oxford University Press
Ruskin Coll
Worcester
St Barnabas CE First Sch
Jericho St Barnabas Com Ctr
Isis Lock
Leckford Place Sch
A4165
A4144
BANBURY RD
WOODSTOCK RD
ST GILES'
PARKS RD
ST CROSS RD
MANSFIELD RD
SOUTH PARKS RD
SIBTHORP RD
HINSHELWOOD ROAD
DOROTHY HODGKIN RD
KEBLE RD
BLACKHALL RD
MUSEUM RD
JOWETT WLK
SAVILE RD
WESTON BLDGS
NORHAM GDNS
BRADMORE RD
WINCHESTER RD
BEVINGTON RD
BELSYRE CT
OBSERVATORY ST
ADELAIDE ST
WALTON MANOR CT
ST BERNARD'S RD
ARTHUR GARRARD CL
PLANTATION RD
LECKFORD PL
LECKFORD RD
HART-SYNNOT HO
KINGSTON RD
LONGWORTH RD
WALTON WELL RD
JUXON ST
VENABLES CL
CRANHAM ST
CRANHAM TERR
BLOMFIELD PL
1 SHIRLEY PL
2 GRANTHAM HO
CARDIGAN ST
KING ST
JERICHO ST
MOUNT PL
HART ST
ALBERT ST
VICTOR ST
CANAL ST
ST BARNABAS ST
GREAT CLARENDON ST
WELLINGTON ST
SCHOOL CT
NELSON ST
WALTON ST
LITTLE CLARENDON ST
WALTON CRES
RICHMOND RD
WALTON LA
WORCESTER PL
WELLINGTON SQ
WELLINGTON PL
PUSEY ST
PUSEY LA
ST JOHN ST
BEAUMONT ST
BEAUMONT PL
BEAUMONT BLDGS
BEAUMONT LA
PO
P

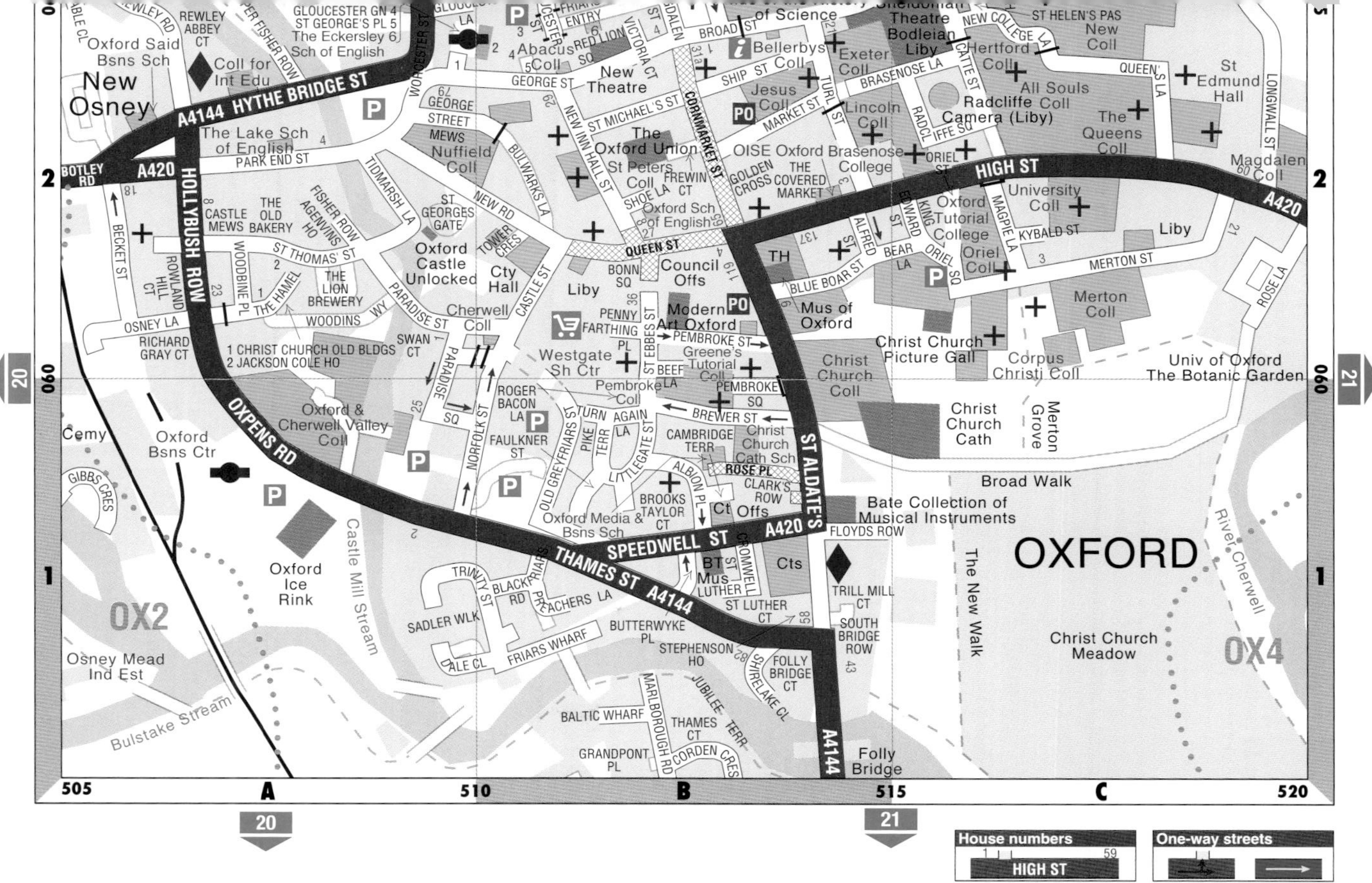

OXFORD
OX4
OX2
River Cherwell
Christ Church Meadow
The New Walk
Broad Walk
Merton Grove
Univ of Oxford The Botanic Garden
Christ Church Cath
Christ Church Coll
Christ Church Picture Gall
Corpus Christi Coll
Merton Coll
MERTON ST
ROSE LA
Magdalen Coll
LONGWALL ST
St Edmund Hall
QUEEN'S LA
The Queens Coll
New Coll
ST HELEN'S PAS
NEW COLLEGE LA
All Souls Coll
Hertford Coll
Radcliffe Camera (Liby)
CATTE ST
Bodleian Liby
Theatre
RADCLIFFE SQ
BRASENOSE LA
Exeter Coll
Lincoln Coll
Brasenose College
TURL ST
University Coll
KYBALD ST
MAGPIE LA
Oriel Coll
ORIEL ST
ORIEL SQ
Oxford Tutorial College
KING EDWARD ST
BEAR LA
ALFRED ST
BLUE BOAR ST
Mus of Oxford
HIGH ST
A420
ST ALDATE'S
Bate Collection of Musical Instruments
FLOYDS ROW
TRILL MILL CT
SOUTH BRIDGE ROW
Folly Bridge
A4144
Cts
CROMWELL ST
ST LUTHER CT
FOLLY BRIDGE CT
SHIRELAKE CL
JUBILEE TERR
CORDEN CRES
THAMES CT
MARLBOROUGH RD
STEPHENSON HO
BUTTERWYKE PL
GRANDPONT PL
BALTIC WHARF
of Science
Bellerbys
Jesus Coll
SHIP ST
BROAD ST
MARKET ST
CORNMARKET ST
OISE Oxford
GOLDEN CROSS
THE COVERED MARKET
TH
QUEEN ST
Council Offs
Modern Art Oxford
PEMBROKE ST
PEMBROKE SQ
Greene's Tutorial Coll
BREWER ST
Christ Church Cath Sch
ROSE PL
CLARK'S ROW
Ct Offs
SPEEDWELL ST
BT
Mus
LUTHER
ALBION PL
CAMBRIDGE TERR
BROOKS TAYLOR CT
ST EBBES ST
BEEF LA
Pembroke Coll
LITTLEGATE ST
TURN AGAIN LA
PIKE TERR
OLD GREYFRIARS ST
Oxford Media & Bsns Sch
THAMES ST
PENNY FARTHING PL
Westgate Sh Ctr
Liby
BONN SQ
The Oxford Union
St Peters Coll
FREWIN CT
Oxford Sch of English
SHOE LA
NEW INN HALL ST
ST MICHAEL'S ST
New Theatre
VICTORIA CT
RED LION SQ
GEORGE ST
Abacus Coll
BULWARKS LA
NEW RD
CASTLE ST
TOWER CRES
Cty Hall
Oxford Castle Unlocked
ST GEORGES GATE
Nuffield Coll
MEWS
GEORGE STREET
WORCESTER ST
Cherwell Coll
PARADISE SQ
PARADISE ST
NORFOLK ST
ROGER BACON LA
FAULKNER ST
TIDMARSH LA
SWAN CT
WYE
BREWERY
WOODINS
THE LION
Oxford & Cherwell Valley Coll
1 CHRIST CHURCH OLD BLDGS CT
2 JACKSON COLE HO
Castle Mill Stream
Oxford Ice Rink
OXPENS RD
FISHER ROW
AGENVINS HO
ST THOMAS' ST
THE HAMEL
THE OLD BAKERY
CASTLE MEWS
WOODBINE PL
HOLLYBUSH ROW
ROWLAND HILL CT
OSNEY LA
RICHARD GRAY CT
BECKET ST
Oxford Bsns Ctr
Cemy
GIBBS CRES
Osney Mead Ind Est
Bulstake Stream
The Lake Sch of English
PARK END ST
HYTHE BRIDGE ST
Coll for Int Edu
REWLEY ABBEY CT
REWLEY RD
Oxford Said Bsns Sch
New Osney
BOTLEY RD
GLOUCESTER GN 4
ST GEORGE'S PL 5
The Eckersley 6 Sch of English
BLACKFRIARS RD
PREACHERS LA
FRIARS WHARF
TRINITY ST
SADLER WLK
DALE CL
505
510
515
520
A
B
C
1
2
060
House numbers
HIGH ST
One-way streets

20

21

20

21

Index

Street names are listed alphabetically and show the locality, the Postcode district, the page number and a reference to the square in which the name falls on the map page

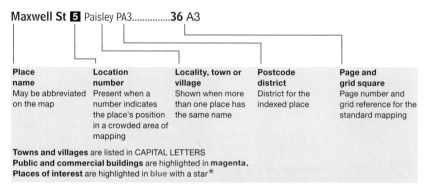

Maxwell St 5 Paisley PA3..............36 A3

Place name	Location number	Locality, town or village	Postcode district	Page and grid square
May be abbreviated on the map	Present when a number indicates the place's position in a crowded area of mapping	Shown when more than one place has the same name	District for the indexed place	Page number and grid reference for the standard mapping

Towns and villages are listed in CAPITAL LETTERS
Public and commercial buildings are highlighted in **magenta.**
Places of interest are highlighted in blue with a star*

Abbreviations used in the index

Acad	**Academy**	Ct	**Court**	Hts	**Heights**	Pl	**Place**
App	**Approach**	Ctr	**Centre**	Ind	**Industrial**	Prec	**Precinct**
Arc	**Arcade**	Ctry	**Country**	Inst	**Institute**	Prom	**Promenade**
Ave	**Avenue**	Cty	**County**	Int	**International**	Rd	**Road**
Bglw	**Bungalow**	Dr	**Drive**	Intc	**Interchange**	Recn	**Recreation**
Bldg	**Building**	Dro	**Drove**	Junc	**Junction**	Ret	**Retail**
Bsns, Bus	**Business**	Ed	**Education**	L	**Leisure**	Sh	**Shopping**
Bvd	**Boulevard**	Emb	**Embankment**	La	**Lane**	Sq	**Square**
Cath	**Cathedral**	Est	**Estate**	Liby	**Library**	St	**Street**
Cir	**Circus**	Ex	**Exhibition**	Mdw	**Meadow**	Sta	**Station**
Cl	**Close**	Gd	**Ground**	Meml	**Memorial**	Terr	**Terrace**
Cnr	**Corner**	Gdn	**Garden**	Mkt	**Market**	TH	**Town Hall**
Coll	**College**	Gn	**Green**	Mus	**Museum**	Univ	**University**
Com	**Community**	Gr	**Grove**	Orch	**Orchard**	Wk, Wlk	**Walk**
Comm	**Common**	H	**Hall**	Pal	**Palace**	Wr	**Water**
Cott	**Cottage**	Ho	**House**	Par	**Parade**	Yd	**Yard**
Cres	**Crescent**	Hospl	**Hospital**	Pas	**Passage**		
Cswy	**Causeway**	HQ	**Headquarters**	Pk	**Park**		

Index of towns, villages, streets, hospitals, industrial estates, railway stations, schools, shopping centres, universities and places of interest

Aba–Ali

A

Abacus Coll OX1 .....**59** B2
Abberbury Ave OX4 ..**32** C2
Abberbury Rd OX4 ..**32** B2
Abbey Cl OX14 ....**49** B1
Abbey Ctr OX14 ......**49** C1
Abbey Fishponds Nature
Reserve* OX14......**50** B3
Abbey Mdws Outdoor
Pool OX14 ....**49** C1
Abbey Rd
Oxford OX2 ....**20** B3
Witney OX28 ....**56** B4

Abbey Wlk OX1 ......**20** B3
Abbots Wood OX3....**23** C2
Abbott Rd OX14......**49** B2
ABINGDON **49** A1
Abingdon Bsns Pk
OX14 ....**48** B1
Abingdon Com Hospl
OX14 ....**48** B1
Abingdon County Hall
Mus* OX14 ....**49** B1
Abingdon Rd
Cumnor OX2 ....**28** A2
Kennington OX1......**31** C2
Oxford OX1 ....**31** C4
Abingdon Sch OX14 ..**49** A1
Abingdon Science Pk
OX14 ....**50** A1

Abingdon & Witney Coll
(Abingdon Campus)
OX14................**49** A3
Abingdon & Witney Coll
(Witney Campus) 9
OX28 ....**54** C1
Ablett Cl OX4 ....**22** B2
Acacia Ave OX4 .....**41** C3
Acland Cl OX3 ....**23** A3
Acre Cl OX3 ....**24** A1
Acremead Rd OX33...**26** A2
Addison Cres OX4....**32** B4
Addison Dr OX4......**33** B1
Adelaide St OX2 .....**58** A4
Agenvins Ho OX1 ....**59** A2
Agnes Ct OX4........**33** B4
Alan Bullock Cl OX4..**21** C3

Albert St OX2........**58** A3
Albion Pl OX1........**59** B1
Aldbarton Dr OX3....**16** C2
Alden Cres OX3......**17** A2
Aldrich Rd OX2 ......**9** C2
Aldsworth Ct OX28 ...**54** A1
Alec Issigonis Way
OX4 ....**33** C4
Alesworth Gr OX3....**15** C3
Alexander Cl
Abingdon OX14 ......**45** C1
Kidlington OX5.......**7** A4
Alexandra Rd OX2....**20** A3
Alfred St OX1........**59** B2
Alhambra La OX4 ....**21** C2
Alice Smith Sq OX4 ..**41** A4
Alison Clay Ho OX3...**23** A4

Allder Cl OX14 . . . . 49 B4
Allin Cl OX4 . . . . 34 A1
All Saints Rd OX3 . . 23 A4
All Soul's Cl OX1 . . 59 C2
Alma Pl OX4 . . . . 22 A2
Almhouses OX28 . . . . . 55 B2
Almond Ave OX5 . . . . . . 6 C4
Almshouses The OX5 . . 4 A4
Alpha Ave OX44 . . . . . . 43 A3
Ambassador Ave OX4 34 A2
Ambleside Dr OX3 . . . 15 C2
Ambrose Rise OX33 . . 27 A2
Amey Cres OX13 . . . . . 44 A4
Amory Cl OX4 . . . . 33 C1
Amyce Cl OX14 . . . . . . 50 A4
Andersey Way OX14 . . 53 B2
Andersons Cl OX5 . . . . 3 B2
Andover Ct ◨1 OX5 . . . . 4 A2
Andromeda Cl OX4 . . 42 A3
Anemone Cl OX4 . . . . 41 C2
Angelica Cl OX4 . . . . 42 A3
Anna Pavlova Cl
  OX14 . . . . 48 C1
Anne Greenwood Cl
  OX4 . . . . 32 C2
Annesley Rd OX4 . . . . 32 C2
Annora Cl OX4 . . . . . . 32 C3
Anson Cl OX33 . . . . . . 27 A2
Apley Way OX28 . . . . . 54 A1
Appleford Dr OX14 . . 50 A4
Appletree Cl OX4 . . . 42 A2
Apsley Rd OX2 . . . . 9 B2
Argentan Cl OX14 . . . 52 C2
Argyle St OX4 . . . . 32 B4
Aristotle La OX2 . . . . . 13 B2
Arlington Dr OX3 . . . 14 C3
Armstrong Rd OX4 . . 40 C3
Arnold Rd OX4 . . . . . . 32 B4
Arnold's Way OX2 . . . . 19 A1
Arthray Rd OX2 . . . . . 19 B2
Arthur Garrard Cl
  OX2 . . . . 58 A4
Arthur St OX2 . . . . 20 B3
Ash Cl OX5 . . . . 3 C1
Ashcombe Cl OX28 . . 54 C1
Ashcroft Cl OX2 . . . . . 18 C3
Ashdale Ave OX28 . . . 55 C4
Ashenden Cl OX14 . . . 49 B3
Ashgate OX14 . . . . 53 A2
Ash Gr OX3 . . . . 16 B2
Ashlong Rd OX3 . . . . . 15 B3
Ashmolean Mus★
  OX1 . . . . 58 B3
Ashmole Pl OX4 . . . . . 34 B1
Ashmole Rd OX14 . . . 53 A2
Ashurst Way OX4 . . . . 32 C1
Ashville Way OX4 . . . . 34 B1
Aspen Sq OX4 . . . . 41 C3
Asquith Rd OX4 . . . . . 32 C1
Astley Ave OX5 . . . . 7 A4
Aston Cl OX14 . . . . . . 49 B1
Aston St OX4 . . . . 22 A1
Atkinson Cl OX3 . . . . . 16 C3
Atkyns Rd OX3 . . . . . . 23 C2
Atwell Pl ◨5 OX3 . . . . . 23 B3

Aubrey Ct OX4 . . . . 32 C2
Audlett Dr OX14 . . . . . 50 A2
Augustine Way OX4 . . 32 C3
Austin Pl OX14 . . . . . . 49 A4
Avens Way OX4 . . . . . . 41 C3
Avenue Four OX28 . . . 57 A4
Avenue La OX4 . . . . . . 22 A2
Avenue One OX28 . . . 56 C3
Avenue The
  Kennington OX1 . . . . . 39 C2
  Wheatley OX33 . . . . . 27 A1
Avenue Three OX28 . . 57 A3
Avenue Two OX28 . . . 57 A3
Avery Ct OX2 . . . . 9 C2
Avon Rd OX13 . . . . 48 B4
Awgar Stone Rd OX3 . 24 A1
Axtell Cl OX5 . . . . 3 B3
Aysgarth Rd OX5 . . . . . 5 C4
Azalea Ave OX5 . . . . 6 C4
Azor's Ct OX4 . . . . 32 C2

◼ B

Back La OX29 . . . . 57 A1
Badger La OX1 . . . . 31 A1
Badgers Copse OX14 . 51 A4
Badgers Wlk OX4 . . . . 33 B4
Bagley Cl OX1 . . . . 39 B4
Bagley Wood Rd OX1 39 B1
Bailey Rd OX4 . . . . 33 C2
Bailie Cl ◨2 OX14 . . . . 53 A4
Bainton Rd OX2 . . . . . . 13 B3
Baker Cl OX3 . . . . 24 A4
Baker Rd OX14 . . . . . . 53 B3
Bakers La OX4 . . . . 32 B2
Bakers Piece OX28 . . . 55 A3
Balfour Rd OX4 . . . . . . 34 A1
Ballard Chase OX14 . . 45 C1
Balliol Coll OX1 . . . . . . 58 B3
Balliol Ct OX2 . . . . 13 B2
Baltic Wharf OX1 . . . . 59 B1
Bampton Cl OX4 . . . . . 33 C1
Banbury Ct ◨1 OX14 . . 49 B1
Banbury Rd
  Cutteslowe OX2 . . . . . . 9 B3
  Kidlington OX5 . . . . 3 B3
  Oxford OX2 . . . . 13 C4
Banbury Road Rdbt
  OX2 . . . . 9 B3
Banjo Rd OX4 . . . . 33 B3
Bankside
  Kidlington OX5 . . . . 3 A4
  Oxford OX3 . . . . 16 C1
Bannister Cl OX4 . . . . 21 C1
Bardwell Ct OX2 . . . . . 14 A2
Bardwell Rd OX2 . . . . 14 A2
Barfleur Cl OX14 . . . . 46 A1
Barleycott La OX1 . . . 31 B2
Barlow Cl OX33 . . . . . . 26 A2
Barn Cl
  Kidlington OX5 . . . . 3 B2
  Oxford OX2 . . . . 29 A4
Barnet St OX4 . . . . 22 B1
Barns Cl OX33 . . . . . . 26 C3
Barns Hay OX3 . . . . . . 15 A4

Barns Ho OX4 . . . . 33 B2
Barn's Rd OX4 . . . . . . 33 C2
Barracks La OX4 . . . . . 22 C1
Barrett St OX2 . . . . 20 B3
Barrington Cl
  Oxford OX3 . . . . 23 A4
  Witney OX28 . . . . 56 A4
Barrow Hill Cl OX14 . . 50 B4
BARROW HILLS 50 C3
Barrow Rd OX13 . . . . . 48 A2
Bartholomew Ave OX5 5 C3
Bartholomew Cl
  OX29 . . . . 57 A1
Bartholomew Rd OX4 33 B2
Bartlemas Cl OX4 . . . . 22 B1
Bartlemas Rd OX4 . . . 22 B2
Bartlett Cl OX28 . . . . . 54 C1
BARTON 16 C2
Barton La
  Abingdon OX14 . . . . . . 50 A1
  Oxford OX3 . . . . 16 B2
Barton Pool OX3 . . . . . 17 A2
Barton Rd OX3 . . . . . . 16 C2
Barton Village Rd
  OX3 . . . . 16 C3
Bassett Rd OX3 . . . . . . 17 A2
Basset Way OX5 . . . . . . 4 A2
Bate Collection of
  Musical Instruments★
  OX1 . . . . 59 B1
Bateman St OX3 . . . . . 23 B4
Bath Ct OX14 . . . . 49 B1
Bathing Pl La OX28 . . 54 C2
Bath Pl OX1 . . . . 59 C2
Bath St
  Abingdon OX14 . . . . . . 49 A2
  Oxford OX4 . . . . 22 A3
Batt CE Prim Sch
  OX28 . . . . 54 C1
Batten Pl OX4 . . . . 40 B3
Bayards Hill Prim Sch ◨
  OX3 . . . . 17 A2
Bayswater Farm OX3 17 B2
Bayswater Farm Rd
  OX3 . . . . 17 B2
Bayswater Rd
  Blenheim OX33 . . . . . . 25 A1
  Oxford OX3 . . . . 17 A2
  Rissinghurst OX3 . . . . . 24 B3
Bay Tree Cl OX4 . . . . . 32 C2
BAYWORTH 38 B1
Bayworth La OX1 . . . . 38 A2
Bayworth Pk OX13 . . . 38 A1
Beagle Cl OX14 . . . . . . 50 B4
Beagles OX5 . . . . 4 B1
Beanhill Cl OX29 . . . . 56 C2
Beanhill Rd OX29 . . . 56 C2
Bear La OX1 . . . . 59 C2
Bears Hedge OX4 . . . . 32 C2
Beauchamp La OX4 . . 33 A2
Beauchamp Pl OX4 . . 33 A2
Beaulieu Ct OX13 . . . 45 B3
Beaumont Bldgs OX1 58 A3
Beaumont Ct OX1 . . . . 39 C3
Beaumont La OX1 . . . 58 B3

Beaumont Pl OX1 . . . . 58 B3
Beaumont Rd OX3 . . 17 A1
Beaumont St OX1 . . . 58 B3
Becket St OX1 . . . . 59 A2
Bedford St OX4 . . . . . . 32 B4
Bedwells Heath OX1 . 37 B3
Beech Cl OX13 . . . . . . 36 B1
Beech Cres OX5 . . . . . . 7 A4
Beech Croft Rd OX2 . . 13 C4
Beeches The OX3 . . . . 16 C2
Beechey Ave OX3 . . . 15 A2
Beechgate OX28 . . . . 56 C3
Beeching Way OX33 . 26 A2
Beech La OX14 . . . . . . 49 B4
Beech Lodge OX3 . . . 16 A1
Beech Pl OX3 . . . . 15 C1
Beech Rd
  Oxford, Botley OX2 . . . 19 B1
  Oxford, Headington
  OX3 . . . . 16 A1
  Wheatley OX33 . . . . . . 26 C1
  Witney OX28 . . . . 54 B1
Beechwood OX4 . . . . . 32 C3
Beechwood Ho OX3 . 16 C2
Beef La OX1 . . . . 59 B2
BEGBROKE 2 C2
Begbroke Cres OX5 . . 2 B3
Begbroke La
  Begbroke OX5 . . . . 2 B3
  Kidlington OX5 . . . . 3 A3
Begbroke Science Pk
  OX5 . . . . 2 C1
Belbroughton Rd
  OX2 . . . . 14 A3
Belgrove Cl OX5 . . . . . 3 B2
Bellenger Way OX5 . . 3 B2
Bellerbys Coll OX1 . . 59 B2
Bell La OX33 . . . . 26 C2
Belsyre Ct OX2 . . . . . 58 A4
Belvedere Rd OX4 . . . 22 B1
Ben Cl OX5 . . . . 3 C3
Benmead Rd OX5 . . . . 3 C3
Bennett Cres OX4 . . . 33 C3
Benouville Cl OX4 . . 34 A4
Benson Pl OX2 . . . . . . 14 B2
Benson Rd
  Abingdon OX14 . . . . . . 49 A4
  Oxford OX3 . . . . 23 B2
Bergamont Pl ◨6 OX4 41 C3
Bergen Ave OX14 . . . . 52 C2
Berkeley Rd OX1 . . . . 37 C3
Bernard Cl OX5 . . . . . . 6 A3
Bernwood Rd OX3 . . 16 C2
Berry Cl OX4 . . . . 34 B1
Berry Croft OX14 . . . . 49 A3
Berrymere Rd OX13 . 36 B1
Bertie Pl OX1 . . . . 31 C2
Bertie Rd OX2 . . . . . . 28 B3
Besselsleigh Rd OX13 36 A2
Beta Bvd OX44 . . . . . . 43 A3
Betty La OX1 . . . . 31 B1
Between Towns Rd
  OX4 . . . . 33 B3

Beverley Cl OX14.....**49** A3
Bevington Rd OX2...**58** B4
Bhandari Cl OX4.....**33** A4
Bicester Rd OX5......**4** A1
Bickerton Rd OX3...**23** A4
Bigwood Cvn Pk
OX14................**47** A4
BINSEY.............**12** C2
Binsey La OX2.......**19** C4
Binswood Ave OX3...**23** C4
Birchfield Cl OX4....**41** C4
Birch Rd OX44.......**43** B4
Biscoe Ct OX33......**27** A2
Bishop Kirk Pl OX2..**9** B1
Blackberry La OX4...**42** B2
BLACKBIRD LEYS..**42** A4
Blackbird Leys L Ctr
OX4................**42** A4
Blackbird Leys Rd
OX4................**41** B4
Blackfriars Coll OX1..**58** B3
Blackfriars Rd OX1...**59** B1
Blackhall Rd OX1....**58** B3
Blacklands Way OX14 48 B1
Blackman Cl OX1...**39** C4
Blacknall Rd OX14...**53** A3
Blacksmiths Mdw **11**
OX4................**42** A3
Blackstock Cl OX3...**23** C1
Blackthorn Cl OX3...**16** C2
Bladon Cl OX2......**9** A2
Blake CE Prim Sch The
OX28..............**55** B1
Blakes Ave OX28.....**57** C4
Blandford Ave OX2...**9** B3
Blandford Rd OX5....**3** B4
Blay Cl OX4.........**34** A1
Bleache Pl OX4......**33** C3
BLENHEIM
Garsington...........**43** B4
Horspath............**25** A1
Blenheim Ct
2 Kidlington OX5......**4** A2
Oxford OX2..........**9** B2
Blenheim Dr
Oxford OX2..........**9** B1
Witney OX28.........**56** A4
Wolvercote OX2......**9** A2
Blenheim La OX33....**26** B2
Blenheim Rd
Horspath OX33.......**25** A1
Kidlington OX5........**4** A2
Blenheim Way OX33..**25** A1
Blewitt Ct OX4.......**40** C4
Blomfield Pl OX2....**58** A4
Blossoms Glade OX14 47 A4
Bluebell Ct **4** OX4...**42** A3
Bluebell Ride OX14...**39** C1
Blue Boar St OX1....**59** B2
BOARS HILL.........**37** B3
Bobby Fryer Cl OX4..**34** A2
Bodleian Liby★ OX1..**59** C2

Bodleian (New Liby)★
OX1................**58** C3
Bodley Pl OX2.......**9** C2
Bodley Rd OX4.......**33** B1
Bonar Rd OX3........**23** C3
Bonn Sq OX1........**59** B2
Boreford Rd OX14....**50** A4
Borough Wlk OX14...**49** A3
Borrowmead Rd OX3 15 C3
Borwood Ct OX5......**7** A4
Bostock Rd OX14....**49** A1
Boswell Rd OX4......**33** C2
Botanic Garden The
(Univ of Oxford)★
OX1................**59** C2
BOTLEY............**19** B2
Botley Intc OX2......**19** B4
Botley Prim Sch OX2.**19** B3
Botley Rd OX2.......**20** A3
Botley Works OX2....**19** B3
Boulevard The OX5...**2** C4
Boulter Dr OX14.....**45** C1
Boulter St OX4.......**22** A3
Boults Cl OX3........**15** A3
Boults La OX3........**15** A3
Boundary Brook Rd
OX4................**32** C4
Bourlon Wood OX14..**48** C3
Bourne Cl OX2......**9** C3
Bourton Cl OX28....**54** A1
Bowerman Cl OX5....**3** B2
Bowgrave Copse
OX14..............**50** B3
Bowness Ave OX3...**15** B2
Bowyer Cl OX14.....**51** B4
Bowyer Rd OX14....**49** B2
Boxhill Rd OX14.....**49** B2
Boxhill Wlk OX14....**49** B2
Boxwell Cl OX14....**50** A4
Bracegirdle Rd OX3..**23** C3
Bradlands OX3.......**10** C1
Bradmore Rd OX2....**14** A2
Brake Hill OX4......**42** B3
Bramble Bank OX28..**55** C3
Brambles The **2** OX3 23 A4
Brambling Way OX4..**41** B4
Bramley Hts OX28....**54** B1
Brampton Cl OX14...**49** A3
Brampton Rd OX3...**17** A2
Bramwell Pl OX4....**22** A2
Brandon Cl OX5......**3** B2
Brasenose Coll OX1..**59** C2
Brasenose Dr OX5...**4** A3
Brasenose Driftway
OX4................**34** A4
Brasenose La OX1...**59** C2
Brewers Ct **11** OX14..**53** B4
Brewer St OX1.......**59** B1
Briar Cl OX5.........**3** A4
Briar End OX5.......**3** A4
Briar Way OX4.......**34** B1
Brick Alley **6** OX14..**53** B4
Bridges Cl OX14.....**52** B3
Bridge St
Abingdon OX14.......**53** B4

Bridge St continued
Oxford OX2..........**20** B3
4 Witney OX28......**55** A2
Brindley Cl OX2.....**13** B2
Broad Cl
Kidlington OX5.......**3** B2
Oxford OX2..........**18** C3
Broad Field Rd OX5...**2** C1
Broadfields OX4.....**41** B4
Broadhead Pl OX3...**15** C3
Broad Hill OX28....**55** B3
Broadhurst Gdns OX4 40 B3
Broad Oak OX3.....**23** C2
Broad St
Abingdon OX14.......**49** B1
Oxford OX1..........**59** B2
Broadway The OX5...**7** A4
Brocklesby Rd OX4...**40** B4
Brode Cl OX14......**50** A4
Brogden Cl OX2.....**19** C1
Brome Pl OX3.......**16** C2
Brookfield Cres OX3..**15** B3
Brooklime Wlk **3**
OX4................**41** C3
Brookside
Abingdon OX14.......**49** B3
Oxford OX3..........**23** A4
Brook St OX1.......**21** A1
Brooks Taylor Ctr OX1 59 B1
Brook View OX4.....**42** B4
Broughtons Cl OX3...**15** A3
Browns Cl OX2.......**18** B2
Brumcombe La OX1,
OX13................**38** A2
Bryony Cl OX4.......**42** B4
Buckingham St **11**
OX1................**21** A1
Buckland Ct OX5....**4** A1
Buckland Mews **3**
OX14..............**48** C1
Buckler Pl OX4.....**40** B3
Buckler Rd OX2......**9** C2
Bucklers Bury Rd
OX14..............**46** A1
Buckles Cl **11** OX14..**48** C1
Bulan Rd OX3.......**23** C2
Bullingdon Rd OX4...**22** A1
Bullsmead OX13.....**45** A3
Bullstake Cl OX2....**20** A3
Bulrush Rd OX4.....**42** A3
Bulwarks La OX1....**59** B2
Burbush Rd OX4....**34** A3
Burchester Ave OX3..**16** C2
Burdell Ave OX3.....**17** B2
Burford Lodge **4**
OX1................**21** A1
Burgan Cl OX4.......**33** C2
Burgess Cl **7** OX14..**49** B1
Burgess Mead OX2...**13** B3
Burlington Cres OX3 .**17** B1
Burra Cl OX4........**40** B1
Burrows Cl OX3......**16** B1
Bursill Cl OX3........**17** B1
Burton Cl OX14.....**52** C4
Burton Pl OX4......**34** A4

Burton Taylor Studio★
OX1................**59** B2
Burwell Cl OX28.....**56** A4
Burwell Ct OX28.....**56** B4
Burwell Dr OX28.....**56** B4
Burwell Mdw OX28...**56** B3
Burycroft The OX14..**53** C1
Buryhook Cnr OX33..**27** A4
Bury St OX14.......**49** B1
Buscot Dr OX14.....**50** A4
Bushey Leys Cl OX3..**16** C3
Bushnell Cl OX3.....**17** A1
Bushy Cl OX2.......**18** C3
Butchers Ct OX28....**54** C1
Butler Cl
Horspath OX33.......**35** C4
Oxford OX2..........**13** C2
Butler Ho OX4......**33** A1
Buttercross The★
OX28..............**55** A1
Buttercup Sq **10** OX4 .**42** A3
Butterwort Pl **1** OX4 42 A4
Butterwyke Pl OX1...**59** B1
Butts La OX3........**11** A1
Butts Rd OX33......**35** B4
Byron Cl OX14......**52** B3

C

Calcot Cl OX3.......**23** C3
CALDECOTT **53** A4
Caldecott Chase
OX14..............**53** A3
Caldecott Cl OX14...**52** C4
Caldecott Prim Sch
OX14..............**52** C3
Caldecott Rd OX14...**53** A4
Calves Cl OX5.......**3** B2
Cambridge Terr OX1..**59** B1
Cameron Ave OX14...**50** B4
Campbell Rd OX4....**32** C4
Campden Cl OX28...**54** A2
Campion Cl **18** OX14..**42** A3
Campion Rd OX14...**50** A2
Campion Way OX28 .**55** C3
Canal St OX2.......**58** A3
Candy Way OX13....**44** A4
Canning Cres OX1....**32** A3
Cannons Field OX3...**15** A4
Canterbury Rd OX2..**13** C2
Capel Cl OX2.......**9** C2
Captains Mill OX28...**55** A4
Cardigan St
Oxford OX2..........**58** A3
Oxford OX2..........**58** A4
Cardinal Cl OX4.....**33** A4
Cardwell Cres OX3...**22** C3
Carey Cl OX2.......**9** A3
Carlton Rd OX2.....**9** C3
Caroline St OX4.....**21** C3
Carpenter Cl OX4...**41** A4
Carpenters Sq **2**
OX28..............**54** C2
Carse Cl OX14......**46** A1
Carswell Ct **2** OX14..**49** A1

Carswell Prim Sch
OX14 . . . . .49 A1
Carter Cl OX3 . . . . .24 A4
Cassington Rd OX5. . . . 5 C2
Castle Mews OX1 . . . .59 A2
Castle Mill OX1 . . . . . .20 B4
Castle Mill Ho OX2 . . .13 B1
Castle St OX1 . . . . .59 B2
Catharine Cl OX14. . . .47 B1
Catherine St OX4 . . . .22 B1
Catte St OX1. . . . . .59 C2
Catwell Cl OX4. . . . . . .33 A4
Cavell Rd OX4 . . . . . . .32 C3
Cavendish Dr OX3. . . .14 C3
Cavendish Rd OX2 . . . .9 C2
Cave St OX4 . . . . .22 A3
Cecil Sharpe Cl OX3. .23 A4
Cedar Ct OX4 . . . . .33 B3
Cedar Dr OX28. . . . . . .55 C3
Cedar Rd OX2. . . . . . . .19 B1
Celandine Pl 6 OX4. .42 A3
Cemetery Rd OX14 . . .48 C1
Centaury Pl OX4 . . . . .42 B4
Centremead OX2. . . . .20 B2
Centre Rise OX33 . . . .35 C4
Century Row OX2 . . . . .9 C1
Chadlington Rd OX2. .14 A3
Chaffinch Wlk OX4 . . .42 A3
Chain Alley OX1. . . . . .59 A2
Chalcroft Cl OX29 . . . .56 C2
Chalfont Rd OX2 . . . . .13 C3
Challenor Cl OX14. . . .53 A2
Chamberlain Pl OX5. . .3 A3
Champion Way OX4 . .33 A1
Champs Cl OX14 . . . . .50 B4
Chancellor Ct OX4 . . .33 C2
Chandlers Cl OX14 . . .50 B3
Chandlings Manor Sch
OX1 . . . . .38 C1
Chapel La OX4 . . . . . . .40 C4
Chapel St OX4 . . . . . . .22 A2
Chapel Way OX2 . . . . .19 B3
Charlbury Cl OX5 . . . . .3 B4
Charlbury Rd OX2. . . .14 A3
Charles St OX4. . . . . . .32 B4
Charney Ave OX14. . . .50 B4
Charter The 8 OX14. .49 B1
Chatham Rd OX1. . . . .31 C3
Chaunterell Way
OX14 . . . . .52 C4
CHAWLEY 28 C4
Chawley La OX2. . . . . .28 C4
Checker Wlk OX14 . . .49 B1
Chedworth Dr OX28 . .54 A1
Cheney La OX3. . . . . . .22 B3
Cheney Sch OX3 . . . . .22 C3
Cheney Student Village
OX3 . . . . .22 B3
Chequers Pl OX3. . . . .16 C1
Cherry Cl
Kidlington OX5. . . . . . .3 C1
Sandford-on-Thames
OX4 . . . . .42 A3
Cherry Tree Ct OX2 . .19 B1
Cherry Tree Dr OX13. .48 B4

Cherwell Ave OX5. . . . . 4 B2
Cherwell Bsns Ctr OX5 3 A4
Cherwell Cl OX14 . . . .50 A3
Cherwell Coll (Bradmore
Hall) OX2 . . . . .58 B4
Cherwell Coll
(Greyfriars) OX1. . . . .59 B2
Cherwell Ct OX5 . . . . . . 3 B3
Cherwell Dr
Headington OX3 . . . . . .15 B3
Marston OX3. . . . . .15 A3
Cherwell Lodge OX2 .10 A2
Cherwell Sch The
OX2. . . . . .14 A4
Cherwell St OX4 . . . . .22 A3
Chester St OX4 . . . . . .22 A1
Chestnut Ave
Oxford OX3 . . . . .16 B2
Radley OX14 . . . . .47 A2
Chestnut Cl OX28 . . . .55 A3
Chestnut Ct OX4 . . . . .33 B1
Chestnut Rd OX2. . . . .19 B1
Chestnuts The OX14 . .50 B3
Chestnut Tree Cl
OX13 . . . . .48 B3
Cheyney Wlk OX14 . . .49 A3
Childrey Way OX14 . . .50 A4
Chillingworth Cres
OX3 . . . . .23 C2
Chillingworth Ct OX3 23 C2
Chilswell La
Boars Hill OX1. . . . . . . .30 B1
Sunningwell OX1. . . . . .38 B4
Chilswell Rd OX1. . . . .21 A1
Chilswell Valley Nature
Reserve* OX1. . . . . . . .30 C2
Chiltern Bsns Ctr
OX4 . . . . .34 A2
Chilterns The OX1. . . .59 B2
Chilton Cl OX14 . . . . . .50 A3
Cholesbury Grange
OX3 . . . . .15 B2
Cholsey Cl OX4 . . . . . .33 B2
Cholswell Ct OX13 . . .44 B1
Cholswell Rd OX13 . . .48 B4
Chorefields OX5 . . . . . . 3 B3
Choswell Spring OX4 41 C3
Christ Church Cath*
OX1 . . . . .59 C1
Christ Church Cath Sch
OX1 . . . . .59 B1
Christ Church Coll
OX1 . . . . .59 B2
Christ Church Old Bldgs
OX1 . . . . .59 A2
Christ Church Picture
Gall* OX1 . . . . .59 C2
Church Cl OX1. . . . . . .31 A3
Church Cowley Rd
OX4 . . . . .33 A4
Church Cowley St James
Prim Sch 6 OX4 . . . .33 B2
CHURCH END 57 B1
Church Gn OX28 . . . . .57 A4
Church Hill Rd OX4. . .33 A2

Churchill Dr OX3. . . . .23 A3
Churchill Hospl The
OX3 . . . . .23 A2
Churchill Pl OX2 . . . . . .9 A2
Churchill Rd OX5. . . . . .3 C2
Church La
Marston OX3. . . . . .15 A4
Witney OX28 . . . . .55 B1
Wolvercote OX2 . . . . . . .9 A2
Yarnton OX5 . . . . .5 C2
Church Rd
Horspath OX33 . . . . . . .35 B4
Radley OX14 . . . . .47 A1
Sandford-on-Thames
OX4 . . . . .40 B2
Wheatley OX33 . . . . . . .26 C2
Church St
Ducklington OX29 . . . . .57 A1
Kidlington OX5. . . . . . . .4 A1
Church View Rd OX28 56 B4
Church Way
Oxford, Dean Court
OX2 . . . . .19 B3
Oxford, Iffley OX4. . . . .32 B2
Church Wlk OX2 . . . . .13 C2
Cinnaminta Rd OX3 . .23 C2
Circus St OX4. . . . . . . .21 C2
Clarendon Cl OX14. . .50 A2
Clark's Row OX1. . . . . .59 B1
Claymond Rd OX3. . . .17 A2
Clays Cl OX3. . . . . .15 B3
Cleavers Sq 4 OX4 . .41 C3
Clematis Pl OX4. . . . . .42 A4
Clevedon Ct 3 OX5 . . 4 A2
Cleveland Cl OX5 . . . . . 4 B1
Cleveland Dr OX4 . . . .33 B3
Clevelands OX14 . . . . .49 C3
Clifford Pl OX2. . . . . . . .8 B2
Clifton Dr OX14 . . . . . .49 B2
Clinton Cl OX4. . . . . . .32 B1
Clive Rd OX4. . . . . .33 B3
Cloisters The 3 OX1 .21 A1
Closes The OX5 . . . . . . .3 C3
Clover Cl OX2. . . . . . . .29 A4
Clover Pl OX4. . . . . . . .42 A4
Cobden Cres OX1 . . . .21 A1
COGGES. 55 B1
Cogges Hill Rd OX28 .57 C4
Cogges Manor Farm
Mus* OX28 . . . . .55 B1
COLD HARBOUR 31 C3
Colegrove Down OX2 28 C4
Colemans Hill OX3 . . .16 C1
Coleridge Cl OX4 . . . .33 C3
Coleridge Dr OX14 . . .52 C3
Collcutt Cl OX33 . . . . .25 A1
College Cl OX33. . . . . .27 A3
College Flats OX4. . . .40 C4
College for Int Ed
OX1 . . . . .59 A2
College La OX4 . . . . . .40 C4
College Way OX33. . . .35 A4
Colley Wood OX1 . . . .39 B4
Collingwood Cl OX14 49 B3
Collins St 4 OX4. . . . .22 A2

Collinwood Cl OX3 . . .17 A1
Collinwood Rd OX3 . .17 A1
Colterne Cl OX3. . . . . .15 B3
Coltsfoot Sq 5 OX4. .42 A3
Columbine Gdns OX4 42 B3
Colwell Dr
Abingdon OX14 . . . . . .48 C1
Oxford OX3 . . . . .17 B2
Witney OX28 . . . . .56 B3
Combe Rd OX2. . . . . . .20 B4
Combewell OX44. . . . .43 A4
Comfrey Rd OX4 . . . . .34 B1
Compass Cl 4 OX4. . .33 B2
Complins Cl OX2. . . . .13 B4
Compton Dr OX14. . . .50 A4
Compton Way OX28 . .55 B2
Conduit House (North
Hinksey)* OX2. . . . . .20 A1
Conduit Rd OX14. . . . .49 A1
Conifer Cl OX2. . . . . . .19 A2
Coniston Ave OX3 . . . .15 B2
Conway Rd OX13. . . . .48 C4
Coolidge Cl 1 OX3. . .23 B3
Cooper Mews 5
OX28 . . . . .54 C1
Cooper Pl OX3 . . . . . . .17 A1
Coopers Cl OX33 . . . . .26 A2
Coopers La OX14 . . . . .53 A4
Copcot Cl OX33 . . . . . .35 C4
Cope Cl OX2. . . . . .19 B2
Copenhagen Dr OX14 48 C3
Coppock Cl OX3 . . . . .23 C4
Copse La OX3. . . . . . . .15 B3
Copse The OX14. . . . . .50 B3
Copthorne Rd OX5 . . . .3 C1
Cordrey Gn OX4. . . . . .32 B2
Coriander Way 9
OX4 . . . . .42 A3
Corn Avill Cl OX14. . . .50 B4
Corn Bar OX28 . . . . . . .54 B1
Corndell Gdns 4
OX28 . . . . .54 C1
Cornfield Cl OX28 . . . .56 A4
Cornmarket St OX1 . .59 B2
Corn St OX28 . . . . .54 C1
Cornwallis Cl OX4. . . .32 C3
Cornwallis Rd OX4 . . .32 C3
Coromandel OX14. . . .52 C2
Corpus Christi Coll
OX1 . . . . .59 C2
Corunna Cres OX4 . . .34 A4
Cosin Cl OX4. . . . . .22 B2
Costar Cl OX4. . . . . . . .33 C1
Cotman Cl OX14 . . . . .53 A3
Cot's Gn OX5 . . . . .3 B3
Cotswold Cres OX3. . .15 A3
Cotswold Rd OX2 . . . .29 A4
Cottesmore Rd OX4 . .32 C3
Cotton Grass Cl OX4. .41 C3
County Trad Est OX4. .34 B2
Court Cl OX5. . . . . .3 B2
Court Farm Rd OX4 . .32 B1
Courtland Rd OX4. . . .32 C2

Court Place Gdns
OX4 . . . . .32 B1
Courts Gdns OX28. . . . .55 C1
Court The OX14 . . . . . .49 A3
Covent Cl OX14 . . . . . .46 A1
Coverley Rd OX3 . . . . .23 B1
Cow La OX1 . . . . .39 C3
COWLEY. 34 A3
Cowley Bsns Ctr OX4 34 B1
Cowley Junc OX4 . . . .34 A2
Cowley Pl OX4. . . . . . .21 C2
Cowley Rd
Oxford, Littlemore
OX4 . . . . .40 C4
Oxford OX4 . . . . .22 B1
Coxís Ground OX2. . . .13 B3
Cox's Alley OX3 . . . . . .16 C1
Crabtree Pl OX14. . . . .50 A1
Crabtree Rd OX2. . . . .19 B2
Cranbrook Ct OX28. . . .56 C3
Cranbrook Dr OX1 . .39 C1
Cranesbill Way 8
OX4 . . . . .41 C3
Cranham St OX2 . . . .58 A4
Cranham Terr OX2 . . .58 A4
Cranley Rd OX3 . . . . . .17 A2
Cranmer Rd OX4. . . . .34 A4
Cranston Ct 1 OX4 . .33 A1
Craufurd Rd OX4. . . . .34 A4
Crawley Rd OX28. . . . .54 C1
Crescent Cl OX4 . . . . .33 C4
Crescent Ct OX4 . . . . .33 C4
Crescent Rd OX4. . . . .33 C4
Crescent The
Oxford OX2 . . . . .13 B1
Sandford-on-Thames
OX4 . . . . .41 A2
Witney OX29 . . . . .55 B3
Cress Hill Pl OX3. . . . .17 A2
Cricket Rd OX4 . . . . . .33 A4
Crick Rd OX2 . . . . .14 A2
Cripley Pl OX2 . . . . . . .20 B3
Cripley Rd OX2. . . . . . .20 B3
Croasdell Cl OX14. . . .53 A2
Croft Ave OX5. . . . . .4 A2
Croft Cl OX3 . . . . .15 A2
Crofters Mews 6
OX28 . . . . .54 C1
Croft Rd OX3 . . . . .15 A2
Crofts The OX28. . . . . .56 C4
Croft The OX3. . . . . . . .16 A1
Cromwell Cl OX3. . . . .15 A2
Cromwell St OX1. . . . .59 B1
Cromwell Way OX5. . . .4 B1
Crosslands Dr OX14 . .49 A3
Cross St OX4. . . . . .22 A2
Crotch Cres OX3 . . . . .15 B2
Crowberry Rd OX4 . .42 A4
Crowell Rd OX4 . . . . . .33 B2
Crown Mews 3 OX14 49 A1
Crown Rd
Kidlington OX5. . . . . .3 B2
Wheatley OX33 . . . . . .26 C2

Crown Sq OX33 . . . . . .26 C2
Crown St OX4. . . . . . . .22 A2
Croxford Gdns OX5. . . .6 C4
Crozier Cl OX2 . . . . . . .19 B2
Cuddesdon Way OX4 .42 A4
Culham Cl OX14. . . . . .49 C3
Cullerne Cl OX14. . . . .45 C1
Cullum Ho OX33 . . . . .27 A2
Cullum Rd OX33 . . . . .27 A1
Cumberland Rd OX4. .22 C1
Cumberlege Cl OX3 . .10 C1
Cummings Cl OX3. . . .23 C4
Cumnor CE Prim Sch
OX2 . . . . .28 A3
CUMNOR HILL 19 A1
Cumnor Hill OX2. . . . .18 C1
Cumnor Rd OX1. . . . . .36 B2
Cumnor Rise Rd OX2 19 A2
Cunliffe Cl OX2 . . . . . .14 A4
Curbridge Rd
Ducklington OX29 . . . .56 C1
Witney OX28 . . . . .56 A4
Curtis Ave OX14. . . . . .50 A1
Curtis Rd OX5. . . . . .3 C3
Curtyn Cl OX14. . . . . .48 C2
CUTTESLOWE. 9 C4
Cutteslowe Prim Sch
OX2 . . . . .10 A3
Cygnet Ct OX14 . . . . .53 A4
Cyprus Terr OX2. . . . . . .9 A2

D

Daisy Bank OX14 . . . . .50 A2
Dale Cl OX1. . . . . .59 A1
Dale Pl OX5. . . . . .3 C3
Dale The OX3 . . . . .17 B2
Dale Wlk OX29. . . . . . .56 C2
Danvers Rd OX4. . . . . .32 C1
Dark La
Sunningwell OX13 . . . . .45 A3
Witney OX28 . . . . .54 C2
Darrell Way OX14 . . . .49 B3
Dart Rd OX13 . . . . .44 B1
Dashwood Ave OX5 . . .5 C3
Dashwood Rd OX4. . . .32 C1
Daubeny Ct OX2. . . . . . .9 B3
Davenant Ct OX2. . . . . .9 B3
Davenant Rd OX2 . . . . .9 B2
Davenport Rd OX28 . .54 B2
David Nicholls Cl
OX4 . . . . .40 C4
David Walter Cl OX2. . .9 C3
Dawson St 1 OX4. . . .21 C2
DEAN COURT 18 C2
Dean Court Rd OX2 . .18 C1
Deanfield Rd OX2. . . . .18 C3
Dearlove Cl OX14 . . . .49 A4
Deaufort Cl OX5 . . . . . .3 C3
Deer Wlk OX4. . . . . . . .42 A3
Delamare Way OX2. . .18 C1
Delbush Ave OX3. . . . .17 C2
Dene Rd OX3 . . . . .23 B2
Dene Rise OX28. . . . . .54 B1
Denman's La OX2. . . . .28 A3

Denmark St OX4 . . . . .22 A1
Denton Cl
Abingdon OX14 . . . . . .50 A2
Oxford OX2 . . . . .18 B2
Dents Cl OX3 . . . . .15 B3
Derwent Ave OX3 . . . .15 B2
Derwent Cl OX13. . . . .48 B4
Desborough Cres
OX4 . . . . .32 C1
Desmesne Furze OX3 23 A3
Des Roches Sq OX28 .57 A4
Devereux Pl OX4. . . . .32 C1
Diamond Ct OX2 . . . . .13 C4
Diamond Pl OX2 . . . . .13 C4
Divinity Rd OX4 . . . . . .22 B2
Dodgson Rd OX4. . . . .33 B2
Dodson Ct OX14 . . . . .49 B2
Don Boscoe Cl 5
OX4 . . . . .33 C4
Donnington Bridge Rd
OX4 . . . . .32 B4
Donnington Lodge
OX4 . . . . .32 B4
Don Stuart Pl OX4. . . .22 C1
Dora Carr Cl OX3. . . . .15 B3
Dorchester Ct OX3 . . .24 A3
Dorchester Cres
OX14 . . . . .49 C3
Dorchester Ct
4 Kidlington OX5. . . . . .4 A2
Oxford OX2 . . . . .13 C4
Doris Field Cl OX3 . . .15 B1
Dorothy Hodgkin Rd
OX1. . . . . .58 C3
Douglas Downes Cl
OX3. . . . . .23 C4
Dove House Cl OX2. . . .9 A2
D'Overbroeck's Coll
OX2 . . . . .13 C3
Dover Cl OX2 . . . . .19 A1
Downside End OX3. . . .17 B1
Downside Rd OX3. . . . .17 B1
Doyley Rd OX2. . . . . . .20 B2
Dragon Sch OX2 . . . . .14 A2
Drake La OX28 . . . . . . .55 C2
Drayman's Wlk 7
OX14 . . . . .53 A4
Drayton Rd OX14. . . . .52 C3
Drewett Ct OX2 . . . . . . .8 C2
Drift Ctr OX4 . . . . .34 B4
Drove Acre Rd OX4. . .22 B1
Druce Way OX4 . . . . . .34 B1
Drysdale Cl OX14 . . . .51 A4
DUCKLINGTON. 56 C1
Ducklington La OX28 56 B4
Dudgeon Dr OX4. . . . .40 C4
Dudley Ct OX2 . . . . .9 C1
Dudley Gdns OX4 . . . .22 A3
Duffield Cl OX14 . . . . .50 A4
Dukes Rd OX5 . . . . .4 A2
Duke St OX2 . . . . .20 A3
Dundas Cl OX14. . . . . .50 A2
Dunmore Prim Sch
OX14 . . . . .49 B3
Dunmore Rd OX14 . . .49 A4

Dunnock Way OX4 . . .42 A3
Dunstan Rd OX3 . . . . .16 A2
Dynham Pl OX3 . . . . . .23 B3

E

Eagle Ind Est OX28. . .54 C1
Earl St OX2 . . . . .20 A3
Early Rd OX28 . . . . . . .55 C3
Eason Dr OX14. . . . . . .50 B3
East Ave OX4 . . . . .22 B2
Eastchurch OX4. . . . . .32 B1
Eastern Ave OX4 . . . . .33 A1
Eastern By-Pass Rd OX3,
OX4 . . . . .34 A3
Eastern Ho OX4. . . . . .33 A1
East Field Cl OX3. . . . .23 C1
Eastfield Pl OX4. . . . . .34 B4
Eastfield Rd OX8,
OX28 . . . . .55 A4
East Oxford Prim Sch
OX4 . . . . .22 A2
East St Helen St OX14 53 B4
East St OX2 . . . . .20 B3
Eaton Ct OX2 . . . . .10 A2
Eckersley Sch of English
The OX1 . . . . .59 A2
Eden Croft OX14 . . . . .49 C4
Eden Dr OX3. . . . . .15 C2
Eden Rd OX3 . . . . .15 B2
Edgecombe Rd OX3. .17 A2
Edgeway Rd OX3. . . . .15 A1
Edinburgh Dr OX5. . . . .4 B2
Edith Ct OX1. . . . . .39 B3
Edith Rd OX1 . . . . .21 A1
Edmund Halley Rd
OX4 . . . . .40 C3
Edmund Rd OX4 . . . . .33 B3
Edward Feild Prim Sch
OX5 . . . . .4 A1
Edward Rd OX1 . . . . . .39 C4
Edward St OX14. . . . . .48 C1
Edwin Ct OX2 . . . . .20 A3
EF International
Language Sch OX3 . .22 B4
Egerton Rd OX4. . . . . .32 C2
Egrove Cl OX1 . . . . . . .32 A2
Eighth Ave OX3 . . . . . .24 A2
Elder Way OX4. . . . . . .42 A3
Eldridge Cl OX14. . . . .49 B4
Eleanor Cl OX4 . . . . . .33 A2
Electric Ave OX2 . . . . .20 B2
Elizabeth Ave OX14. . .50 B4
Elizabeth Jennings Way
OX2 . . . . .13 B4
Ellesmere Rd OX4. . . .32 C2
Elm Cl
Wheatley OX33 . . . . . .27 A1
Witney OX28 . . . . .54 A1
Elm Dr OX44. . . . . .43 B4
Elm Gr OX5 . . . . .7 A4
Elms Dr OX3 . . . . .15 B3
Elms Par OX2 . . . . .19 B3
Elms Rd OX2. . . . . .19 B3
Elmthorpe Rd OX2 . . . .8 C2

Elm Tree Cl OX4......33 A1
Elm Tree Wlk OX13...48 B3
Elsfield Rd OX3......15 A4
Elsfield Way OX2......9 C3
Elton Cl OX3.........17 C2
Elton Cres OX33......27 A1
Elwes Cl OX14........50 A2
Ely Cl OX14..........52 B4
Emden Ho OX3.......16 B2
Emmanuel Christian Sch
OX4................40 C4
Emperor Gdns OX4...41 C3
Eney Cl OX14........50 B4
English at Oxford
OX1................58 A3
Erica Cl OX4.........34 B1
Essex St OX4.........22 B1
Ethelhelm Cl OX14...46 B1
Ethelred Ct OX3......16 A2
Eton Cl OX28.........57 C4
Evans Ct OX5.........4 A2
Evans La OX5.........4 A2
Evelin Rd OX14......49 A3
Evelyn Cl OX2........18 C2
Evenlode Cres OX5...2 B4
Evenlode Ct OX28....55 A1
Evenlode Pk OX14...50 A3
Evenlode Twr OX4...41 C4
Everard Cl **2** OX3...23 B3
Ewert Pl OX2........13 C4
Ewin Cl OX3.........15 A3
Ewin Ct OX3.........15 A3
Exbourne Rd OX14...48 C1
Exeter Coll OX1.....59 B2
Exeter Ct **5** OX5......4 A2
Exeter Rd OX5........3 C3
Eynsham Rd OX2.....18 C2
Eyot Pl OX4..........21 C1
Eyston Way OX14.....48 B1

F

Faber Cl OX4.......41 A4
Fairacres OX14......48 B1
Fairacres Rd OX4....32 B4
Fairacres Shopping &
Trad Est OX14......52 B4
Fairfax Ave OX3....14 C2
Fairfax Ctr OX5......7 A4
Fairfax Gate OX33...27 A2
Fairfax Rd
Kidlington OX5........7 A4
Oxford OX4..........34 A4
Fairfield Dr OX28...56 B4
Fairfield Pl OX14....49 B2
Fairlawn End OX2....9 A2
Fairlawn Flats OX2...9 A2
Fairlawn Wharf OX14 53 B4
Fairlie Rd OX4.......33 A1
Fair View OX3.......23 B1
Fairways OX1........39 C1
Falcon Cl OX4.......41 B4
Fallowfield Cres
OX28................55 C2
Fane Rd OX3........14 C3

Fanshawe Pl OX4....34 A3
Faringdon Rd OX14...48 C2
Farm Cl
Kidlington OX5.........4 A4
Sandford-on-Thames
OX4................42 A3
Farm Close La OX33..26 C2
Farm Close Rd OX33..26 C2
Farmer Pl OX3.......15 A2
Farmers Cl OX28.....55 A3
Farmhouse Mdw
OX28................56 A4
Farmington Dr OX28.54 A1
Farm Mill La OX28...57 A4
Farm Rd OX14.......49 B4
Farndon Rd OX2.....13 C2
Farnham Ct **6** OX5.....4 A2
Farriers Mews OX14..49 C1
Faulkner St OX1.....59 B1
Feilden Cl OX29.....57 A1
Feilden Gr OX3......15 B1
Fennel Way OX14....50 B2
Ferguson Pl OX14....50 B2
Fernhill Cl OX5.......3 B2
Fernhill Rd OX5......2 B2
Fern Hill Rd OX4....34 A3
Ferny Cl OX14.......47 A1
Ferry Ct OX14.......53 B4
Ferry Hinksey Rd OX2 20 B3
Ferry Mills OX2......20 B2
Ferry Pool Rd OX2...14 A4
Ferry Rd OX3........15 A1
Ferry Sports Ctr
OX26................13 C4
Ferry Wlk OX14......53 B4
Fettiplace Rd
Oxford OX3..........16 C3
Witney OX28.........54 A1
Field Ave OX4.......42 A4
Field Cl
Kidlington OX5.........4 A2
Yarnton OX5.........5 C4
Fieldfare Rd OX4....41 C2
Field Ho OX2........19 A2
Field House Dr OX2...9 B2
Fieldmere Cl OX28...54 B1
Fieldside OX14......48 C3
Fiennes Rd OX4......32 C1
Finch Cl OX3.......23 A3
Finmore Cl **3** OX14..49 A2
Finmore Rd OX2.....19 B2
Firs Mdw **3** OX4.....42 A3
First Ave OX3.......24 A2
Firs The OX2.........9 C2
First Turn OX2.......9 A2
Fir Trees OX14......39 C1
Fishermans Wharf
OX14................53 B2
Fisher Row OX1.....59 A2
Fitchett Yd OX14....49 A2
Fitzharry's Rd OX14..49 B2
Fitzharrys Sch OX14..49 B3
Fitzherbert Cl OX4...32 B2
Five Mile Dr OX2.....9 B3
Flatford Pl OX5......3 A4

Flaxfield Rd OX4.....42 A4
Fletcher Cl OX5.......5 C3
Fletcher Rd OX4.....34 A4
Flexney Pl OX3......23 B3
Florence Cl OX5......4 A2
FLORENCE PARK...33 A3
Florence Park Rd
OX4................33 A3
Floyd's Row OX1....59 B1
Fogwell Rd OX2.....18 C3
Follets Cl OX5........5 C3
Folly Bridge Ct OX1..59 B1
Fords Cl OX33.......35 B4
Foresters Tower OX3.23 C3
Forest Rd OX3.......17 A1
Forest Side OX1.....39 B4
Forget-me-not Way **1**
OX4................42 A3
Forster La OX2.......28 A2
Fortnam Cl OX3.....15 C1
Foster Rd OX14......45 B1
Fountain Ct OX14....49 B2
Fourth Ave OX3.....24 A2
Foxborough Rd OX14 51 A4
Fox Cl OX44.........43 B4
Foxcombe Ct OX14...48 B2
FOXCOMBE HILL....38 A2
Foxcombe La OX1...38 B3
Foxcombe Rd
Boars Hill OX1.......38 A3
Sunningwell OX1......38 B4
Fox Cres OX1.......32 A3
Foxdown Cl OX5......3 C3
Fox Furlong OX4....40 B3
Foxglove Cl **7** OX4...41 C3
Foxglove Rd OX5.....2 C2
Fox La OX1.........37 B1
Foxton Cl OX2.......9 A3
Foxwell Dr OX3.....16 A3
Francis Little Dr
OX14................52 C4
Frank Cook Ct OX5...4 A3
Franklin Cl OX5......4 A3
Franklin Rd OX3.....15 C1
Franklyn Cl OX14....49 B4
Frederick Rd OX4....33 C2
Freeborn Cl OX5......4 A4
Freelands Rd OX4....32 B3
Frenchay Rd OX2....13 B3
French Cl OX28......56 B4
Frewin Ct OX1......59 B2
Friars' Entry OX1.....59 B2
Friars Wharf OX1....59 B1
Friday La OX33......26 C2
Frieze Way OX5......7 A2
Frys Hill OX4........41 C3
Fullwell Cl OX14.....49 A3
Furlong Cl OX4......33 C1
Fyfield Rd OX2.......14 A2

G

Gainsborough Gn
OX14................53 A3
Gaisford Rd OX4.....33 B2

Elm – Gol   65

Gall Cl OX14.........50 B2
Galley Field OX14....50 A2
Galpin Cl OX4.......22 B1
GARDEN CITY........6 C3
Gardiner Cl
Abingdon OX14.......50 B2
Wheatley OX33......26 C2
Gardiner St OX3.....23 B4
Garford Cl OX14.....50 A4
Garford Rd OX2.....14 A3
GARSINGTON.......43 C3
Garsington CE Prim Sch
OX44................43 C4
Garsington Rd OX4...34 A2
Garth The
Oxford OX2..........19 B2
Yarnton OX5..........5 C4
Gateley OX33.......35 C4
Gathorne Rd OX3...23 B4
Gentian Rd OX4......42 A4
Geoffrey Barbour Rd
OX14................49 B2
George Moore Cl
OX4................32 C4
George Morland Ho **8**
OX14................53 B4
George St OX1......59 B2
George Street Mews
OX1................59 A2
Gerard Pl OX4.......33 B3
Gibbs Cres OX2.....59 A1
Gibson Cl OX14.....45 C1
Gidley Way OX33....25 B1
Giles Cl OX4.........40 C4
Giles Rd OX4.......41 A4
Gillians Way OX4....33 A4
Ginge Cl OX14.......50 A4
Gipsy La OX3.......22 C3
Girdlestone Cl OX3...23 B3
Girdlestone Rd OX3..23 B3
Gladstone Ct OX3...16 C1
Gladstone Rd OX3...16 C1
Glanville Rd OX4....22 C1
Glean Cotts OX28...55 C2
Glebelands OX3.....23 B1
Glebe Rd OX2.......28 A3
Glebe St OX4........22 A3
Glebe The
Cumnor OX2.........28 A3
Wheatley OX33......26 C2
Gloucester Court Mews
OX28................55 A2
Gloucester Gn OX1...59 B2
Gloucester La OX1...59 B2
Gloucester Pl OX28..55 A2
Gloucester St OX1...59 B2
Glyme Cl OX14......50 A3
Godfrey Cl
6 Abingdon OX14...53 A4
Oxford OX3.........23 C3
Godstow Rd OX2.....8 B2
Godwyn Cl OX14....49 A2
Golafre Rd OX14....53 A3

Golden Cross OX1....59 B2
Golden Rd OX4 ......22 B1
Goodey Cl OX4.......33 B1
Goodson Wlk OX3...15 A1
Gooseacre OX14 .....51 A4
Goose Green Cl OX2...8 C2
Gordon Cl OX3.......15 A3
Gordon Dr OX14 .....50 B3
Gordon St OX1.......31 C4
Gordon Way OX28....56 C4
Gordon Woodward Way
OX1................31 C3
Goring Lodge **7** OX1 21 A1
Gorse Leas OX3......15 C3
GOSFORD 4 A1
Gosford Cl OX5 .....7 A4
Gosford Hill Ct OX5 ...4 A1
Gosford Hill Sch OX5..4 A1
Goslyn Cl **3** OX3.....23 B3
Gouldland Gdns OX3 .15 C3
GRANDPONT........21 B1
Grandpont Pl OX1...59 B1
Grange Ct OX2.......18 C2
Grange Rd OX4 ......40 C4
Grangers Pl OX28 ....55 A4
Grantham Ho OX2...58 A4
Grants Mews **2** OX4 .22 A2
Granville Ct OX3 .....22 B3
Grates The OX4 ......33 B2
Gravel Pits La OX5 ....5 C4
Grays Rd OX3........22 C4
Great Clarendon St
OX2................58 A3
Great Close Rd OX5 ...6 A3
Great Mead OX1 .....58 A3
Grebe Cl
Abingdon OX14 ......53 B3
Sandford-on-Thames
OX4 ....41 C3
Green Cnr OX28......55 B3
Greene's Tutorial Coll
OX1................59 B2
Greenfinch Cl OX4 ...42 A3
Green Hill OX4.......42 B4
Green La
Oxford OX2 ....18 B2
Sunningwell OX13.....45 C4
Green Pl OX1 ....31 C4
Green Rd
Kidlington OX5.........3 C2
Oxford OX3 ....17 A1
Green Ridges OX3....17 B2
Green St OX4 ....22 B1
Green Templeton Coll
OX2................58 A4
Green The
Culham OX14........53 C1
Garsington OX44......43 C4
Horspath OX33 ......35 B3
Grenoble Rd
Oxford OX4 ....42 B3
Sandford-on-Thames
OX4 ....41 B3

Greycotes Oxford High
Sch **1** OX2 ....14 A2
Grey La OX28 ....55 C2
Greystones Ct OX5 ....3 B3
Grimbly Pl OX2 ....9 C2
Grosvenor Rd OX2 ...30 A4
Grove Ct OX4 ....32 C3
Grovelands OX5.......3 B2
Grovelands Rd OX3...24 B4
Grove St OX2 ....9 C1
Grove The OX14 .....50 A4
Grundy Cl OX14......50 A2
Grundy Cres OX1.....39 C3
Grunsell Cl OX3......16 A3
Guelder Rd OX4......41 B3
Guildford Ct **7** OX5 ...4 A2
Gurden Pl OX3.......16 C2
Gurl Cl OX3..........16 C2
Gwyneth Rd OX4.....40 B4

H

Hadland Rd OX14 ....50 B2
Hadow Rd OX3.......15 B2
Hailey Rd OX8, OX28 ..55 A4
Haldane Rd OX4 .....41 C4
Halliday Hill OX3.....15 C3
Halls Cl OX2 ....18 C1
Hamble Dr OX14 .....50 A3
Hamels La OX1 ....38 A3
Hamel The OX1 ......59 A2
Hamilton Rd OX2 .....9 C1
Hampden Dr OX5 .....7 A4
Hampden Rd OX4 ....33 B2
Handlo Pl OX3 ....17 A2
Hanson Rd OX14 .....45 B1
Harberton Mead
Marston OX3 ....15 A1
Oxford OX3 ....15 B1
Harbord Rd OX2 ......9 C4
HARCOURT HILL ...30 A4
Harcourt Hill OX2....30 A4
Harcourt Terr OX3....22 C4
Harcourt Way OX14 ..49 B3
Harding Rd OX14.....48 C2
Hardings Cl OX4 .....33 A1
Hardwick Ave OX5 ....3 C1
Harebell Rd OX4.....42 A4
Harefields OX2........9 C3
Harley Rd OX2 ....20 A3
Harlow Way OX3.....11 A1
Harolde Cl OX3 ......16 B2
Harold Hicks Pl OX4..32 B4
Harold White Cl OX3 .24 A4
Harpes Rd OX2 ....9 C2
Harpsichord Pl OX4 ..22 A3
Harris Manchester Coll
OX1................58 C3
Harrow Rd OX4 ......34 B1
Hart Cl OX14.........50 B2
Harts Cl OX5..........3 B2
Hart St OX2..........58 A3
Hart-Synnot Ho OX2 .58 A4
Harwell Cl OX14 .....49 C3
Haslemere Gdns OX2..9 B4

Hastoe Grange OX3 ..15 B2
Hathaways OX33.....26 C2
Havelock Rd OX4 ....33 B3
Hawkins St **1** OX4 ...22 A1
Hawkins Way OX13...44 A4
Hawksmoor Rd OX2...9 C3
Hawkswell Gdns OX2 10 A1
Hawkswell Ho OX2...10 A1
Hawlings Row OX4...42 B3
Hawthorn Ave OX3...16 B1
Hawthorn Cl OX2 ....19 B2
Hawthorne Ave OX13 48 B4
Hawthorn Way OX5 ...3 C1
Hayes Cl OX3 ....15 A1
Hayes The OX1.......59 B2
Hayfield Rd OX2 .....13 C3
Haynes Rd OX3 ......14 C3
Hayward Rd OX2......9 C4
Hazel Cl OX14........49 A3
Hazel Cres OX5 ....7 A4
Hazel End OX44......43 B4
Hazelnut Path OX14 ..39 C1
Hazel Rd OX2 ....19 A3
Hazel Wlk OX5........7 A4
HEADINGTON 16 A2
HEADINGTON HILL ..22 B4
Headington Prep Sch **1**
OX3................23 A4
HEADINGTON
QUARRY 23 C4
Headington Rd OX3 ..22 B4
Headington Rdbt OX3 17 A1
Headington Sch OX3 .22 C4
Headley Ho OX3 .....15 B2
Headley Way OX3....15 C1
Healey Cl OX14 ......53 A4
Hean Cl OX14........50 A4
Heath Cl OX3 ....23 B2
Heathcote Pl OX14...50 B4
Heather Pl OX3 ......15 A2
Hedgemead Ave
OX14...............50 B4
Hedges Cl OX3.......16 C1
Helen Rd OX2........20 A3
Hellebourine Cl OX4 .42 A3
Helwys Pl OX5 ....3 B4
Hendred Ho OX4.....33 A4
Hendred St OX4......33 A4
Hendred Way OX14...50 A3
Hengrove Cl OX3.....16 B3
Henley Ave OX4......32 C3
Henley Rd OX4 ......40 C2
Henley St OX4 ....22 A1
Henor Mill Cl OX14...50 A4
Henry Box Cl OX28...56 C4
Henry Box Sch The
OX28...............56 C4
Henry Rd OX2........20 A3
Henry Taunt Cl OX3..16 C3
HENWOOD..........36 B3
Henwood Cotts OX1..36 A3
Henwood Dr OX1 ...36 B3
Herbert Cl OX4 ......22 C1
Herman Cl OX14.....50 A2
Hermitage Rd OX14 ..53 A4

Hernes Cl OX2 ....9 C2
Hernes Cres OX2.....9 C2
Hernes Rd OX2 ......9 C2
Heron Ct OX14.......53 B2
Herons Pl OX2 ....9 C2
Heron's Wlk OX14....49 B3
Herschel Cres OX4 ...33 B1
Herschel Ct OX4 .....33 B1
Hertford Coll OX1....59 C2
Hertford Ct **8** OX5 ....4 A2
Hertford St OX4......22 B1
Heyford Hill La OX4 ..40 A4
Heyford Hill Rdbt
OX4................40 A4
Heyford Mead **2** OX5 .3 B3
Hid's Copse Rd OX2 ..18 C1
High Cross Way OX3..16 C3
Highfield Ave OX3....23 A3
High St
Abingdon OX14 ......49 B1
Kidlington OX5........3 C3
Oxford OX1 ....59 C2
Wheatley OX33......26 C2
Witney OX28 ....55 A1
Highworth Pl OX28...56 C4
Hillary Way OX33.....27 A1
Hilliard Ho OX14 .....53 A3
Hill Rise OX33 ....35 C4
Hillsborough Cl **3**
OX4................33 A1
Hillsborough Rd OX4 33 A2
Hillside OX2.........29 A4
Hill The OX44 ....43 C3
Hilltop Ct OX4 ....22 C2
Hill Top Rd OX4 .....22 C2
Hill View OX3 ....17 B2
Hill View La OX1 .....36 B2
Hillview Rd
Abingdon OX14 ......49 B4
Oxford OX2 ....20 B3
Hinksey Bsns Ctr OX2 19 B3
Hinksey Hill OX1.....31 A1
Hinksey Hill Interchange
OX1................31 B1
Hinksey Pool (Outdoor)
OX26...............31 B4
Hinshelwood Rd OX1 58 C3
Hitching Ct OX14.....48 B1
Hive Mews **3** OX14 ..53 B4
Hobbs Cl OX14.......50 A2
Hobby Ct OX4........42 A3
Hobson Rd OX2 ......9 C1
Hockmore St OX4....33 B2
Hodge Ct OX1.......21 A1
Hogarth Pl OX14.....53 A3
Holford Rd OX28 ....56 B4
Holland Pl OX3 ......23 C2
Holland Rd OX14.....49 C4
Holley Cres OX3......16 C1
Hollis Cl OX28 ....57 C4
Holloway Rd
Wheatley OX33 ......26 C2
Witney OX28 ....54 C1
Hollow Way OX3, OX4 33 C4
Hollybush Row OX1 ..59 A2

Holly Cl OX5 . . . . 3 C1
Holly Ct OX4 . . . . 34 A1
HOLTON 27 A4
Holt The OX14. . . . . 49 B2
Holt Weer Cl OX2 . . . . . 9 C3
Holyoake Rd OX3 . . . . 16 B1
Holywell Bsns Ctr
OX2 . . . . 20 B2
Holywell Cl OX14. . . . . 50 B4
Holywell Music Room★
OX1 . . . . 58 C3
Holywell St OX1. . . . . . 58 C3
Home Cl
Kidlington OX5. . . . . 3 C3
Wolvercote OX2 . . . . 8 B2
Wootton OX13. . . . . . . 36 C1
Homestall Cl OX2 . . . . . 18 C3
Homestead The OX5. . . 3 B2
Honeybottom La
OX13 . . . . 44 A3
Honeysuckle Gr OX4 . 42 B4
Honor Cl OX5 . . . . 4 A2
Hopkins Ct 4 OX4 . . . 33 C4
Hornbeam Dr OX4 . . . 42 B4
Horseman Cl OX3 . . . . 15 B3
Horsepath Park Cvn Site
OX33 . . . . 35 C4
HORSPATH. 35 C4
Horspath Athletics &
Sports Gd OX4 . . . . . 34 C4
Horspath CE Prim Sch
OX33 . . . . 25 A1
Horspath Driftway
OX3 . . . . 23 C1
Horspath Rd OX4 . . . . 34 A4
Horspath Rd Ind Est
OX4 . . . . 34 B4
Horwood Cl OX3 . . . . . 16 A1
Hosker Cl OX3 . . . . 17 B1
Hound Cl OX14. . . . . . . 50 B4
Howard St OX4 . . . . . . 32 C4
Howe Cl OX33. . . . . 26 B2
Hoyle Cl OX28. . . . . 54 C4
Hubble Cl OX3 . . . . 16 C3
Hugh Allen Cres OX3 15 A1
Hughes Ho OX4 . . . . . . 22 A2
Hugh Price Ho OX4 . . 22 C1
Humfrey Rd OX3 . . . . . 17 A2
Hunder Ct OX1. . . . . . . 39 B4
Hundred Acres Cl
OX3 . . . . 23 C1
Hunsdon Rd OX4. . . . . 32 C2
Hunter Cl
Abingdon OX14 . . . . 46 A1
Oxford OX4 . . . . 34 A4
Hurst La OX2 . . . . 29 A4
Hurst Rise Rd OX2 . . . 19 A2
Hurst St OX4. . . . . 22 A1
Hutchcombe Farm Cl
OX2 . . . . 19 A1
Hutchcomb Rd OX2 . . 19 A2
Huxley Cl OX13 . . . . . .44 A4
Hyacinth Wlk OX4. . . . 41 C2
Hyde Mdw View 3
OX28 . . . . 54 C2

Hyde Pl
Abingdon OX14 . . . . 52 C3
Oxford OX2 . . . . 9 B1
Hyde The OX14. . . . . . . 52 C3
Hythe Bridge St OX1 . 59 A2

I

IFFLEY 32 B2
Iffley Mdw Nature
Reserve★ OX1. . . . . 32 A3
Iffley Mead Sch OX4. . 32 B3
Iffley Rd OX4 . . . . 22 A1
Iffley Turn OX4 . . . . . . 32 C3
Ilsley Rd OX3 . . . . 16 C2
Ingle Cl OX3 . . . . 15 C2
Inkerman Cl OX14. . . . 48 C3
Inott Furze OX3 . . . . . . 23 B1
Inst of Virology &
Experimental
Microbiology OX1 . . . 58 C3
Iqra Sch OX4 . . . . 40 C4
Isis Bsns Ctr OX4 . . . . 34 B4
Isis Cl
Abingdon OX14 . . . . 50 A3
South Hinksey OX1 . . . . 32 A3
Islip Rd OX2 . . . . 9 C2
Ivy Cl OX4 . . . . 33 C3
Ivy La OX3 . . . . 16 A2

J

Jack Argent Cl 16
OX4 . . . . 42 A3
Jackdaw La OX4 . . . . . 21 C1
Jackies La OX33 . . . . . 27 A1
Jackman Cl OX14 . . . . 49 C1
Jackson Cole Ho OX1 59 A2
Jackson Dr OX1. . . . . . 39 B4
Jackson Rd OX2 . . . . . . 9 C3
Jack Straw's La OX3 . 15 B1
Jacobs Cl OX28 . . . . . . 55 A2
James St OX4. . . . . 22 A2
James Wolfe Rd OX4 23 C1
Janaway OX4 . . . . 40 B3
Jane Seaman Ct OX4 42 B3
Jarn Way OX1. . . . . 37 B3
Jasmine Cl OX4. . . . . . 34 B1
Jenyns Ct OX14 . . . . . . 52 B4
JERICHO 58 A3
Jericho St OX2. . . . . . . 58 A4
Jersey Rd OX4 . . . . 32 C1
Jessops Cl
Marston OX3 . . . . 14 C3
Oxford OX3 . . . . 15 B3
Jesus Coll OX1. . . . . . . 59 B2
Jeune Hall 1 OX4 . . . 22 A2
Jeune St OX4 . . . . 22 A2
Joan Lawrence Pl
OX3 . . . . 23 C3
John Allen Ctr OX4. . . 33 B3
John Buchan Rd OX3 15 C3
John Garne Way OX3 22 B4
John Henry Newman
Prim Sch OX4 . . . . . . 40 C4

John Kallie Ho OX4 . . 33 A4
John Mason Rd OX14 49 C2
John Mason Sch
OX14 . . . . 49 A2
John Morris Rd OX14 53 A3
John Piers La OX1 . . . 31 B3
John Radcliffe Hospl
OX3 . . . . 15 C2
John Radcliffe Hospl Sch
OX3 . . . . 16 A2
John Smith Dr OX4. . . 33 C2
John Snow Pl OX3 . . . 16 C1
Johnson Cl OX44. . . . . 43 B4
John Towle Cl OX1. . . 31 C3
John Watson Sch
OX33 . . . . 26 B2
Jordan Hill OX2 . . . . 9 B4
Jordan Hill Rd OX2. . . . 9 B4
Jordon Hill Bsns Pk
OX2 . . . . 9 B4
Jourdain Rd OX4. . . . . 34 B1
Jowett Wlk OX1. . . . . . 58 B4
Jubilee Terr OX1 . . . . . 59 B1
Judds Cl OX28 . . . . 55 C1
Judges Cl OX5 . . . . 3 B2
Junction Rd OX4. . . . . 33 C4
Juniper Ct 4 OX14. . . 48 C1
Juniper Dr OX4 . . . . . . 42 A4
Juxon St OX2 . . . . 58 A4

K

Kames Cl OX4 . . . . 33 A3
Kassam Stad (Oxford Utd
FC) OX4 . . . . 41 B3
Keble Coll OX1. . . . . . . 58 B4
Keble Rd OX1. . . . . 58 B4
Keene Cl OX4 . . . . 40 C2
Kelburne Rd OX4. . . . . 33 A2
Kelham Hall Dr OX33 26 C1
Kellogg Coll (Norham
Manor) OX2. . . . . 14 A2
Kellogg Coll (Rewley
House) OX1. . . . . 58 B3
Kelly's Rd OX33 . . . . . . 26 A2
Kempson Cres OX4. . . 40 B4
Kempster Cl OX14 . . . 50 A2
Kendall Cres OX2 . . . . . 9 C3
Kenilworth Ave OX4. . 22 C1
Kenilworth Ct OX4 . . . 22 B1
Kenilworth Rd OX2. . . 28 A2
Kennedy Cl OX4. . . . . . 23 C1
Kennet Rd OX14. . . . . . 50 A3
Kennett Rd OX3. . . . . . 23 B4
KENNINGTON 39 C1
Kennington Rd
Kennington OX1. . . . . . . 39 C4
Kennington OX1, OX14 .47 A4
Kennington Rdbt OX1 31 C1
Kensington Cl OX14 . . 53 A2
Kent Cl
Abingdon OX14 . . . . 50 A2
Oxford OX4 . . . . 34 A1
Kenville Rd OX1. . . . . . 39 B4
Kersington Cres OX4 . 33 C1

Kestrel Cres OX4. . . . . 41 B4
Keydale Rd OX33. . . . . 26 A2
KIDLINGTON 3 B1
Kidlington Ctr The 8
OX5 . . . . 3 C3
Kidlington & Gosford
Sports Ctr OX5 . . . . . . 4 A1
Kiln Cl OX4 . . . . 41 A2
Kiln La
Garsington OX44. . . . . . 43 A4
Oxford OX3 . . . . 24 A4
Wheatley OX33. . . . . . . 26 B2
Kimber Cl OX33 . . . . . . 26 C2
Kimber Rd OX14 . . . . . 48 B1
Kineton Rd OX1. . . . . . 21 A1
King Edward St OX1. . 59 C2
Kingfisher Cl OX14 . . . 53 B3
Kingfisher Dr OX28. . . 56 C3
Kingfisher Gn OX4 . . . 42 A3
Kingfisher Sch OX14 50 A2
King's Cross Rd OX2 . 9 C1
Kingsfield Cres OX28 55 B2
Kingsgate OX4. . . . . . . 33 C2
Kings Meadow Ind Est
OX2 . . . . 20 B2
King's Mill La OX3 . . . 22 A4
King's School Oxford 5
OX4 . . . . 33 C4
King's Sch The (Primary)
OX29 . . . . 55 C4
King's Sch The (Seniors)
OX28 . . . . 55 A1
King St OX2 . . . . 58 A4
Kingston Cl OX14 . . . . 49 B2
Kingston Ct OX2 . . . . . 58 A4
Kingston Rd OX2. . . . . 13 C2
Kingsway Dr OX5 . . . . . 4 B2
Kirby Pl OX4 . . . . 33 C3
Kirk Cl
Cutteslowe OX2. . . . . 9 B3
Kennington OX1. . . . . . . 39 C2
Knapp Cl OX14 . . . . . . 48 C2
Knights Ho OX3 . . . . . . 24 A4
Knights Rd OX4. . . . . . 41 C4
Knolles Rd OX4 . . . . . . 33 B3
Knollys Cl OX14 . . . . . . 45 C1
Kybald St OX1 . . . . 59 C2
Kysbie Cl OX14. . . . . . . 45 B1

L

Laburnum Ave OX13. . 48 B3
Laburnum Cres OX5. . . 6 C4
Laburnum Rd OX2. . . . 19 B1
Ladder Hill OX33. . . . . 26 B1
Ladenham Rd OX4 . . . 34 A1
Ladygrove Paddock
OX14 . . . . 52 C4
Ladygrove Rd OX14 . . 52 C4
Lady Margaret Hall Coll
OX2 . . . . 14 B2
Lakefield Rd OX4. . . . . 40 C3

Lake Sch of English The
OX1 . . . .**59** A2
Lakeside
Cutteslowe OX2. . . . .**9** A4
Witney OX28 . . . .**56** C3
Lakesmere Cl OX5. . . . .**3** A4
Lake St OX1 . . . .**31** C4
Lamarsh Rd OX2 . . . .**19** C3
Lamborough Hill
OX13 . . . .**44** A4
Lambourn Rd OX4. . . .**32** C1
Lambrick Way OX14 . .**53** A2
Lambs Cl OX5. . . . .**3** C4
Lambton Cl OX4 . . . . .**23** C1
Lammas Cl OX14 . . . . .**49** B3
Lancut Rd OX28. . . . . .**54** A2
Landseer Wlk OX14 . .**53** A3
Lane Cl OX5 . . . .**3** B2
Langdale Ct OX28 . . . .**55** A1
Langdale Gate OX28. .**55** A1
Langford Bsns Pk The
OX5 . . . .**2** C4
Langford La OX5 . . . . . .**2** B4
Langford Locks OX5. . .**3** A4
Langley Cl OX3 . . . . . .**23** B4
Langley Rd OX14 . . . . .**49** B4
Lanham Way OX4 . . . .**40** C4
Larch Cl OX2. . . . .**19** B2
Larch End OX44. . . . . .**43** B4
Larches The OX3 . . . . .**17** B1
Larch La OX28 . . . .**55** C2
Larkfields OX3. . . . . . .**23** C4
Lark Hill OX2 . . . .**13** B4
Larkhill Pl OX14. . . . . .**48** C3
Larkhill Rd OX14 . . . . .**49** A2
Larkins La OX3. . . . . . .**16** B2
Larkmead Sch OX14. .**48** B2
Larkrise First Sch
OX4 . . . .**32** C4
Lashford La OX13 . . . .**36** A1
Lathbury Rd OX2 . . . .**13** C3
Latimer Grange OX3 .**23** A4
Latimer Rd OX3 . . . . . .**23** A4
Laurel Ct OX4. . . . .**22** B2
Laurel Farm Cl OX3 . .**16** A2
Lavender View OX28. .**55** C3
Lawrence Rd OX4 . . . .**33** B3
Leafield Rd OX4. . . . . .**33** B4
Leander Way OX1 . . . .**32** A2
Leckford Pl OX2 . . . . . .**58** A4
Leckford Pl Sch OX2 .**58** A4
Leckford Rd OX2. . . . .**58** A4
Ledgers Cl OX4 . . . . . .**41** A4
Lee Ave OX14 . . . .**50** A2
Lee Cl OX5 . . . .**3** B4
Leiden Rd OX3. . . . . . .**23** C2
Leigh Croft OX13. . . . .**36** B1
Lely Cl OX14 . . . .**53** A3
Lenthall Rd
Abingdon OX14 . . . . . .**49** B2
Oxford OX4 . . . .**32** B1
Leoline Jenkins Ho
OX4 . . . .**22** C1

Leon Cl OX4 . . . .**22** A2
Leopold St OX4 . . . . . .**22** B1
Letcombe Ave OX14 . .**49** B2
Levery Cl OX14. . . . . . .**50** B2
Lewell Ave OX3 . . . . . .**15** A2
Lewin Cl **1** OX4. . . . . .**33** B2
Lewis Cl OX3 . . . .**24** B4
Leyshon Rd OX33 . . . .**27** A1
Leys Pl OX4. . . . .**22** B1
LEYS THE **56** C4
Leys Villas OX28. . . . . .**56** C4
Liddell Rd OX4. . . . . . .**33** B2
Liddiard Cl OX1 . . . . . .**39** C2
Lime Rd OX2. . . . .**19** B1
Lime Wlk OX3 . . . .**23** A4
Linacre Coll OX1 . . . . .**58** C3
Linacre Ct OX3. . . . . . .**24** A4
Lincoln Coll OX1 . . . . .**59** B2
Lincoln Rd OX3 . . . . . .**31** C3
Lincombe La OX1 . . . .**37** C1
Lincraft Cl OX5 . . . .**3** C1
Linden Cl OX3 . . . .**16** B1
Lindsay Dr OX14 . . . . .**50** A4
Linkside Ave OX2 . . . . .**9** A4
Links Rd OX1 . . . .**39** C2
Link The
Marston OX3 . . . .**14** C2
Oxford OX3 . . . .**17** A1
Linnet Cl OX4. . . . .**41** B4
Linton Rd OX2 . . . .**14** A3
Lion Brewery The
OX1 . . . .**59** A2
Little Acreage OX3 . . .**15** A4
LITTLE BLENHEIM. . . .**5** B3
Little Blenheim OX5. . .**5** C3
Little Brewery St OX4 **22** A3
Little Bury OX4 . . . . . .**42** B4
Little Clarendon St
OX1 . . . .**58** B3
Little Field OX3 . . . . . .**33** C1
Littlegate St OX1. . . . .**59** B1
Littlehay Rd OX4 . . . . .**33** A3
Little Howe Cl OX14 . .**47** A1
LITTLE LONDON. **39** B2
LITTLEMORE. **41** A3
Littlemore Rd OX4 . . .**33** B2
Littlemore Rdbt OX4 .**33** A1
LITTLEWORTH **26** A1
Littleworth Bsns Ctr
OX33 . . . .**26** A1
Littleworth Ind Est
OX33 . . . .**26** A1
Littleworth Pk OX33. .**26** A2
Littleworth Rd OX33. .**26** B2
Livingstone Cl OX5. . . .**2** C1
Lobelia Rd OX4 . . . . . .**42** A4
Lock Cres OX5 . . . .**6** C3
Lockheart Cres OX4. .**33** C2
Loddon Cl OX14. . . . . .**50** A3
Lodge Cl OX3 . . . .**11** A1
Lodge Hill OX14. . . . . .**46** A2
Lodge Hill Intc OX14 .**46** A3
Lombard St **5** OX14. .**49** B1
London Ct OX3. . . . . . .**23** A4
London Pl OX4. . . . . . .**22** A3

London Rd
Oxford OX3 . . . .**16** B1
Wheatley OX33 . . . . . .**27** B1
Long Alley Almshouses
10 OX14 . . . .**53** B4
Long Cl
Oxford, Dean Court
OX2 . . . .**18** C3
Oxford, New Headington
OX3 . . . .**23** C2
Longfellow Dr OX14. .**52** B3
Long Ford Cl OX1 . . . .**21** A1
Long Furlong Prim Sch
OX14 . . . .**45** C1
Long Furlong Rd
OX13 . . . .**44** C2
Long Ground OX4 . . . .**41** C3
Long La OX4. . . . .**33** B1
Longlands Rd OX4 . . .**34** A1
Longmead OX14 . . . . .**49** A3
Long Tow OX13. . . . . .**48** C4
Longwall OX4. . . . .**33** A1
Longwall St OX1 . . . . .**59** C2
Longworth Rd OX2. . .**58** A4
Lonsdale Rd OX2. . . . . .**9** C1
Lovelace Cl OX14 . . . .**45** C1
Lovelace Dr OX5 . . . . . .**4** B2
Lovelace Rd OX2. . . . . .**9** B3
Lovelace Sq OX2. . . . . .**9** B3
Lovell Cl OX29. . . . .**57** A1
Lowell Pl OX28. . . . . . .**54** C1
LOWER RADLEY. **47** C1
Lower Radley Cvn Pk
OX14 . . . .**51** B4
LOWER WOLVERCOTE **8** B1
Loyd Cl OX14 . . . .**45** C1
Lucas Pl OX4 . . . .**32** B3
Lucca Dr OX14 . . . .**52** C2
Lucerne Rd OX2 . . . . . .**10** A2
Lumberd Rd OX14. . . .**50** A4
Luther Ct OX1 . . . .**59** B1
Luther St OX1. . . . .**59** B1
Lydia Cl OX3 . . . .**17** A2
Lye Valley OX3 . . . .**23** B1
Lye Valley Nature
Reserve★ OX3. . . . . . .**23** B2
Lyford Way OX14. . . . .**50** A4
Lynams Sch OX2 . . . . . .**9** B1
Lyndworth Cl OX3. . . .**16** C2
Lyndworth Mews
OX3 . . . .**16** C1
Lyneham Cl OX28 . . . .**54** A2
Lyne Rd OX5. . . . .**3** B3
Lynges Cl OX14 . . . . . .**50** A4
Lynn Cl OX3 . . . .**15** A2
Lyon Cl OX14 . . . .**49** C3
Lytton Rd OX4 . . . .**33** A3

M

Mabel Prichard Sch
OX4 . . . .**41** C4
Maberley Cl OX14 . . . .**52** B4
McCabe Pl OX3 . . . . . .**15** B1
Macray Rd OX29 . . . . .**57** A1

Madley Brook Prim Sch
OX28 . . . .**55** C3
Magdalen Coll OX1. . .**21** C3
Magdalen Coll Sch
OX4 . . . .**21** C2
Magdalene Quarry
Nature Reserve★
OX3 . . . .**16** C1
Magdalen Rd OX4. . . .**22** A1
Magdalen St OX1 . . . .**59** B2
Magnette Cl OX14. . . .**49** B1
Magnolia Cl OX5 . . . . . .**3** C1
Magpie La OX1 . . . . . .**59** C2
Maidcroft Rd OX4. . . .**33** B3
Maidley Cl OX28 . . . . .**55** B3
Main Ave OX4. . . . .**41** A4
Malford Rd OX3. . . . . .**17** A2
Mallard Cl OX4. . . . . . .**41** B4
Mallard Dr OX28 . . . . .**56** C3
Mallinson Ct OX2 . . . .**20** B3
Maltfield Rd OX3. . . . .**15** C3
Mandeville Cl OX14 . .**49** C4
Mandlebrote Dr OX4 .**40** C3
Manor Ct OX14. . . . . . .**53** A4
Manor Dr OX33 . . . . . .**35** B4
Manor Farm Rd OX33 **35** B4
Manor Gr OX1 . . . .**39** C1
Manor Ho★ OX5 . . . . . .**5** C2
Manor Hospl The
OX3 . . . .**16** A1
Manor Pk OX3 . . . .**16** A1
Manor Pl OX1. . . . .**21** C4
Manor Prep Sch
OX13 . . . .**48** B3
Manor Rd
Ducklington OX29 . . . .**56** C1
Oxford OX1 . . . .**21** C4
South Hinksey OX1 . . .**31** A3
Witney OX28 . . . .**57** B4
Wootton OX13. . . . . . .**36** B1
Manor Way OX5. . . . . . .**4** A4
Mansfield Coll OX1. . .**58** C3
Mansfield Rd OX1. . . .**58** C3
Manzil Way OX4 . . . . .**22** B2
Maple Ave OX5 . . . .**4** A1
Maple Cl OX2. . . . .**19** B2
Maple Ct OX5 . . . .**4** A1
Marcham Rd OX14 . . .**52** B4
Margaret Rd OX3 . . . .**23** C4
Marigold Cl **12** OX4 . .**42** A3
Marina Way OX14 . . . .**53** B2
Marjoram Cl OX4 . . . .**42** B4
Market Pl **4** OX14 . . .**49** B1
Market Sq OX28. . . . . .**55** A1
Market St OX1 . . . .**59** B2
Mark Rd OX3 . . . .**23** C4
Marlborough Ave OX5. **3** C4
Marlborough Cl
Kidlington OX5. . . . .**3** B4
Oxford OX4 . . . .**40** C4
Marlborough Ct **20** A3
Marlborough La
OX28 . . . .**54** C1
Marlborough Rd OX1 **21** A1
Marriott Cl OX2. . . . . . .**9** C3

Marriotts Cl OX28 . . . . **55** A1
Marshall Rd OX4 . . . . . **33** C4
Marsh Cl OX5 . . . . **6** A3
Marsh Ct OX14 . . . . **49** B2
Marsh La
  Marston OX3 . . . . **15** B3
  Witney OX28 . . . . **55** A2
Marsh Rd OX4 . . . . **33** B4
MARSTON **14** C4
Marston Ferry Ct OX2 **14** A4
Marston Ferry Rd
  OX2 . . . . **14** B4
Marston Rd OX3, OX4 . **15** A1
Marston St OX4 . . . . . . **22** A2
Martin Ct OX2 . . . . **9** C1
Mary Price Cl OX3. . . . **15** B1
Mascall Ave OX3 . . . . . **23** C1
Masefield Cres OX14 . **52** B3
Masey Cl **4** OX3 . . . . . **23** B3
Masons Rd OX3 . . . . . . **23** C3
Mathematical Inst Univ
  of Oxford OX1. . . . . . . **58** B3
Mather Rd OX3 . . . . . . **17** A2
Mathews Way OX3 . . . **44** A4
Matthew Arnold Sch
  OX2 . . . . **19** A1
Mattock Cl OX3 . . . . . . **23** B4
Mattock Way OX14 . . . **46** A1
Maud Hale Cotts **11**
  OX14 . . . . **53** B4
Mayfair Rd OX4 . . . . . . **33** A2
Mayfield Rd OX2 . . . . . . **9** C1
Mayott's Rd **1** OX14 . **49** A1
Meaden Hill OX3 . . . . . **15** C3
Mead La OX28 . . . . **55** A2
Meadow La
  Oxford OX4 . . . . **21** C1
  Oxford OX4 . . . . **32** B3
  6 Witney OX28 . . . . . **54** C2
Meadow Prospect OX2 **8** B2
Meadowside OX14 . . . **53** A4
Meadowside Ct **1**
  OX14 . . . . **53** A4
Meadow View
  Kidlington OX5. . . . . **3** C4
  Oxford OX2 . . . . **10** A2
  Witney OX28 . . . . **55** B1
Meadow View Rd
  OX1 . . . . **40** A2
Meadow Way OX5. . . . . **6** A3
Mead Rd OX5 . . . . **6** A2
Mead Way OX5. . . . . **3** C4
Medhurst Way OX4. . . **40** C4
Medlicott Dr OX14 . . . **52** B4
Medway Cl OX13 . . . . . **44** B1
Medway Rd OX13 . . . . **44** B1
Mercury Rd OX4 . . . . . **42** B4
Mere Rd OX2 . . . . **9** A2
Merewood Ave OX3 . . **17** B2
Merlin Rd
  Abingdon OX13 . . . . . . **48** A4
  Oxford OX4 . . . . **41** C4
Merrivale Sq OX2 . . . . **13** B2
Merton Coll OX1 . . . . **59** C2
Merton Ct OX2. . . . . . . **13** B2

Merton St OX1 . . . . **59** C2
Merton Way OX5 . . . . . . **5** C3
Metcalfe Cl OX14 . . . . **53** A2
Meyseys Cl OX3 . . . . . . **23** C1
Middle Way OX2 . . . . . . **9** C1
Midget Cl OX14 . . . . . . **52** C3
Mileway Gdns OX3 . . **23** A3
Milking La OX28, OX29 **54** C4
Millbank OX2 . . . . **20** B2
Millbuck Ind Est
  OX28 . . . . **57** A3
Mill End OX5. . . . . **4** B3
Miller Rd OX33. . . . . . . **27** A1
Miller's Acre **1** OX2 . . **9** C3
Millers Mews OX28. . . **55** A2
Mill La
  Marston OX3 . . . . **10** C2
  Marston OX3 . . . . **11** A1
  Oxford OX4 . . . . **32** B2
Mill Paddock **7** OX14 **53** B4
Mill Rd
  Abingdon OX14 . . . . . . **52** B3
  Wolvercote OX2 . . . . **8** B2
Mill St
  Kidlington OX5. . . . . **4** A3
  Oxford OX2 . . . . **20** B3
  Witney OX28 . . . . **54** C2
Millstream Ct OX2 . . . . **8** B2
Millway Cl OX2 . . . . **9** A2
Milne Pl OX3 . . . . **15** C3
Milton Rd OX4 . . . . **33** A4
Milvery Way OX4. . . . . **33** A1
Minchery Farm Cotts
  OX4 . . . . **41** A3
Minchery Rd OX4 . . . . **41** A3
Minchins Cl OX14 . . . . **50** B2
Minster Rd OX4 . . . . . . **22** B2
Mirfield Rd OX28. . . . . **54** A1
Mistletoe Gn OX4 . . . . **41** C3
Mitchell Cl OX13 . . . . . **36** B1
Moberly Cl OX4 . . . . . . **22** A2
Modern Art Oxford*
  OX1. . . . . **59** B2
Mole Pl
  Oxford OX4 . . . . **42** B3
  17 Sandford-on-Thames
  OX4 . . . . **42** A3
Monard Terr **2** OX4 . . **22** A1
Monks Cl OX4. . . . . **41** B4
Monmouth Rd OX1. . . **31** C3
Mons Way OX14. . . . . . **48** C3
Montagu Rd OX2. . . . . **19** B2
Moody Rd OX3 . . . . **15** A1
Moor Ave OX28 . . . . . . **54** C2
Moorbank OX4. . . . . . . **41** C4
Moorhen Wlk OX4 . . . **41** C3
Moorland Cl OX28. . . . **54** B2
Moorland Rd OX28 . . . **54** B1
Moorlands The OX5 . . . **3** C4
Moors Cl OX29 . . . . **56** C2
MOORS THE. **56** C2
Moors The OX5 . . . . **3** B4
Moreton Rd OX2 . . . . . **13** C4
Morland Cl OX33. . . . . **26** C2
Morrell Ave OX4 . . . . . **22** B2

Morrell Cl OX5 . . . . **3** B2
Morrell Cres OX4 . . . . **40** B4
Morris Cres OX4 . . . . . **33** A4
Morris Ho OX4 . . . . **33** B2
Mortimer Dr OX3 . . . **15** A2
Mortimer Rd OX4 . . . . **32** B1
Morton Ave OX5 . . . . . . **3** C1
Morton Cl
  Abingdon OX14 . . . . . . **50** B2
  Kidlington OX5. . . . . **3** C2
Motte The OX14 . . . . . **49** B1
Mountfield Rd OX28. . **56** B4
Mount Pl OX2. . . . . **58** A3
Mount St OX2. . . . . **20** B4
Mulberry Ct OX2 . . . . . . **9** B2
Mulberry Dr OX3. . . . . **26** C2
Mulcaster Ave OX5 . . . . **4** A2
Mullard Way OX14 . . . **49** A1
Murray Ct OX2 . . . . **14** A2
Museum of the History
  of Science* OX12 . . . **59** B2
Museum Rd OX1 . . . . . **58** B3
Mus of Oxford* OX1 . **59** B2
Musson Cl **3** OX14. . . **53** A4

N

Napier Ct OX14 . . . . . . **50** A1
Napier Rd OX4 . . . . **33** C3
Narrow Hill OX28 . . . . **55** A3
Nash Ct OX4 . . . . **33** C2
Nash Dr OX14. . . . . **52** B4
Navigation Way OX2. . **13** B3
Neave Mews **9** OX14 **53** B4
Nelson St OX2 . . . . **58** A3
Nene Rd OX13 . . . . **48** B4
Nether Durnford Cl
  OX3 . . . . **24** A1
Netherwoods Rd OX3 **24** A4
Nettlebed Mead OX4 . **41** C3
NEW BOTLEY **19** C3
New Bridge St OX28. . **55** A2
New Close La OX28. . . **56** B2
New Coll OX1. . . . . **59** C2
New College La OX1. . **59** C2
New College Sch
  OX1. . . . . **58** C3
Newcombe Ct OX2 . . . . **9** B1
New Cross Rd OX3 . . . **16** C1
NEW HEADINGTON . . **23** A3
New High St OX3. . . . . **23** A4
NEW HINKSEY **31** C4
New Hinksey CE Prim
  Sch OX1 . . . . **31** B4
New Inn Hall St OX1. . **59** B2
NEWLAND **55** C1
Newland OX28 . . . . **55** B2
Newland Mill OX28. . . **55** B2
Newlin Cl OX4 . . . . **32** B1
Newman Ct OX4 . . . . . **22** A3
Newman Rd OX4 . . . . . **33** A1
NEW MARSTON **15** A2
New Marston Prim Sch
  OX3 . . . . **15** B3
Newmill La OX28. . . . . **54** B3

New Mill Mews **1**
  OX28 . . . . **54** C2
NEW OSNEY **59** A2
Newport Cl OX5. . . . . . . **3** B1
New Rd
  Oxford OX1 . . . . **59** B2
  Radley OX14 . . . . **51** A4
New St OX14. . . . . **49** B1
Newtec Pl OX4. . . . . . . **22** A1
New Theatre* OX1 . . . **59** B2
Newton Rd OX1. . . . . . **21** A1
Nicholas Ave OX3 . . . . **15** A2
Nicholson Rd OX3. . . . **15** A1
Nightingale Ave OX4 . **42** A3
Ninth Ave OX3, OX4 . . **24** A1
Nixon Rd OX4. . . . . **32** B3
Nobles Cl OX2 . . . . **18** B2
Nobles La OX2 . . . . **18** B2
Nor Brook Cl OX14 . . . **50** B4
Norfolk Cl OX14. . . . . . **51** A4
Norfolk St OX1. . . . . . . **59** B1
Norham End OX2 . . . . **14** A2
Norham Gdns OX2 . . . **58** B4
NORHAM MANOR . . . **58** C4
Norham Rd OX2. . . . . . **14** A2
Norman Ave OX14 . . . **14** A3
Normandy Cres OX4. . **34** A3
Norman Smith Rd **14**
  OX4 . . . . **42** A3
Norreys Ave OX1 . . . . **31** C4
Norreys Rd OX2. . . . . . **28** B3
Norris Cl OX14 . . . . **50** A4
Northampton Rd OX1 **31** C3
North Ave OX14 . . . . . . **49** C4
Northbrook Ho **1**
  OX4 . . . . **41** C4
NORTHCOURT **49** C3
Northcourt La OX14 . . **49** C3
Northcourt Mews
  OX14 . . . . **49** B3
Northcourt Rd OX14. . **49** B3
Northcourt Wlk OX14 **49** C2
Northern By-Pass Rd
  Cutteslowe OX2. . . . . **8** C3
  Oxford OX3 . . . . **16** A3
Northern House Sch
  OX2 . . . . **9** C1
Northfield Cl OX4 . . . . **41** A4
Northfield Rd
  Abingdon OX14 . . . . . . **45** C1
  Oxford OX3 . . . . **16** C2
  Woodgreen OX28 . . . . . **55** C2
Northfield Row **1**
  OX28 . . . . **55** C2
Northfield Sch OX4. . . **41** B3
Northfield Sq OX28. . . **55** C2
North Hinksey CE Prim
  Sch OX2 . . . . **19** C2
North Hinksey La
  OX2 . . . . **19** C2
NORTH HINKSEY
  VILLAGE **19** C2

North Hinksey Village
OX2 . . . .**20** A1
North Kidlington Prim
Sch **4** OX5 . . . .**3** B3
North Lodge OX2 . . . .**19** B3
North Manor OX44 . . . .**43** C4
North Manor Estate The
OX44 . . . .**43** C4
Northmoor Pl OX2 . . . .**14** A3
Northmoor Rd OX2 . . . .**14** A3
North Parade Ave
OX2 . . . .**14** A2
North Pl OX3 . . . .**16** B1
North Quay OX14 . . . . .**53** B2
North St OX2 . . . .**20** B3
North Way
Cutteslowe OX2 . . . .**9** B3
Oxford OX3 . . . .**16** C2
Norton Cl OX3 . . . .**23** B4
Nowell Rd OX4 . . . .**32** C1
Nuffield Coll OX1 . . . .**59** A2
Nuffield Ind Est OX4 . .**41** A4
Nuffield Orthopaedic Ctr
OX3 . . . .**23** B3
Nuffield Rd OX3 . . . . . .**24** A3
Nuffield Way OX14 . . . .**48** B1
Nuneham Sq OX14 . . . .**49** B2
Nunnery Cl OX4 . . . . . .**41** B4
Nurseries Rd OX5 . . . .**3** B2
Nursery Cl OX3 . . . . . .**23** A3
Nuthatch Cl **1** OX4 . .**41** C3
Nyatt Rd OX14 . . . .**50** B2
Nye Bevan Cl OX4 . . . .**22** B2

O

Oak Ave OX14 . . . .**47** A4
Oakdale Rd OX28 . . . . .**55** C4
Oak Dr OX5 . . . .**4** A3
Oakfield Pl OX28 . . . . .**57** A4
Oakmead OX28 . . . . . .**55** C3
Oakthorpe Pl OX2 . . . .**13** C4
Oakthorpe Rd OX2 . . . .**13** C4
Oatlands Rd OX2 . . . . .**20** A3
Observatory St OX2 . .**58** A4
Ockham Ct OX2 . . . . . .**14** A2
Ock Meadow Nature
Reserve★ OX4 . . . .**52** A3
Ock Mews **5** OX14 . . . .**49** A1
Ock Mill Cl OX14 . . . . .**52** C4
Ock St OX14 . . . .**52** C4
OISE Oxford OX1 . . . . .**59** B2
Old Bakery The OX1 . .**59** A2
Old Barn Ground OX3 24 A1
OLD BOARS HILL **37** B2
Old Boars Hill
Boars Hill OX1 . . . .**37** B3
Wootton OX1 . . . .**37** A2
Old Chapel Cl OX5 . . . .**3** C3
Old Coachyard The **1**
OX28 . . . .**55** A2
Old Farm Cl OX14 . . . . .**50** B2
Old Greyfriars St OX1 59 B1

Old High St OX3 . . . . . .**16** B1
Old London Rd OX33 . .**27** B2
Old Marston Rd OX3 . .**15** A2
Old Nursery View
OX1 . . . .**31** C1
Old Pound The OX13 . .**44** A4
Old Rd
Littleworth OX33 . . . . . .**25** C2
Oxford OX3 . . . .**23** C3
Old Rectory Mews
OX28 . . . .**56** C4
Old School The OX4 . .**33** B4
Old Stables The OX3 . .**16** A2
Old Station Yd **6**
OX14 . . . .**49** B1
Old Warehouse Flats The
OX28 . . . .**55** B2
Oliver Rd OX4 . . . .**34** A3
Onley Ct **8** OX1 . . . . . .**21** A1
Orchard Cl
Abingdon OX14 . . . .**49** C3
Wheatley OX33 . . . .**26** C1
Orchard Ct OX4 . . . . . .**33** A2
Orchard La OX1 . . . . . .**37** A3
Orchard Meadow Prim
Sch OX4 . . . .**41** C4
Orchard Rd OX2 . . . . . .**18** B2
Orchard Way
Kidlington OX5 . . . .**4** A2
Oxford OX4 . . . .**33** B1
Witney OX28 . . . .**54** C1
Oriel Coll OX1 . . . .**59** C2
Oriel Sq OX1 . . . .**59** C2
Oriel St OX1 . . . .**59** C2
Orkney Pl OX28 . . . . . .**54** B1
Orpwood Way OX14 . .**52** B4
Osberton Rd OX2 . . . . .**9** B1
Osborne Cl
Kidlington OX5 . . . .**3** B1
Wolvercote OX2 . . . .**9** A2
Osler Rd OX3 . . . .**16** A1
OSNEY **20** B3
Osney La
Oxford OX1 . . . .**20** B3
Oxford OX1 . . . .**59** A2
Osney Mead OX2 . . . . .**20** B2
Osney Mead Ind Est
OX2 . . . .**20** B2
Osney Mews OX2 . . . . .**20** B3
Oswestry Rd OX1 . . . . .**31** C3
Otters Reach OX1 . . . .**39** C3
Otwell Cl OX14 . . . .**50** A4
Our Lady of Lourdes RC
Prim Sch **1** OX28 . . . .**56** A4
Our Ladys Convent Jun &
Senior Sch OX14 . . . .**49** C2
Our Ladys RC Prim Sch
OX4 . . . .**33** C3
Ouseley Cl OX3 . . . . . .**15** A2
Outram Rd OX4 . . . . . .**33** A3
Oval The OX4 . . . .**32** C1
Overbrooke Gdns
OX4 . . . .**42** B4
Overdale Cl OX3 . . . . .**16** C2
Overmead OX14 . . . . . .**53** A2

Overmead Gn OX4 . . .**41** C4
Owens Way OX4 . . . . .**33** B4
Owlington Cl OX2 . . . .**19** A3
Ox Cl OX14 . . . .**49** C2
Oxeye Ct OX4 . . . .**41** C2
OXFORD **59** C1
Oxford Acad OX4 . . . . .**41** A4
Oxford Brookes Univ
(Harcourt Hill Campus)
OX2 . . . .**29** C4
Oxford Brookes Univ
(Headington
Campus:Gipsy La)
OX3 . . . .**22** C4
Oxford Brookes Univ
(Headington
Campus:Headington
Hill) OX3 . . . .**22** B4
Oxford Brookes Univ
(Marston Road Site)
OX3 . . . .**15** B1
Oxford Brookes Univ
(Wheatley Campus)
OX33 . . . .**27** A2
Oxford Bsns Ctr The
OX1 . . . .**59** A1
Oxford Bsns Park N
OX4 . . . .**33** C3
Oxford Bsns Park S
OX4 . . . .**33** C2
Oxford Bsns Pk OX2 . . .**9** B4
Oxford Castle
Unlocked★
OX1 . . . .**59** A2
Oxford & Cherwell Valley
Coll (Blackbird Leys
Campus) OX4 . . . .**41** C4
Oxford & Cherwell Valley
Coll (Oxford Campus)
OX1 . . . .**59** A1
Oxford English Ctr The
4 OX2 . . . .**14** A2
Oxford High Sch OX2 14 A4
Oxford Hill OX28,
OX29 . . . .**55** C1
Oxford House Sch of
English OX33 . . . .**26** C2
Oxford Ice Rink★
OX1 . . . .**59** A1
Oxford Int Coll of Beauty
2 OX28 . . . .**55** A2
Oxford Media & Bsns
Sch OX1 . . . .**59** B1
Oxford Motor Pk OX5 . .**2** C4
Oxford Playhouse★
OX1 . . . .**58** B3
Oxford Rd
Abingdon OX1, OX13,
OX14 . . . .**46** A3
Cumnor OX2 . . . .**28** B3
Cutteslowe OX2 . . . .**7** B1
Garsington OX44 . . . . . .**43** A4
Horspath OX33 . . . .**35** A4
Kidlington OX5 . . . .**4** A1
Marston OX3 . . . .**15** A3

Oxford Rd continued
Oxford, Littlemore OX4 **33** A1
Oxford, Temple Cowley
OX4 . . . .**33** B3
South Hinksey OX1 . . . .**38** C4
Oxford Retail Pk OX4 **34** A2
Oxford Said Bsns Sch
OX1 . . . .**59** A2
Oxford Sch OX4 . . . . . .**22** C1
Oxford Sch of English
OX1 . . . .**59** B2
Oxford Science Pk The
OX4 . . . .**41** A2
Oxfordshire Hospital Sch
6 OX3 . . . .**23** B3
Oxford Sta OX2 . . . . . .**20** B3
Oxford Study Ctr OX2 . .**9** B3
Oxford Tutorial Coll
OX1 . . . .**59** C2
Oxford Union The★
OX1 . . . .**59** B2
Oxford Univ OX2 . . . . .**58** B4
Oxford University Press
OX2 . . . .**58** A3
Oxford Univ Inst Of
Experimental
Psychology OX1 . . . . .**58** C3
Oxford Univ Mus of
Natural History The★
OX1 . . . .**58** B3
Oxlease OX28 . . . .**55** B1
Oxpens Rd OX1 . . . . . .**59** A1
Ozone L Pk OX4 . . . . . .**41** B3

P

Paddocks The OX5 . . . .**5** C3
Paddock The OX1 . . . . .**39** C1
Paddox Cl OX2 . . . .**9** B2
Paddox The OX2 . . . . . .**9** B2
Paget Rd OX4 . . . .**34** A4
Pagisters Rd OX14 . . . .**50** B4
Painswick Cl OX28 . . . .**54** A2
Palladian Ct OX4 . . . . .**33** A4
Palmer Pl OX14 . . . . . .**53** A3
Palmer Rd OX3 . . . .**23** C3
Parade The
Kidlington OX5 . . . .**7** A4
Oxford OX3 . . . .**16** B1
Paradise Sq OX1 . . . . .**59** A1
Paradise St OX1 . . . . . .**59** A2
Park Ave OX5 . . . .**3** B4
Park Cl
Cutteslowe OX2 . . . .**9** C4
Yarnton OX5 . . . .**5** C2
Park Cres OX14 . . . . . .**49** A1
Park End Pl OX1 . . . . . .**59** A2
Park End St OX1 . . . . . .**59** A2
Parker St OX4 . . . .**32** B4
Park Hill OX33 . . . .**26** C3
Park Hospl for Children
OX3 . . . .**23** A3
Parklands OX3 . . . .**23** C3
Park Rd
Abingdon OX14 . . . .**49** A1

Park Rd *continued*
Ducklington OX29 . . . . .**56** C1
Witney OX28 . . . .**54** B2
Parkside OX28 . . . .**57** A3
Park Sports Ctr The
OX33 . . . .**26** C3
Parks Rd OX1 . . . .**58** B3
Park The OX2 . . . .**28** A2
PARK TOWN **14** B2
Park Town OX2 . . . .**14** A2
Park View Rd OX28 . . .**55** C2
Park Way OX3 . . . .**11** A1
Parkway Ct OX4 . . . . . .**33** C2
Parma Ho OX2 . . . .**9** C1
Parry Cl OX3 . . . .**15** A1
Parsons Mead OX14 . .**49** A4
Parsons Pl OX4 . . . . . .**22** B2
Partridge Pl OX5 . . . . . .**3** A3
Partridge Wlk OX4 . . .**42** B3
Pattison Pl OX4 . . . . . .**32** C1
Pauling Rd OX3 . . . . . .**23** C3
PEACHCROFT **50** B4
Peachcroft Rd OX14 . .**50** A4
Peacock Rd OX3 . . . . .**15** A1
Peartree Cl 2 OX4 . . .**42** A3
Peartree Interchange
OX2 . . . .**8** C4
Peat Moors OX3 . . . . .**23** B2
Peeble Hill Mobile Home
Pk OX14 . . . .**47** A4
Peel Cl OX29 . . . .**57** A1
Peel Pl OX1 . . . .**31** C3
Peep-O-Day La OX14 **53** B1
Pegasus Ct 5 OX1 . . .**21** A1
Pegasus First Sch
OX4 . . . .**42** A4
Pegasus Rd OX4 . . . . .**42** A4
Pembroke Coll OX1 . .**59** B1
Pembroke Ct 3 OX4 .**22** A2
Pembroke Sq OX1 . . . .**59** B1
Pembroke St OX1 . . . . .**59** B2
Penfold Ct OX3 . . . . . .**15** C3
Pen La OX13, OX14 . . .**45** B3
Penlon Pl OX14 . . . . . .**49** C1
Penn Cl OX14 . . . .**50** B4
Pennycress Rd OX4 . .**42** B4
Pennyfarthing Pl OX1 **59** B2
Pennywell Dr OX2 . . . . .**9** C3
Pensclose OX28 . . . . . .**55** B2
Penson's Gdns OX4 . .**21** C3
Pentagon The OX14 . .**50** A1
Peppercorn Ave OX3 .**23** C2
Percy St OX4 . . . .**32** B4
Peregrine Rd OX4 . . . .**41** B4
Periwinkle Pl 3 OX4 **42** A4
Perkins OX1 . . . .**39** B4
Perrin St OX3 . . . .**23** A4
Peterley Rd OX4 . . . . .**34** B4
Peter's Way OX4 . . . . .**33** B1
Pether Rd OX3 . . . .**23** C3
Petre Pl OX5 . . . .**4** A3
Pettiwell OX44 . . . .**43** B2
Pheasant Wlk OX4 . . .**40** B3
Phelps Pl OX4 . . . .**22** A3
Phelps The OX5 . . . .**3** B2

Phipps Rd OX4 . . . .**33** C2
Phoebe Ct OX2 . . . . . .**13** B3
Pickett Ave OX3 . . . . .**23** C1
Picklers Hill OX14 . . . .**49** C4
Pike Terr OX1 . . . .**59** B1
Pilcher Ct OX4 . . . .**22** A3
Pimpernel Cl OX4 . . . .**42** B4
Pine Cl
Garsington OX44 . . . . . .**43** A4
Oxford OX4 . . . .**34** B1
Pine Rise OX28 . . . . . .**55** C3
Pinnocks Way OX2 . . .**18** C2
Piper St OX3 . . . .**23** B4
Pipit Cl OX4 . . . .**41** C3
Pipkin Way OX4 . . . . . .**32** C4
Pipley Furlong OX4 . .**40** C4
Pitt Rivers Mus * OX1 **58** B3
Pitts Rd OX3 . . . .**16** C1
Pixey Pl OX2 . . . .**9** A2
Plain The OX4 . . . .**21** C2
Plantation Rd OX2 . . .**58** A4
Plater Dr OX2 . . . .**13** B2
Playfield Rd OX1 . . . . .**39** C1
Plough Cl OX2 . . . .**9** A2
Ploughley Cl OX5 . . . . .**3** B2
Plover Dr OX4 . . . .**41** C3
Pochard Pl 8 OX4 . . .**42** A3
Polstead Rd OX2 . . . . .**13** C2
Pond Cl OX3 . . . .**17** B1
Ponds La OX3 . . . .**15** A4
Pony Rd OX4 . . . .**34** B4
Pope's Piece OX28 . . .**54** B2
Poplar Cl
Garsington OX44 . . . . . .**43** A4
Kidlington OX5 . . . .**4** A1
Poplar Gr OX1 . . . .**39** C2
Poplar Rd OX2 . . . .**19** A3
Poppy Cl OX5 . . . .**2** C1
Portland Rd OX2 . . . . . .**9** C1
Potenger Way OX14 . .**52** C4
Pottery Piece OX4 . . .**41** C3
Pottle Cl OX2 . . . .**18** C3
Poulton Pl OX4 . . . . . .**34** B1
Pound Cl
Ducklington OX29 . . . . .**57** A1
Yarnton OX5 . . . .**5** C3
Pound Field Cl OX3 . .**16** C3
Pound Way 7 OX4 . . .**33** B2
Preachers La OX1 . . . .**59** B1
Prestidge Pl OX5 . . . . . .**4** A2
Preston Rd OX14 . . . . .**53** A2
Prestwich Pl OX2 . . . .**20** A3
Prichard Rd OX3 . . . . .**15** B1
Primrose Dr 20 OX4 . .**42** A3
Prince Gr OX14 . . . . . .**45** C1
Princes St OX4 . . . .**22** A2
Prior's Forge OX2 . . . . .**9** C3
Priory Ct OX2 . . . .**9** C3
Priory Rd OX4 . . . .**41** A4
Prospect Pk OX33 . . . .**25** A1
Prunus Cl OX4 . . . .**34** B1
Puck La OX28 . . . .**55** A2
Pudsey Cl OX4 . . . .**53** A2
Pulker Cl OX4 . . . .**33** B2
Pullens Field OX3 . . . .**22** B4

Pullens La OX3 . . . . . .**22** B4
Purcell Rd OX3 . . . . . .**15** A1
Purland Cl OX4 . . . . . .**33** B4
Purslane OX14 . . . .**50** A2
Pusey La OX1 . . . .**58** B3
Pusey St OX1 . . . .**58** B3
Pykes Cl OX14 . . . .**50** A4
Pytenry Cl OX14 . . . . . .**46** A1

Q

Quadrangle The OX2 . .**9** A2
Quadrant The OX14 . .**50** A1
Quakers Ct 10 OX14 . .**49** B1
Quarry End OX5 . . . .**2** C2
Quarry High St OX3 . .**16** C1
Quarry Hollow OX3 . .**23** C4
Quarry Rd
Oxford OX3 . . . .**23** C4
Sunningwell OX13 . . . . .**38** A1
Witney OX28 . . . .**54** C3
Quarry School Pl OX3 **23** C4
Quarry The OX13 . . . . .**38** A1
Quartermain Cl OX4 . .**32** C4
Queen Elizabeth Ho
OX1 . . . .**58** B3
Queen Emma's Dyke
OX28 . . . .**54** B1
Queens Ave OX5 . . . . . .**4** B2
Queens Cl OX2 . . . .**18** C2
Queens Coll The OX1 **59** C2
Queens Dyke Prim Sch
OX28 . . . .**56** B4
Queen's La OX1 . . . . . .**59** C2
Queen St
Abingdon OX14 . . . .**49** B1
Oxford OX1 . . . .**59** B2
Quercus Ct OX2 . . . . . .**13** C4

R

Rackham Pl OX2 . . . . .**13** B2
Radcliffe Camera Liby
OX1 . . . .**59** C2
Radcliffe Rd OX4 . . . . .**32** B3
Radcliffe Science Liby
OX1 . . . .**58** B3
Radcliffe Sq OX1 . . . . .**59** C2
Radford Cl OX4 . . . . . .**32** B1
RADLEY **47** A1
Radley CE Prim Sch
OX14 . . . .**47** A1
Radley Coll OX14 . . . . .**46** C2
Radley Ct OX14 . . . . . .**50** A3
Radley Ho OX2 . . . .**14** A4
Radley Rd OX14 . . . . . .**50** B3
Radley Road Ind Est
OX14 . . . .**50** A3
Radley Sta OX14 . . . . .**51** B4
Rahere Rd OX4 . . . .**33** B2
Railway La OX4 . . . . . .**40** C4
Rainbow Way OX14 . .**46** A1
Raleigh Park Rd OX2 .**19** C1
Rampion Cl OX4 . . . . . .**42** B4
Ramsey Rd OX3 . . . . . .**16** C1

Ramsons Way OX14 . .**50** B2
Randolph St 7 OX4 . .**22** A2
Rawlings Gr OX14 . . . .**48** C2
Rawlinson Rd OX2 . . . .**13** C3
Rawson Cl OX2 . . . .**9** A3
Raymund Rd OX3 . . . .**15** A3
Rayson Ho OX3 . . . . . .**15** C2
Reade Ave OX14 . . . . .**50** A2
Rectory Rd OX4 . . . . . .**22** A2
Red Bridge Hollow
OX1 . . . .**31** B2
Red Copse La OX1 . . .**38** B4
Rede Cl OX3 . . . .**23** C3
Redland Rd OX3 . . . . . .**15** C3
Red Lion Sq OX1 . . . . .**59** B2
Redmoor Cl OX4 . . . . .**41** A4
Redwood Cl OX4 . . . . .**42** B4
Reedmace Cl OX4 . . . .**42** B4
Regal Cl 11 OX14 . . . .**49** B1
Regent Sch OX2 . . . . . .**14** A3
Regents Park Coll
OX1 . . . .**58** B3
Regent St OX4 . . . .**22** A2
Reliance Way OX4 . . . .**22** C1
Remy Pl OX4 . . . .**32** B3
Renault Ho OX4 . . . . . .**32** B4
Rest Harrow 2 OX4 . .**22** A4
Rewley Abbey Ct OX1 **59** A2
Rewley Rd OX1 . . . . . .**59** A2
Reynolds Way OX14 . .**53** A3
Rhodes Ho OX1 . . . . . .**58** C3
Richard Gray Ct OX1 .**59** A2
Richards La OX2 . . . .**9** B1
Richardson Ct OX4 . . .**22** A3
Richards Way OX3 . . . .**24** A4
Richmond Rd OX1 . . . .**58** A3
Rickyard Cl OX1 . . . . . .**58** A3
Riddell Pl OX2 . . . .**9** B3
Ridgefield Rd OX4 . . . .**22** B1
Ridgemont Cl OX2 . . . .**9** B1
Ridgeway OX1 . . . .**37** B3
Ridgeway Rd OX3 . . . .**17** A1
Ridings The
Kidlington OX5 . . . .**3** A3
Oxford OX3 . . . .**24** A2
Ridley Rd OX4 . . . .**34** A4
Riley Cl OX14 . . . .**52** C4
Riley Ho OX4 . . . .**33** B2
Rimmer Cl OX3 . . . . . .**15** A3
Ringwood Rd OX3 . . . .**17** B1
Rippington Dr OX3 . . .**15** A2
RISINGHURST **17** B1
Rissington Dr OX28 . .**54** A1
River Cl OX14 . . . .**53** A3
Rivermead Rd OX4 . . .**32** B1
Riverside Ct OX1 . . . . .**21** A1
Riverside Gdns OX28 .**55** C2
Riverside Rd OX2 . . . .**20** A3
River View
Kennington OX1 . . . .**39** C3
Sandford-on-Thames
OX4 . . . .**40** B1
River View Terr OX14 .**53** A4

Rivy Cl OX14 . . . . **50** B2
Robert Robinson Ave
OX4 . . . . **41** A3
Roberts Cl OX3 . . . . . . **17** B2
Robin Cl OX14 . . . . **48** C2
Robin Pl OX4 . . . . **41** C3
Robinson Rd OX1 . . . **36** B1
Robsart Pl OX2 . . . . . . **28** A2
Rock Edge OX3 . . . . . . **23** B4
Rock Edge Nature
Reserve* OX3. . . . . **23** B3
Rock Farm La OX4 . . . . **40** C2
Roger Bacon La OX1 . **59** B1
Roger Dudman Way OX1,
OX2 . . . . **20** B4
Rogers St OX2 . . . . **9** C1
Rolfe Pl OX3 . . . . **15** B1
Roman Rd OX33. . . . . . **27** A1
Roman Way OX4 . . . . **34** B3
Rookery Cl OX13 . . . . . **48** A3
Rookery Ho OX44 . . . . **43** C3
Rookery The 1 OX5 . . . **3** B3
Roosevelt Dr OX3 . . . . **23** A3
Rosamund Rd OX2 . . . . **8** C2
Rose Ave OX14 . . . . **45** B1
Rose Ct 2 OX4 . . . . . . **33** A1
Rose Gdns OX2 . . . . . . **19** A2
ROSE HILL **32** C2
Rose Hill OX4 . . . . **33** A2
Rose Hill Prim Sch
OX4 . . . . **32** C1
Rose La OX1 . . . . **59** C2
Rosemary Ct OX4 . . . . **22** A1
Rose Pl OX1 . . . . **59** B1
Ross Ct OX1 . . . . **39** C3
Rotha Field Rd OX2 . . . **9** B3
Roundham Cl OX5. . . . . **3** B3
Roundway The OX3. . **17** A1
Routh Rd OX3. . . . . **17** A2
Rowan Cl OX5 . . . . **3** C1
Rowan Gr OX4 . . . . **42** B3
Rowel Dr OX5. . . . . **2** C3
Rowland Cl OX2. . . . . . **8** B2
Rowland Hill Ct OX1. .**59** A2
Rowlands Ho OX3 . . . . **17** B1
Rowles Cl OX1 . . . . **39** C3
Rowney Pl OX4 . . . . . . **32** C2
Rupert Rd OX4. . . . . . . **34** A4
Rush Common Prim Sch
OX14 . . . . **50** A3
Rushmead Copse
OX14 . . . . **50** B4
Ruskin Ave OX14 . . . . **53** A3
Ruskin Coll
Oxford, Headington
OX3 . . . . **16** A2
Oxford OX1 . . . . **58** A3
Russell Ct OX2 . . . . . . **13** C2
Russell St OX2 . . . . . . **20** B3
Rutherford Cl OX14 . . **49** C3
Rutherway OX2 . . . . . . **13** B1
Rutten La OX5 . . . . **5** B4
Rutters Cl OX5 . . . . **3** B2

Ryder Cl
Summertown OX2 . . . . **13** B4
Yarnton OX5 . . . . **5** C4
Rye St Antony Sch
OX3 . . . . **15** C1
Rylands OX3 . . . . **15** A3
Rymers La OX4 . . . . . . **33** A3

S

Sackler Liby OX1. . . . . .**58** B1
Sadlers Croft OX44. . .**43** C3
Sadlers Ct OX14. . . . . .**46** A1
Sadler Wlk OX1 . . . . . .**59** A1
Saffron Ct OX14. . . . . .**50** A2
Sage Wlk 7 OX4 . . . .**42** A3
St Aldate's OX1 . . . . . .**59** B1
St Aloysius RC Prim Sch
OX2 . . . . **13** C2
St Amand Dr OX14 . .**53** A4
St Andrews CE Prim Sch
OX3 . . . . **16** B1
St Andrews Cl OX14 . .**50** B4
St Andrew's La OX3 . .**16** B2
St Andrew's Rd OX3. .**16** A2
St Anne's Coll OX2 . .**58** B4
St Anne's Rd OX3 . . . .**23** B4
St Antony's Coll OX2 .**58** A4
St Barnabas CE First Sch
OX2 . . . . **58** A3
St Barnabas St OX2 . .**58** A3
St Bernard's Rd OX2 .**58** A4
St Catherines Coll
OX1 . . . . **21** C4
St Catherines Ho OX4 **21** C3
St Christophers CE First
Sch OX4 . . . .**33** B4
St Christopher's Pl
OX4 . . . . **33** B4
St Clares Bardwell Rd
Ctr 2 OX2 . . . .**14** A2
St Clares Oxford OX2 **13** C4
St Clement's St OX4. .**22** A3
St Cross Bldg OX1. . . .**58** B1
St Cross Coll OX1 . . . .**58** B3
St Cross Coll (Annexe)
OX1 . . . . **58** C3
St Cross Rd OX1 . . . . .**58** C3
St Ebbe's CE Prim Sch
OX1 . . . . **21** A1
St Ebbes St OX1. . . . . .**59** B2
St Edmund Hall OX1. .**59** C2
St Edmund's La 4
OX14 . . . . **53** B4
St Edmunds RC Prim Sch
OX14 . . . . **49** C2
St Edward's Ave
Oxford OX2 . . . . **9** B1
Summertown OX2 . . . .**13** B4
St Edwards Ct OX2 . . .**13** C4
St Edwards Sch
Oxford OX2 . . . . **9** B1
Oxford OX2 . . . . **13** C4
SS Mary & John CE Prim
Sch 1 OX4 . . . .**22** B1

SS Philip & James CE
Prim Sch OX2 . . . .**13** B2
St Francis CE Prim Sch
OX4 . . . . **34** A4
St Francis Ct OX3 . . . .**23** C1
St Georges Gate OX1 **59** A2
St George's Pl OX1. . .**59** B2
St Giles' OX1 . . . .**58** B3
St Gregory the Great RC
Sec Sch OX4 . . . .**32** C4
St Helen's Ct OX14 . . .**53** B4
St Helen's Mews 6
OX14 . . . . **53** B4
St Helen's Mill 12
OX14 . . . . **53** B4
St Helen's Pas OX1. . .**59** C2
St Helen's Wharf
OX14 . . . . **53** B4
St Hildas Coll OX4. . . .**21** C2
St Hugh's Coll OX2 . . .**13** C2
St James Rd OX14. . . .**47** A1
St James Terr OX14. . .**51** A4
St John Fisher Prim Sch
OX4 . . . . **33** C1
St John's Coll OX1 . . .**58** B3
St Johns Dr OX5 . . . . . **4** A3
St John's Rd OX14 . . . .**49** C2
St John St OX1. . . . . . .**58** B3
St Josephs RC Prim Sch
OX3 . . . . **15** B2
St Lawrence Rd OX1. .**31** A3
St Leonard's Rd OX3 .**16** B1
St Luke's Rd OX4. . . . .**33** C3
St Margaret's Rd OX2 **13** C2
St Martin's Rd OX4. . .**32** C1
St Maryís Ho OX33 . . .**26** C2
St Marys CE Inf Sch
OX28 . . . . **57** A4
St Mary's Cl
Kidlington OX5. . . . . . . **3** C4
Oxford OX4 . . . .**40** C4
Wheatley OX33 . . . . . .**26** C2
St Mary's Ct OX28 . . .**56** C4
St Mary's Gn OX14 . . .**49** B3
St Marys Mead OX28 .**57** A4
St Mary's Rd OX4 . . . .**22** A1
St Michael's Ave
OX14 . . . . **49** A1
St Michaels CE First Sch
OX3 . . . . **22** A4
St Michael's La OX5. . **2** A2
St Michael's St OX1 . .**59** B2
St Nicholas' Gn OX14 **49** B3
St Nicholas Pk (Cvn Pk)
OX3 . . . . **11** A4
St Nicholas Prim Sch
OX3 . . . . **15** A3
St Nicholas Rd OX4 . .**41** A4
St Nicolas CE Prim Sch
OX14 . . . . **49** B2
St Omer Rd OX4. . . . . .**33** B3
St Paul's Cres OX2 . . .**19** B2
St Peter's Cl OX13. . . .**44** A4
St Peter's Coll OX1. . .**59** B2

St Peter's Rd
Abingdon OX14 . . . .**50** B3
Wolvercote OX2 . . . . . . **9** A2
St Swithuns CE Prim Sch
OX1 . . . . **39** C2
St Swithun's Rd OX1 .**39** C2
St Thomas More RC
Prim Sch 1 OX5 . . . . . **3** C1
St Thomas' St OX1. . . .**59** A2
Salegate La OX4 . . . . .**33** C3
Salesian Gdns OX4. . .**33** C4
Salesian Ro 1 OX4 . .**33** C4
Salford Rd OX3 . . . . . .**14** C2
Salisbury Cres OX2. . . **9** C2
Salter Cl OX1 . . . .**21** A1
Samphire Rd OX4 . . . .**42** A4
Sandfield Rd OX3 . . . .**15** C1
Sandford Cl OX14 . . . .**50** A4
Sandford La OX1. . . . .**40** A1
SANDFORD-ON-
THAMES **40** C1
Sandford Rd OX4. . . . .**40** B3
Sandhill Rd OX5 . . . . . . **2** B2
SANDHILLS **17** C2
Sandhills Prim Sch
OX3 . . . . **17** C2
Sandleigh Rd OX13. . .**36** B1
Sands Cl OX2 . . . .**28** A3
Sandy La
Boars Hill OX1. . . . .**37** A4
Oxford OX4 . . . .**34** A1
Yarnton OX5 . . . . **3** A1
Sandy Lane W OX4 . . .**33** C1
Saunders Rd OX4 . . . .**33** A4
Savile Rd OX1. . . . .**58** C3
Sawpit Rd OX4. . . . . . .**34** A1
Saxifrage Sq 5 OX4. .**41** C3
Saxon Ct OX3 . . . .**16** A1
Saxon Way
Oxford OX3 . . . .**15** C2
Witney OX28 . . . .**56** C4
Saxton Rd OX14 . . . . .**53** A3
Sch of Geography
OX1 . . . . **58** C3
Schofield Ave OX28 . .**54** C4
Schofield Gdns OX28 **54** C4
Scholar Pl OX2. . . . . . .**19** A1
Scholar's Mews OX2 .**13** C4
Schongau Cl OX14 . . .**52** C2
School Ct OX2 . . . .**58** A3
School of St Helen & St
Katherine OX14 . . . . .**48** C2
School Pl OX1 . . . .**31** C4
School Rd OX5. . . . . **3** C3
Science Oxford*
OX4 . . . . **22** A3
Scott Cl OX5. . . . . **3** B2
Scott Rd OX2 . . . . **9** C2
Scrutton Cl OX3. . . . . .**16** C1
Seacourt Rd OX2. . . . .**19** C3
Sealham Rd OX29 . . . .**57** A1
Sefton Rd OX3 . . . .**16** C1
Sellwood Rd OX14 . . .**49** B3
Selwyn Cres OX14. . . .**51** A4
Sermon Cl OX3 . . . . . .**24** A4

Seventh Ave OX3.....24 A2
Severn Rd OX13......48 C4
Sewell Cl OX14.......50 B3
Shaftesbury Rd OX3..16 C3
Shaw's Copse OX14..51 B4
Sheepway Ct OX4....32 C2
Sheldonian Theatre★
OX1...............59 C2
Sheldon Way OX4....33 B1
Shelford Pl OX3......23 B3
Shelley Cl
Abingdon OX14.......49 C3
Oxford OX3..........24 A4
Shelley Rd OX4......33 A4
Shepherd Gdns OX14 52 B4
Shepherds Hill OX4..42 A3
Sheriff's Dr OX2......9 A2
Sherwood Ave OX14..49 C1
Sherwood Pl OX3....16 C2
SHIPPON...........48 B3
Ship St OX1..........59 B2
Shire Lake Cl OX1....59 B1
Shirley Pl OX2.......58 A4
Shoe La OX1.........59 B2
Shorte Cl OX3.......23 C1
Shotover Ctry Pk★
OX3...............24 C2
Shotover Kilns OX3..24 A3
Shotover Trad Est
OX3...............24 A3
Shrieves Cl OX14.....50 A4
Sibthorp Rd OX1.....58 C3
Sidney St OX4.......22 A1
Silkdale Cl OX4......33 C3
Silver Rd OX4........22 B1
Simon Ho OX3.......16 B1
Simon's Cl OX33.....26 B2
Simpsons Way OX1...39 C2
Singletree OX4......33 A2
Sinnet Ct OX4........22 B2
Sint Niklaas Cl OX14..52 C2
Sir William Dunn Sch of
Pathology OX1......58 C4
Skelton Ct OX4.......22 A3
Skene Cl OX3........23 A3
Skylark Pl OX4.......41 B4
Slade Cl OX3.........23 B3
Slade The OX3.......23 C2
Slaymaker Cl OX3....24 A4
Snowdon Mede OX3..15 B2
Sollershott OX2.......9 A4
Somerville Coll OX2..58 A3
Songers Cl OX2......18 C2
Sorrel Rd OX4.......42 B4
South Ave
Abingdon OX14.......49 B4
Kidlington OX5.........7 A4
South Bridge Row
OX1...............59 B1
South Cl OX5.........7 A3
Southcroft OX3......15 A4
Southdale Rd OX2.....9 C2
SOUTHEND.........43 C2
Southend OX44......43 C2
Southern By-Pass Rd
Kennington OX1.......31 C2
Oxford, Botley OX2....19 C2
Southfield Pk OX4...22 C2
Southfield Rd OX4...22 B2
SOUTH HINKSEY....31 B3
Southlawn OX28.....56 B4
Southmoor Pl OX2...13 C2
Southmoor Rd OX2...13 B2
Southmoor Way
OX14..............49 A2
South Par OX2........9 C1
South Park Ct 5 OX4 22 A2
South Parks Rd OX1..58 C3
South Quay OX14....53 B2
South St OX2........20 B2
Sparrow Way OX4....42 A3
Sparsey Pl OX2.......9 C3
Spears The OX5.......5 C4
Speedwell St OX1....59 B1
Spencer Ave OX5.....5 C3
Spencer Cres OX4....33 A2
Spenlove Cl OX14....49 B4
Spey Rd OX13........44 B1
Spindleberry Cl OX4 .41 C4
Spindlers OX5........4 A4
Spinney Field OX4...41 C3
Spinneys Cl OX14....47 B1
Spinney The OX14....48 C3
Spooner Cl OX3......16 C1
Spring Cl OX28.......56 C4
Spring Copse OX1....31 B1
Springfield Dr OX14..49 A2
Springfield Oval
OX28..............54 B3
Springfield Pk OX28..54 B2
Springfield Rd
Kidlington OX5.........4 A2
Oxford OX2..........19 A2
Springfield Sch OX28 55 C3
Spring Gdns OX14....48 C1
Spring Hill Rd OX5....2 A2
Spring La
Horspath OX33.......25 A1
Oxford, Headington Quarry
OX3...............24 A4
Oxford OX4..........41 B4
Spring Rd OX14......48 C1
Springs The OX28....56 C4
Spring Terr 2 OX14..48 C1
Spruce Gdns OX4....41 C2
Spruce Rd OX5.......3 C1
Square The
3 Abingdon OX14....49 B1
Ducklington OX29.....57 A1
Oxford, Botley OX2....19 B3
2 Oxford OX4.......33 B2
Squitchey La OX2.....9 B2
Stable Cl OX1........59 A2
Stainer Pl OX3.......15 A2
Stainfield Rd OX3....15 C3
Standon Ct OX3......23 A4
Stanford Dr OX14....49 B2
Staniland Ct OX14....49 B2
Stanley Cl
Oxford OX2..........19 B2
Yarnton OX5..........2 C1
Stanley Rd OX4......22 A1
Stansfeld Pl OX3.....23 C3
Stansfield Cl OX3....24 A3
Stanton Cl OX28.....54 A1
Stanton Harcourt Rd
Witney, Cogges
OX28..............55 B1
Witney OX28.........57 C4
Stanton Rd OX2......30 A4
Stanville Rd OX2.....18 C1
Stanway Rd OX3.....17 B1
Stapleton Rd OX3....23 A4
Starnham Rd OX29...56 C1
Starwort Path 4 OX4 42 A4
Station App OX5......3 A4
Station Field Ind Est
OX5.................3 A4
Station La OX28......57 A3
Station Rd OX33.....26 C2
Staunton Rd OX3.....15 C1
Staverton Rd OX2....13 C3
Steep Rise OX3......16 A3
Stenter La OX28......54 C2
Stenter Mews 5
OX28..............54 C2
Stenter Rise 4 OX28 54 C2
Stenter Sq OX28.....54 C3
Stenton Cl OX14.....53 A3
Stephen Ct OX3......16 A1
Stephen Rd OX3.....16 A1
Stephenson Ho OX1..59 B1
Sterling Cl OX5.......3 C2
Sterling Rd OX5.......3 C2
Sterling Road App
OX5.................3 C3
Stert St OX14........49 B1
Stevens Cl OX2......13 C2
Stevenson Dr OX14..48 C2
Stewart St OX1......31 B4
Stile Rd OX3.........16 B1
Stimpsons Cl OX2....18 C3
Stockey End OX14....50 B4
Stockleys Rd OX3....15 B3
Stockmore St OX4...22 A2
Stocks Tree Cl OX5....5 C3
Stoke Pl OX3........16 A2
Stone Cl OX2........18 C3
Stonegables OX28...56 C3
Stonehill La OX14....52 C1
Stonehill Wlk OX14...52 C2
Stone Mdw OX2......13 B3
Stone Quarry La OX4 32 C2
Stone St OX4........22 B2
Stonhouse Cres OX14 51 A4
Stonor Pl OX3.......22 C4
Stoutsfield Cl OX5....5 B3
Stowford Ct OX3.....17 A3
Stowford Rd OX3.....17 A2
Stowood Cl OX3.....16 C2
Straignes Cl OX29....57 A1
Stratfield Rd
Kidlington OX5.........6 C4
Stratfield Rd *continued*
Oxford OX2..........13 C4
Stratford St OX4.....22 A1
Stratton Way OX14...49 B1
Strawberry Path OX4 42 A4
Streatley Lodge 6
OX1................21 A1
Stubble Cl OX2......18 B2
Stubbs Ave OX3......23 C1
Sturges Cl OX3.......16 B3
Suffolk Way OX14....52 C4
Sugworth Cres OX14 .47 A4
Sugworth La OX14...46 C4
Summerfield OX1....31 C4
Summerfield Rd OX2..9 C1
Summer Fields OX14 46 A1
Summer Fields Sch
OX2.................9 C1
Summerhill Rd OX2...9 C1
SUMMERTOWN.....10 A1
Summertown Ct OX2..9 B1
Summertown Ho OX2.9 B2
Sunderland Ave OX2..9 B3
Sundew Cl OX4......42 B4
SUNNINGWELL......45 A4
Sunningwell CE Prim
Sch OX13...........45 A4
Sunningwell Rd
Oxford OX1..........31 C4
Sunningwell OX13.....45 A2
SUNNYMEAD........9 C2
Sunnymeade Ct 2
OX2.................9 C3
Sunny Rise OX33.....35 C4
Sunnyside
Oxford OX4..........33 C4
Wheatley OX33.......27 A2
Sutton Cl OX14.......49 B1
Sutton Rd OX3.......15 C3
Swain Ct OX28.......56 C3
Swallow Cl 15 OX4...42 A3
Swan Ct
Oxford OX1..........59 A2
7 Witney OX28......54 C1
Swan Sch of English
OX2...............13 C3
Swan St OX2.........20 B3
Sweet Green Cl OX3..17 C2
Sweetmans Rd OX2..19 C1
Swift Cl
Oxford OX4..........42 B3
19 Sandford-on-Thames
OX4...............42 A3
Swinbourne Rd OX4..40 C4
Swinbrook Ct OX28...57 A4
Swinburne Rd
Abingdon OX14.......49 C2
Oxford OX4..........32 B4
Swingburn Pl OX28..54 C1
Sycamore Cl
Abingdon OX13.......48 B3
Witney OX28.........55 B3
Sycamore Cres OX14 .39 C1

Sycamore Rd OX2 . . . . . .19 B1
Sycamores The OX3 . .16 C2
Sympson Cl 5 OX14. .53 A4

T

Tackley Pl OX2 . . . . . . .13 C2
Taggs Gate OX3 . . . . . .17 A3
Talbot Rd OX2 . . . . .9 B4
Taphouse Ave OX28 . .55 A3
Tarragon Dr OX4 . . . . .42 A3
Tarrant Ave OX28 . . . .55 C3
Tatham Rd OX14 . . . . .49 B3
Taverner Pl OX3 . . . . .15 A2
Tawney St OX4 . . . . . . .22 B2
Taylor Inst Main Liby
 OX1 . . . . .58 B3
Teal Cl OX4 . . . . .42 A3
Templar Ho OX4 . . . . .33 B3
Templar Rd OX2 . . . . . .9 C3
Templars Cl OX33 . . . .26 B2
Templars Square Sh Ctr
 5 OX4 . . . . .33 B2
Temple Cloisters 2
 OX4 . . . . .33 C4
TEMPLE COWLEY . . .33 B3
Temple Cowley Pool &
 Fitness Ctr OX4 . . . . .33 B4
Temple Rd OX4 . . . . . .33 B4
Temple St OX4 . . . . . . .21 C2
Tennyson Dr OX14 . . .52 B3
Tern Wlk OX4 . . . . .41 C3
Terrett Ave OX3 . . . . .17 C2
Terrington Cl OX14. . .49 C4
TF Smith Bldgs OX28 55 B1
Thackley End OX2 . . . .13 C3
Thames Ct
 Abingdon OX14 . . . . . . .49 C1
 Oxford OX1 . . . . .59 B1
Thameside Prim Sch
 OX14 . . . . .52 C3
Thames International 8
 OX28 . . . . .54 C1
Thames St
 Abingdon OX14 . . . . . . .53 B4
 Oxford OX1 . . . . .59 B1
Thames View OX14 . . .49 C1
Thames View Bsns Ctr
 OX14 . . . . .49 C1
Thames View Ind Pk
 OX14 . . . . .49 C1
Thames View Rd OX4 32 B1
Thelwell Ho OX4 . . . .22 C1
Thesiger Rd OX14 . . . .49 B2
Third Acre Rise OX2. .18 C2
Thistlecroft Cl OX14. .50 A4
Thistle Down Cl OX4 .41 C2
Thistle Dr OX4 . . . . . . .42 B4
Thomas Mews OX4 . . .22 A3
Thomas Reade Prim Sch
 OX14 . . . . .50 A2
Thomson Terr OX4 . . .40 B4
Thorncliffe Rd OX2. . .13 C4

Thorne Cl OX5 . . . . .3 A3
Thorney Leys OX28 . . .56 A3
Thorney Leys Ind Pk
 OX28 . . . . .56 B3
Thornhill Wlk OX14 . .49 A3
Three Corners Rd
 OX4 . . . . .42 B4
Three Fields Rd OX3 .23 C2
Thrift Pl OX4 . . . . .42 A4
Thrupp La OX14. . . . . .50 C3
Thurston Cl 4 OX14. .53 A4
Tidmarsh La OX1. . . . .59 A2
Tilbury La OX2 . . . . . . .19 A3
Tilehouse Cl OX3 . . . .16 C1
Tilsley Pk OX14 . . . . . .45 A1
Timothy Way 5 OX4 .42 A4
Titup Hall Dr OX3 . . . .23 C3
Tomkin's Almshouses 4
 OX14 . . . . .49 A1
Toot Hill Butts OX3. . .17 A1
Tower Cl OX14 . . . . . . .52 C4
Tower Cres OX1 . . . . . .59 B2
Tower Ct OX28 . . . . . . .54 B2
Tower Hill OX28 . . . . . .54 B1
Tower Hill Prim Sch
 OX28 . . . . .54 C2
Town Furze OX3 . . . . .23 B1
Town Gn The OX5 . . . . .4 A3
Townsend OX14. . . . . .53 B3
Townsend Sq OX4 . . .32 B4
Toynbee Cl OX2 . . . . . .19 B2
Trafford Rd OX3. . . . . .16 C1
Tree Close Bay OX4 . .32 C2
Treeground Pl OX5 . . . .3 C2
Tree La OX4 . . . . .32 C2
Trefoil Pl OX4 . . . . .42 B4
Trendell Pl OX14 . . . . .49 A3
Trevor Pl OX4 . . . . .33 A3
Trill Mill Ct OX1 . . . . . .59 B1
Trinity Cl OX14. . . . . . .50 A4
Trinity Coll OX1 . . . . . .58 B3
Trinity Rd OX3 . . . . . . .24 A4
Trinity St OX1 . . . . .59 B1
Tristram Rd OX29 . . . .57 A1
Troy Cl OX3 . . . . .23 C1
Tucker Rd OX4 . . . . . . .34 A1
Tudor Cl OX4 . . . . .32 B2
Tudor Ct OX2 . . . . .18 B2
Tumbling Bay Ct OX2 20 B3
Turberville Cl OX14. . .53 A4
Turl St OX1 . . . . .59 B2
Turnagain La OX14 . . .53 B4
Turn Again La OX1 . . .59 B1
Turner Cl OX4 . . . . .33 C4
Turner Ct OX5 . . . . .4 A1
Turner Rd OX14 . . . . . .52 C3
Turners Cl OX14. . . . . .51 B4
Turnpike Rd OX2 . . . . .29 A4
Turret Ho OX3 . . . . . . .16 A1
Twelve Acre Dr OX14 .46 B1
Two Rivers Ind Est
 OX28 . . . . .57 A3
Tyndale Pl OX33. . . . . .27 A2
Tyndale Rd OX4 . . . . . .21 C2
Tyne Rd OX13 . . . . .48 B4

U

Ulfgar Rd OX2 . . . . .9 A2
Underhill Cir OX3 . . . .17 A2
Unicorn Sch The 5
 OX14 . . . . .48 C1
Union St OX4 . . . . .22 A2
Union Way OX28 . . . . .54 B1
University Coll OX1. . .59 C2
University Coll (Annexe)
 OX2 . . . . .13 C3
Upland Park Rd OX2. . .9 B2
Upper Barr 3 OX4 . . .33 B2
Upper Fisher Row
 OX1 . . . . .59 A2
Upper Rd OX1 . . . . . . .39 C4
UPPER WOLVERCOTE 9 A2
Upton Cl
 Abingdon OX14 . . . . . . .49 C3
 Oxford OX4 . . . . .41 A4
Upway Rd OX3 . . . . . . .15 C3

V

Valence Cres OX28 . . .54 A2
Valentia Rd OX3. . . . . .23 A4
Vale Rd OX28 . . . . .54 A1
Van-Dieman's La OX4 33 B1
Vanner Rd OX28. . . . . .55 B3
Venables Cl OX2 . . . . .58 A4
Venneit Cl OX1. . . . . .20 B4
Verbena Way 2 OX4 .41 C3
Vernon Ave OX2. . . . . .30 A4
Vetch Pl OX4 . . . . .42 A4
Vicarage Cl OX4 . . . . .40 C4
Vicarage Ct OX1 . . . . .31 C4
Vicarage La OX1 . . . . .31 B4
Vicarage Rd
 Kidlington OX5. . . . . . . .4 A3
 Oxford OX1 . . . . .31 C4
Victoria Ct
 Oxford, Headington
 OX3 . . . . .22 C4
 Oxford OX1 . . . . .59 B2
Victoria Gate OX2 . . . .9 C2
Victoria Rd
 Abingdon OX14 . . . . . . .48 C1
 Oxford OX2 . . . . .9 C2
Victor St OX2 . . . . .58 A3
Villeboys Cl OX14 . . . .50 B2
Villiers Ct OX4 . . . . . . .33 A2
Villiers La OX4 . . . . . . .33 A2
Viner Cl OX28. . . . . . . .55 B3
Vines The 2 OX14. . . .49 B1
Vineyard OX14 . . . . . . .49 B1
Vintner Rd 9 OX14. . .49 B1
Violet Way OX4 . . . . . .41 C2
Virginia Way OX14 . . .52 C2
Vivienne Ct OX3. . . . . .23 B3

W

Wadard's Mdw OX28 .55 C1
Wadham Coll OX1. . . .58 C3

Waine Rush View
 OX28 . . . . .55 A1
Wallace Cl OX14 . . . . .53 A3
Wallbrook Ct OX2 . . . .19 B3
Walled Gdns OX14 . . .47 A1
Walnut Cl OX28 . . . . . .54 B1
Walter's Row OX4. . . .22 A3
Walton Cres OX1. . . . .58 A3
Walton La OX1 . . . . . . .58 A3
WALTON MANOR 58 A4
Walton Manor Ct
 OX2 . . . . .58 A4
Walton St OX1, OX2. . .58 A3
Walton Well Rd OX2. .13 B1
Warbler Wlk OX4 . . . .41 C3
Warburg Cres OX4 . . .34 B1
Warnborough Rd
 OX2 . . . . .13 C2
Warneford Hospl OX3,
 OX4 . . . . .22 C3
Warneford La OX3,
 OX4 . . . . .22 C3
Warneford Rd OX4 . . .22 B2
Warren The OX14. . . . .50 A2
Warwick Cl OX14. . . . .49 C2
Warwick St OX4. . . . . .22 A1
Water Eaton La OX5. . .4 B1
Water Eaton Rd OX2. .10 A2
Waterford La OX4 . . . .55 C2
Waterford Rd OX28. . .55 C2
Waterloo Way OX28 . .55 A1
Watermans Reach 2
 OX1 . . . . .21 A1
Watermead OX5 . . . . . .4 B2
Watermill Way OX3 . .17 B2
Watlington Rd
 Garsington OX44. . . . . .43 B1
 Oxford OX4, OX44. . . . .42 C4
Watson Cres OX13 . . .36 B1
Watts Way 1 OX5. . . . .3 C3
Waverley Ave OX5. . . . .4 B2
Waxes Cl OX14. . . . . . .50 B4
Wayfaring Cl OX4 . . . .41 C2
Waynflete Rd OX3. . . .17 B2
Weavers Cl OX28. . . . .56 C4
Webb's Cl OX2. . . . . . . .8 B2
Webb's Way OX5. . . . . .4 A3
Weirs La OX1 . . . . .31 C3
Welch Way 2 OX28 . .54 C1
Weldon Rd OX3 . . . . . .15 A1
Welford Gdns OX14 . .49 C4
Welland Cl OX13 . . . . .48 B4
Wellesbourne Cl
 OX14 . . . . .50 A2
Wellington Pl OX1 . . .58 B3
Wellington Sq OX1. . .58 B3
Wellington St OX2 . . .58 A3
Wenman Rd OX28 . . . .54 A1
Wentworth Rd OX2. . . .9 C2
Werrell Dr OX1 . . . . . . .36 B1
Wesley Cl OX4 . . . . . . .34 A1
Wesley Wlk OX28. . . . .55 A1
Wessex Ind Est OX28 .57 A3
West Ave OX14 . . . . . . .49 C4
Westbury Cres OX4. . .33 A2

West End OX28. . . . . . . 55 A3
West End Ind Est
  OX28 . . . . 55 A2
Western By-Pass Rd
  Cutteslowe OX2. . . . . 8 C3
  Wytham OX2 . . . . 12 A3
Western Rd OX1 . . . . . 21 A1
Westfield Cl OX4 . . . . . 33 A4
Westfield Rd
  Wheatley OX33 . . . . 26 B3
  Witney OX28. . . . . 55 A3
Westfields OX14 . . . . . 48 C1
Westgate Sh Ctr OX1 59 B2
West Gr OX2. . . . . 9 C2
West Kidlington Prim
  Sch 🛿 OX5 . . . . 3 C1
Westlands Dr OX3. . . . 15 C3
Westminster Way
  OX2 . . . . 19 C2
Weston Bldgs OX1 . . . 59 B2
West Oxford Prim Sch
  OX2 . . . . 20 B3
West Quay OX14 . . . . . 53 B2
Westrup Cl OX3 . . . . . . 15 A1
West St Helen St
  OX14 . . . . 53 B4
West St OX2 . . . . 20 B3
West View OX4 . . . . . . 32 C2
West Way OX2 . . . . 19 B3
West Witney Cty Prim
  Sch OX28 . . . . 54 A1
Weyland Rd OX3 . . . . . 23 C4
Wharf Cl OX14 . . . . 53 B4
Wharton Rd OX3 . . . . . 16 B1
Wheatcroft Cl OX14 . . 49 C4
WHEATLEY 26 B2
Wheatley Bsns Ctr
  OX33 . . . . 27 A2
Wheatley CE Prim Sch
  OX33 . . . . 28 B2
Wheatley Park Sch
  OX33 . . . . 26 C4
White Barn OX1. . . . . . 37 A4
Whitecross OX13. . . . . 44 C2
White Hart OX3 . . . . . . 15 A4
White Hill La OX1 . . . . 36 B3
White Horse Leisure &
  Tennis Ctr OX14 . . . . . 50 B2
Whitehouse Cl OX13 . 48 B3
Whitehouse Rd OX1. . 21 A1
Whitelock Rd OX14. . . 49 B3
White Rd OX4. . . . . 34 A4
White's La OX14 . . . . . 46 C1
Whitethorn Way 🛿
  OX4 . . . . 41 C4
White Way OX5 . . . . . . 3 C2
Whitson Pl OX4 . . . . . . 22 B1
Whitworth Pl OX2. . . . 20 B4
Wick Cl
  Abingdon OX14 . . . . . . 50 B4
  Oxford OX3. . . . . 16 C2
Wick Farm Pk OX3 . . . 16 C3
Wick Hall OX14 . . . . . . 50 C2
Wilberforce St OX3. . . 23 B4
Wilcote Rd OX3 . . . . . . 17 A2

WILDMOOR 49 B3
Wildmoor Gate OX14 49 A3
Wilkinson Pl OX28 . . . 54 B2
Wilkins Rd OX4 . . . . . . 34 A4
William Fletcher Prim
  Sch OX5 . . . . 5 B3
William Kimber Cres
  OX3 . . . . 16 C1
William Lucy Way
  OX2 . . . . 13 B1
William Orchard Cl
  OX3 . . . . 16 A2
Williams Mews OX28 56 C4
Williamson Way OX4 . 32 C1
William St OX3. . . . . . . 15 A1
Willow Brook OX14. . . 48 C1
Willow Cl
  Garsington OX44. . . . . 43 B4
  Yarnton OX5 . . . . 5 C4
Willows The
  Witney OX28 . . . . 55 B2
  Wootton OX1. . . . . 36 B1
Willow Tree Cl OX13 . 48 B3
Willow Way
  Begbroke OX5 . . . . 2 B3
  Kennington OX14. . . . . 39 C1
  Oxford OX4 . . . . 41 C4
Wilmot Cl OX28 . . . . . 56 B3
Wilsdon Way OX5 . . . . 3 B3
Wilsham Rd OX14 . . . . 53 B3
Winchester Rd OX2. . . 13 C2
Windale Ave OX4. . . . . 41 C3
Windale Ho 🛿 OX4. . . 41 C4
Windale Prim Sch
  OX4 . . . . 41 C3
Windmill La OX33 . . . . 26 A1
Windmill Prim Sch
  OX3 . . . . 23 B4
Windmill Rd OX3. . . . . 23 B4
Windows Ct OX33 . . . . 27 A1
Windrush Cl OX28. . . . 54 A1
Windrush Ct OX14. . . . 48 B1
Windrush L Ctr OX28 55 A1
Windrush Twr OX4 . . . 41 C4
Windrush Valley Rd
  OX28 . . . . 54 A2
Windrush Way OX14. . 50 A3
Windsor Cres OX3. . . . 14 C3
Windsor St OX3. . . . . . 23 B4
Wingate Cl OX4 . . . . . . 34 A1
Wingfield Ct OX4. . . . . 22 A3
Winnyards The OX2 . . 28 A2
Winsmore La 🛿 OX14 53 B4
Winston Cl OX5 . . . . . . 3 C1
Winterborne Rd
  OX14 . . . . 48 C1
Wise Ave OX5. . . . . 3 B3
Witan Pk OX28 . . . . . . 57 A3
Witan Way OX28 . . . . . 55 A1
Withington Ct OX14 . . 49 B1
WITNEY 57 B4
Witney Com Hospl
  OX28 . . . . 54 C1
Witney Com Prim Sch
  OX28 . . . . 54 C4

Witney & District Mus*
  OX28 . . . . 55 A2
Witney Prim Sch
  OX28 . . . . 55 A4
Witney Rd
  Crawley OX29 . . . . 54 B4
  Ducklington OX29 . . . . 56 C2
Wolfson Coll OX2 . . . . 14 A3
Wolsely Ho OX4. . . . . . 33 B2
Wolsey Rd OX2. . . . . . . 9 C3
WOLVERCOTE. 8 C2
Wolvercote Gn OX2 . . 9 A2
Wolvercote Prim Sch
  OX2 . . . . 9 A2
Wolvercote Rdbt OX2 . 9 A3
Woodbine Pl OX1 . . . . 59 A2
Woodcote Way OX14 . 53 A2
Woodcroft OX1 . . . . . . 39 C3
Wood Farm Prim Sch
  OX3 . . . . 23 C3
Wood Farm Rd OX3 . . 23 C3
Woodford Mill OX28. . 54 C2
Woodford Way 🛿
  OX28 . . . . 54 C1
WOODGREEN 55 C3
Woodgreen OX28 . . . . 55 B2
Woodgreen Hill 🛿
  OX28 . . . . 55 A2
Wood Green Sch
  OX28 . . . . 55 C2
Woodhouse Way OX4 32 C2
Woodins Way OX1. . . . 59 A2
Woodland Park Cvn Site
  The OX14 . . . . 39 C1
Woodlands OX5. . . . . . 4 B2
Woodlands Cl OX3 . . . 15 C1
Woodlands Ct OX28 . . 55 B3
Woodlands Rd
  Oxford OX3 . . . . 15 C1
  Witney OX28. . . . . 55 B2
Woodland Wlk OX1 . . 38 A3
Woodley Cl OX14. . . . . 45 B1
Woodman Ct OX4 . . . . 22 A3
Woodman Villas OX3 . 23 A4
Woodpecker Gn 🛚
  OX4 . . . . 42 A3
Woodruff Cl OX4 . . . . . 42 A4
Woodstock Cl OX2 . . . 9 B2
Woodstock Close Flats
  OX2 . . . . 9 B2
Woodstock Ct OX2 . . . 9 B1
Woodstock Rd
  Oxford OX2 . . . . 13 C3
  Witney OX28. . . . . 55 C3
  Wolvercote OX2 . . . . . . 6 B2
Woodstock Road E
  OX5 . . . . 2 A3
Woodstock Road W
  OX20 . . . . 2 A3
Woolgate Sh Ctr
  OX28 . . . . 55 A1
Wootten Dr OX4 . . . . . 32 C2
Wootton Bsns Pk
  OX1 . . . . 36 A1

Wootton CE Prim Sch
  OX1 . . . . 36 C2
Wootton Rd
  Abingdon OX13,
  OX14 . . . . 49 A4
  Abingdon OX14 . . . . . . 49 A2
Wootton Road Ind Est
  OX14 . . . . 49 A3
WOOTTON VILLAGE. . 36 C2
Worcester Coll OX1 . . 58 A3
Worcester Pl OX1 . . . . 58 A3
Worcester St OX1 . . . . 59 A2
Wordsworth Rd OX14 52 C3
Wren Cl OX33 . . . . 26 C3
Wren Rd OX2 . . . . 10 A3
Wrightson Cl OX33 . . . 35 B4
Wyatt Rd 🛿 OX2 . . . . . 9 C3
Wychwood Brewery* 🛅
  OX28 . . . . 54 C1
Wychwood Cl OX28 . . 54 A1
Wychwood La
  Oxford OX3 . . . . 24 B4
  Rissinghurst OX3. . . . . 24 B4
Wychwood Sch 🛿
  OX2 . . . . 14 A2
Wycliffe Hall OX2 . . . . 58 B4
Wykeham Cres OX4 . . 33 A2
Wylie Cl OX3. . . . . 23 B3
Wynbush Rd OX4 . . . . 32 C1
Wyndham Way OX2 . . 9 B2
Wyndyke Furlong
  OX14 . . . . 48 B2
Wytham St OX1 . . . . . . 31 C3

Yarnell's Hill OX2 . . . . 19 B1
Yarnell's Rd OX2 . . . . . 19 C2
YARNTON. 5 B4
Yarnton Ct OX5 . . . . . . 3 C2
Yarnton La OX5 . . . . . . 6 B4
Yarnton Rd OX5 . . . . . . 3 C2
Yarrow Cl OX4 . . . . 41 C3
Yeats Cl OX4 . . . . 34 A4
Yeftly Dr OX4 . . . . 40 B3
Yeld Hall Rd OX14. . . . 50 A4
Yew Cl OX4 . . . . 42 B4
Yewtree Mews OX14. . 49 B1
Yew Tree Mews OX29 57 A1
York Ave OX3 . . . . 23 C3
York Pl OX4. . . . . 21 C3
York Rd OX3 . . . . 23 C4
Ypres Way OX14 . . . . . 48 C3

Zedcor Bsns Pk 🛿
  OX28 . . . . 55 A2

List of numbered locations

In some busy areas of the maps it is not always possible to show the name of every place.

Where not all names will fit, some smaller places are shown by a number. If you wish to find out the name associated with a number, use this listing.

The places in this list are also listed in the Index.

	10		
C1	**2** Sunset Square		
Page number	**Grid square**	**Location number**	**Place name**

3
B3 **1** Rookery The
   2 Heyford Mead
   4 North Kidlington Prim Sch
C1 **1** St Thomas More RC Prim Sch
   2 West Kidlington Prim Sch
C3 **1** Watts Way
   3 Kidlington Ctr The

4
A2 **1** Andover Ct
   2 Blenheim Ct
   3 Clevedon Ct
   4 Dorchester Ct
   5 Exeter Ct
   6 Farnham Ct
   7 Guildford Ct
   8 Hertford Ct

9
C3 **1** Miller's Acre
   2 Sunnymeade Ct
   3 Wyatt Rd

14
A2 **1** Greycotes Oxford High Sch
   2 St Clares Bardwell Rd Ctr
   3 Wychwood Sch
   4 Oxford English Ctr The

17
A2 **1** Bayards Hill Prim Sch

21
A1 **1** Buckingham St
   2 Watermans Reach
   3 Cloisters The
   4 Burford Lodge
   5 Pegasus Ct
   6 Streatley Lodge
   7 Goring Lodge
   8 Onley Ct
C2 **1** Dawson St

22
A1 **1** Hawkins St
   2 Monard Terr

A2 **1** Jeune Hall
   2 Grants Mews
   3 Pembroke Ct
   4 Collins St
   5 South Park Ct
   7 Randolph St
B1 **1** SS Mary & John CE Prim Sch

23
A4 **1** Headington Prep Sch
   2 Brambles The
B3 **1** Coolidge Cl
   2 Everard Cl
   3 Goslyn Cl
   4 Masey Cl
   5 Atwell Pl
   6 Oxfordshire Hospital Sch

33
A1 **1** Cranston Ct
   2 Rose Ct
   3 Hillsborough Cl
B2 **1** Lewin Cl
   2 Square The
   3 Upper Barr
   4 Compass Cl
   5 Templars Square Sh Ctr
   6 Church Cowley St James Prim Sch
   7 Pound Way
C4 **1** Salesian Ho
   2 Temple Cloisters
   3 Don Boscoe Cl
   4 Hopkins Ct
   5 King's School Oxford

41
C3 **1** Nuthatch Cl
   2 Verbena Way
   3 Brooklime Wlk
   4 Cleavers Sq
   5 Saxifrage Sq
   6 Bergamont Pl
   7 Foxglove Cl
   8 Cranesbill Way
C4 **1** Northbrook Ho
   2 Windale Ho
   3 Whitethorn Way

42
A3 **1** Forget-me-not Way
   2 Peartree Cl
   3 Firs Mdw
   4 Bluebell Ct
   5 Coltsfoot Sq
   6 Celandine Pl
   7 Sage Wlk
   8 Pochard Pl
   9 Coriander Way
   10 Buttercup Sq
   11 Blacksmiths Mdw
   12 Marigold Cl
   13 Woodpecker Gn
   14 Norman Smith Rd
   15 Swallow Cl
   16 Jack Argent Cl
   17 Mole Pl
   18 Campion Cl
   19 Swift Cl
   20 Primrose Pl
A4 **1** Butterwort Pl
   2 Rest Harrow
   3 Periwinkle Pl
   4 Starwort Path
   5 Timothy Way

48
C1 **1** Buckles Cl
   2 Spring Terr
   3 Buckland Mews
   4 Juniper Ct
   5 Unicorn Sch The

49
A1 **1** Mayott's Rd
   2 Carswell Ct
   3 Crown Mews
   4 Tomkin's Almshouses
   5 Ock Mews
A2 **3** Finmore Cl
B1 **1** Banbury Ct
   2 Vines The
   3 Square The
   4 Market Pl
   5 Lombard St
   6 Old Station Yd
   7 Burgess Cl
   8 Charter The
   9 Vintner Rd
   10 Quakers Ct
   11 Regal Cl

53
A4 **1** Meadowside Ct
   2 Bailie Cl
   3 Musson Cl
   4 Thurston Cl
   5 Sympson Cl
   6 Godfrey Cl
   7 Drayman's Wlk
B4 **1** Brewers Ct
   2 Winsmore La
   3 Hive Mews
   4 St Edmund's La
   5 St Helen's Mews
   6 Brick Alley
   7 Mill Paddock
   8 George Morland Ho
   9 Neave Mews
   10 Long Alley Almshouses
   11 Maud Hale Cotts
   12 St Helen's Mill

54
C1 **2** Welch Way
   3 Woodford Way
   4 Cordell Gdns
   5 Cooper Mews
   6 Crofters Mews
   7 Swan Ct
   8 Thames International
   9 Abingdon and Witney Coll (Witney Campus)
   10 Wychwood Brewery
C2 **1** New Mill Mews
   2 Carpenters Sq
   3 Hyde Mdw View
   4 Stenter Rise
   5 Stenter Mews
   6 Meadow La

55
A2 **1** Old Coachyard The
   2 Oxford Int Coll of Beauty
   3 Zedcor Bsns Pk
   4 Bridge St
   5 Woodgreen Hill
C2 **1** Northfield Row

56
A4 **1** Our Lady of Lourdes RC Prim Sch